# NOT LIKE ALL THE OTHER BOYS

## AN UNPLANNED JOURNEY INTO FAITH AND IDENTITY

TODD NORMAN RINGNESS

Copyright © 2024 by Todd Norman Ringness. All rights reserved.

No part of this publication may be reproduced, distributed, or transmitted in any form or by any means, including photocopying, recording, or other electronic or mechanical methods, without the prior written permission of the publisher, except in the case of brief quotations embodied in reviews and certain other non-commercial uses permitted by copyright law.

ISBN 13 paperback: 978-1-0688574-0-9

Scripture quotations marked (NLT) are taken from the *Holy Bible*, New Living Translation, copyright ©1996, 2004, 2015 by Tyndale House Foundation. Used by permission of Tyndale House Publishers, Carol Stream, Illinois 60188. All rights reserved.

Scripture quotations marked (NIV) are taken from the Holy Bible, New International Version®, NIV®. Copyright © 1973, 1978, 1984, 2011 by Biblica, Inc.™ Used by permission of Zondervan. All rights reserved worldwide. www.zondervan.com The "NIV" and "New International Version" are trademarks registered in the United States Patent and Trademark Office by Biblica, Inc.™

Scripture quotations marked by (NKJV) are taken from the New King James Version®. Copyright © 1982 by Thomas Nelson. Used by permission. All rights reserved.

Scripture quotations marked (Voice) are taken from The Voice™. Copyright © 2012 by Ecclesia Bible Society. Used by permission. All rights reserved.

*06240705*

www.notlikealltheotherboys.com | coaching@toddnormanringness.com

*For the struggler in all of us,
especially where truth is veiled,
and hope is fading.*

# Contents

Introduction (Spoiler Alert) .................................................................. 3

PART ONE .................................................................................................. 5

The Incident ............................................................................................... 7

PART TWO ................................................................................................ 15

Roots and Wings ..................................................................................... 17

Danny's Lessons ...................................................................................... 29

Tightrope Walking .................................................................................. 45

The Great Escape .................................................................................... 57

Salesman and Soulmate ......................................................................... 67

Coming Home to Change ...................................................................... 77

Fitting In or Stand Out ........................................................................... 87

Longing and Love ................................................................................... 97

Outlasting the First Time ..................................................................... 105

Flickering Lights ................................................................................... 115

House of Mirrors .................................................................................. 129

Breaking Olympic Fever ...................................................................... 139

Embraced and Released ...................................................................... 147

PART THREE ......................................................................................... 155

The Revelation ...................................................................................... 157

PART FOUR ........................................................................................... 161

The Impossible Dream ........................................................................ 163

A Whole New World ........................................................................... 179

Aren't All Homosexuals Anonymous? .............................................. 187

Intimacy Cravings ................................................................................ 195

| | |
|---|---|
| Buddies and Butch | 207 |
| Growing Faith | 217 |
| Overjoyed Over There | 237 |
| Naked for Jesus | 245 |
| Expanding Horizons | 253 |
| Deeper Healing | 269 |
| The Struggle for Obedience | 279 |
| Crossing the Great Divide | 295 |
| Happiest of Christians | 307 |
| My Father Knows Best | 319 |
| Notes | 327 |
| Acknowledgements | 331 |

# Not Like All the Other Boys

# Introduction
(Spoiler Alert)

This book aims to fulfil the desire of my heart: to reach someone who was like me, not happy being gay and not knowing logical explanations existed and choices were available. The moment I heard what rang out as truth from people who cared about me, my thinking changed, and a transformation process began.

If you are the one who was like me, I'm asking that you trust me as I share my story as it happened and as best as I can recall. In the pages ahead, more than a hundred individuals are introduced as real-life characters in my story. However, with the exception of my immediate family, nearly all names have been altered to protect anonymity, because I'm here to tell my story not theirs.

My story includes an account of a very unexpected introduction to the God of the Bible, located in Part Three: The Revelation, which is also when everything I believed to be true about same-sex attractions went up in smoke. Perhaps those two things were connected... or not. A little later I describe my first very real and personal encounter with Jesus in a quite undignified setting. The rest of the book (aka my life) recounts the ups and downs of clarifying my identity as a believer, growing in maturity and following Christ.

For the suspicious one, I wish I could give you a big hug right now because no matter what you've heard, thought, done, or said, I know that you are loved! And to be clear, mine is not a story of self-hatred... I've loved myself probably a little too much in this life. Also, other than possible triggers from descriptions of my behavior, nothing within these pages will cause you or anyone else harm, any more than a book about dieting will cause you to lose weight. As with all things, nothing happens if nothing happens, and ultimately, we are all of us responsible for our own actions (or inactions). Just like those who cared enough to share their stories with me so long ago, I'll let you decide what makes sense and brings you peace.

If you love someone who struggles, I truly hope that you will be encouraged with deeper understanding of the mind and heart of those of us struggling with any degree of same-sex attractions. Perhaps you'll experience renewed compassion and new awareness on how to better support those you care about. Here's a hint: Never stop loving them, right where they're at. It happens to be the same way God loves me—and you as well. His perfect love is the single greatest catalyst for personal transformation and inner peace that I've ever known.

If we *all* did better at the unconditional love thing, our planet could be a vastly different home for *all* of us. Just imagine that love nurturing every human into the awesome fullness of God-given potential. All of creation standing on tiptoe in anticipation, sons and daughters coming into their own, incomparable inner joy and peace becoming the new normal. As Louis Armstrong put it, "What a wonderful world," indeed.

# PART ONE

# The Incident

As the early afternoon sunlight streamed through large open windows, we sprawled ourselves over various wooden projects and tools. A familiar aroma of fresh-cut wood with hints of machinery grease filled the air. Our middle school shop class had begun like the others with the chipper Mr. Jacobs as our mentor. About halfway through, he slunk away for a smoke after optimistically telling all the boys to maintain radio silence.

At an awkward ten years old, hovering a bit under average height and a little over average weight, my meticulous dark brown hair aided a pleasant appearance. Hunched over the battle-scarred shop table, I was shaving pine planks with my classmate.

Even as an outsider in a new school, I was still friendly with almost everyone, and my teachers especially appreciated my attentiveness toward them. But there was one abrasive character, like 24-grit sandpaper on my inner thigh—Arnold, the wisecracking, doughy menace whose bravado overflowed like the rest of him. The mere sight of Arnold caused me to walk the other way.

Treading in swirling pools of masculine insecurity, my ongoing shop class supplied unexpected pleasure. Creativity in wood projects yielded surprising accomplishments from my unmanly hands more suited for the delicate work of lesser men.

Patrick stood taller than me with thick blond hair and an athletic build, also my former best friend. Across the floor of woodchips and shavings, he and his new best buddy Arnold snickered together at their worktable. Soon after The Incident, Patrick began spending more time with that irritation. *Why does he annoy me so freaking much?*

In typical troublemaker fashion, Arnold amplified himself to amuse Patrick and disturb the rest of us. Rules were important to me, prompting a polite duty-bound reminder to Arnold of Mr. Jacob's wishes. Arnold didn't like being challenged in front of everyone and fought back with his loud mouth.

"Yah well, at least I don't feel up my friends while they're sleeping," Arnold brayed across the shop.

His jarring judgment hovered in the sawdust-laden air turning time into tree sap. Confusion and embarrassment clenched my ambushed heart like an over-tightened vice. Accusing stares from all the other boys sentenced me to intense embarrassment for a damaging offense. Even the overhead fluorescent lights stopped buzzing to hear what would happen next.

Not once had I considered what happened with Patrick in such a way and it alarmed me to even consider those condemnatory words. And yet, the implications tangled in my mind as fiery panic ignited shame. A quick-witted reply was crucial to drown the flames.

"Yah, right. You wish," I squeaked, barely louder than a termite's titter. Though rapid, its impact was about as effective as toothpicks in a log-rolling competition.

Meanwhile, wicked worry made its dramatic debut deep rooting itself into my psyche. A driving fear of humiliation established itself as my goblin enemy, and burrowed into my life, only to fully identify itself decades later.

When Mr. Jacobs finally rematerialized, his class resumed as if Arnold's fierce accusation had been imagined. Oh, how I wished it could be true. Burning questions consumed me like careless paper tossed on glowing embers of self-doubt, igniting an identity dilemma and years of desperate, silent struggle.

*Did Patrick actually think I wanted to feel him up?*

*Was it his idea to embarrass me? Or Arnold's?*
*But embarrass me about what? Nothing even happened!*
*But why do I feel so ashamed?*

\* \* \*

What first drew Patrick and I together as friends in Saskatoon, Saskatchewan (say that five times fast, if you dare) remain as mysterious as moths to flames because we didn't share many interests. Like all the other boys, Patrick was sportier and into cars while good grades and books were the logs in my woodshed.

Neither of us had many friends. As outsiders, perhaps we recognized that in each other. He and I often hung out after school including an occasional sleepover.

Bored one night at his place, we stretched a paper streamer across the road between a corner mailbox and a tree. Crouching in shrubbery, we peered through the darkness awaiting our unsuspecting quarry. A car approached, its headlights illuminating our prank just in time for the driver to slam the brakes, screeching to a halt.

Patrick and I thought it was hilarious because we knew the paper would have snapped easier than a brittle twig. Perhaps the puzzled driver didn't know what it was. After a bit, he drove right through the streamer, and sped away into the night.

Time for a reset and an escalation to something more durable: Twine. We hid again nearby and awaited our next victim with the patience of a sneaky spider awaiting its prey.

The next guy didn't spot the dark-colored cord in time, and it struck the front of his car hard. That time, no brakes. The twine's stubborn knot seized the mailbox handle, sending it through the darkness into the street with a mighty crash.

Skidding to a stop, the irate driver threw open his door, forcing various profanities into the cool night air. We started running. He yelled out at us in the dark as we stifled our snickers and hightailed it behind Patrick's house.

Our shameless shenanigan thrilled me much more than my adventure books. It was rare rebellion for a rule follower like me, and a disobedient dark side compelled me for a few reasons.

More developed than me, Patrick emanated an alluring masculinity like a young lumberjack which sparked curiosity. So, during a sleepover with his parents away and his brother out sowing his oats, we played Truth or Dare. I challenged Patrick to strip and run around his house under cover of night. He accepted the charge and headed to the back door to drop his drawers and head outdoors as I observed from the living room window. Even though darkness veiled nearly everything, the scene stoked a sense of exhilaration in me. *I almost saw it!*

The ill-fated events of The Incident occurred at a sleepover at my house. In a conversation about very personal things—including *our* things—Patrick described himself as well-endowed. Compared to my modest proportions, those details inflamed inquisitiveness and disbelief. *How could it be true?*

After lights out, various thoughts foraged through my mind. *Could he truly be so much bigger?* Sure, it made sense with my brothers because they were older. But Patrick and I were the same age. I needed to find out if he was making this up only to impress me.

The windowless basement was pitch dark, and Patrick seemed to be sleeping soundly in our side-by-side fold-up cots. I was certain I could complete my field research with stealth and care without disturbing him. After finding and lifting the edge of his blanket with deliberate bomb-squad slowness, I guided my hand under the covers toward him to confirm—or contradict—his outlandish claims. As I inched closer, careful not to awaken him, my hand recoiled after meeting a gooey mess under the blanket. *Abort!*

Bewildered and concerned, I wasted no time and snuck out of my bed to wash up. Meanwhile, Patrick stirred and announced with pride he had a wet dream, an unknown experience for me. We laughed as we squared everything away, and neither of us ever brought it up again.

\* \* \*

The aftermath of the shop class shaming spectacle left me concerned about my reputation at school. *Are they whispering about me? Do they think I'm a fag?*

Time to launch Project Reputation. I began the work of setting straight the record—and my sexuality—by clarifying Patrick indeed had a nocturnal emission. Otherwise, it raised the possibility Patrick had been awake the whole time. It was damage control to deny the alleged event and let it all fade away. Well, the battle plan wasn't altogether successful.

Patrick wasn't keen on having his sexuality questioned by anyone who may have doubted his ability to remain asleep during uninvited nighttime touching. I'd have probably done the same thing if the situation had been reversed. With tension rising, Mrs. Reynolds's class became the battleground for a sneak attack. This time, Patrick was flying solo without Arnold's lead as others settled into their seats.

"You think you're fooling everybody but you're not," Patrick accused, hostility ringing louder than the recess bell. Everyone turned to view the scarlet expression on my disbelieving face. I couldn't believe my trusted friend was doing this to me in front of our class. Patrick had become my enemy, and my attention shifted to a sharp retaliation to salvage some dignity.

"And you're so stupid…" began my retort precisely when Mrs. Reynolds marched into the room. *Oh, crap.* "You don't even know what you're talking about," I continued, my clenched voice trailing off with the usefulness of a wet match on dry brushwood.

Mrs. Reynolds had zero tolerance for disrespect on her watch which meant there would be consequences. Except for a Grade 1 reprimand when I used a word I didn't understand, my first formal taste of school discipline would be immediate. Patrick and I were hauled into the teacher's workroom as every eye and mouth in the room hung open.

It hardly seemed fair because Patrick had provoked the argument, but Mrs. Reynolds saw no need for an investigation and carried out her verdict. She withdrew the Yardstick of Justice from its hallowed perch. I offered to go first hopeful it might soothe the discord. Mrs. Reynolds swung hard, and it stung like the repeated revenge of hateful wasps like it was supposed to. Then Patrick had his turn, and I felt bad for him.

The whole predicament fueled his anger as he blamed me for being urged out of the backwoods of inconspicuousness into an unpleasant glade of notoriety and conflict. Nobody wants to be shoved into the limelight, especially for the wrong reasons.

One week had passed when a friend told me Patrick was still furious and was planning to take me down after class. Panic coursed through my veins, and my armpits dampened as I contemplated what he could do to me. His strength seemed like a tall, wide timber compared to the wispiness of my masculinity.

As the winter sun prepared for twilight, my intel revealed Patrick lay in ambush for me on my normal route home from school. Unfortunately, word spread like wildfire, so there would be onlookers. Standing in the empty hallway, my guts knotted in on themselves as I considered my options. Remain in the school until the janitor kicks me out. Or choose a back road and leave early to throw off my attacker. *Or maybe there's a hole I can crawl into?*

Even now—decades later—I'm disturbed when I hear footsteps come up behind me with determination. The dreadful sound had filled my ears when Patrick grabbed me by the coat and threw me to the ground where his punching began. In reaction, I let out garbled, whining exclamations of, "What did I ever do to you?" And when it was over, I limped home with a bogus explanation for my parents.

In the end, the wet dream account became popular opinion, assisted by Patrick proving his manliness by beating me up while I maintained my innocence. Our friendship was over, and to my regret, nothing was ever resolved between us.

Life went on at my school. I got involved with computers and made a new ally named Joe, who was also a bit of a tech geek like me. The new Apple II desktop computer had appeared at our school, and Joe and I spent our spare time programming games in simple BASIC language. He had a good sense of humor and helped me realize I was smarter than perhaps I knew as I tried to reach the heights he set in our digital adventures.

Our friendship grew, and we began having sleepovers. A subtle effort was meant to determine if Joe was curious like me. He wasn't, and it was better for me to forget about it because keeping him as my friend meant much more. Joe would choose a different high school affecting our connection. About eleven years later, I really appreciated the invitation to his wedding, though I almost didn't make it.

My insecurities, doubts, and not-quite-fitting-in made me a walking contradiction. I belonged to a loving and functional family with two present and healthy parents providing a firm social foundation and what appeared to be high self-confidence. So, to the outside world, I projected an image of amiability, charisma, competence, and intellect. *Nothing to see here!*

Yet unbeknownst to all (me included), the warden of all fears would seize control of my very being, increasingly having its way. It had weaponized my natural curiosity, triggering deeper insecurities and self-doubt. In time, the battle to extinguish the firestorm would intensify, requiring more complex means and methods driven by desperation to determine—or conceal—my sexual identity.

# PART TWO

# Roots and Wings

My upbringing seemed somewhat normal except for my hidden insecurities and the trio of momentous family moves due to Dad's job changes. Many assumed he was military, but simple random occurrences led to far-flung career opportunities.

Let me introduce you to the man behind those moves, my dad, John Norman. He was the youngest in a big family with four sisters and one brother. His father had known a hard life in Norway before emigrating to Canada in the early 1900s, so our "Boppa" (our name for Dad's dad) had a traditional, stoic, few-words-only demeanor. And guess what? My dad inherited those traits, though thankfully, to a lesser degree.

Not an ordinary guy, my dad. He was handsome and eligible, even though some say he was from the wrong side of the tracks. Dad was compared to a young Elvis in appearance. As was more common back then, he was only nineteen when he popped the question to my seventeen-year-old, British-born mum.

Wanda Natalie has a life story also far from ordinary. My mum's parents treated her like a princess including breakfast in bed, until she married and left home. Mum was an only child whose mum had married a dapper Canadian soldier during World War II. Our "Granch" (our name for Mum's dad) was a real Nova Scotia native with a tough upbringing. Granch joined the military to find purpose and escape. Our "Nan" (Mum's mum) grew up in a large British family where silliness was the norm and laughter ruled the day. *That's where it comes from!*

Nan and Mum lived in England until the day they boarded the *Ascania*, a ship docked in Liverpool, and sailed toward the land of maple syrup to live with Granch's family; he would arrive later. Mum was a fifth grader at the time, and in time they moved west to Calgary, Alberta. Mum grew more beautiful and became popular with the boys, noting her intriguing accent. Some even said she looked like a young Elizabeth Taylor. So, between the two of them, you might think Baby Todd could come along looking like James Dean. But I felt more like Jim Nabors.

After meeting Mum, Dad wasted little time and tied the knot, but their marriage wasn't a walk in the park. Dad worked his butt off with many grueling jobs to make sure we were all taken care of. Our family grew fast—within nine years, they had four healthy children to feed and clothe.

\* \* \*

A bigger family offers both advantages and disadvantages. But on the positive side, our siblings enable us to step outside ourselves and examine the world through their perspective, whether we like it or not. Throughout my journey and to this day, their companionship has made rough patches a little less intimidating. My siblings are a precious gift in my world, so please allow me to introduce them.

John was the first of us to come along. We called him Randy in the early years, based on his given first name. Later in life, he preferred John to signify major changes in his life and honor his namesake. My stalwart oldest brother was headstrong, conscientious, and tenacious in track and field and basketball. Despite his serious nature, John has an endearing, goofy side, quirky tastes in food and music, and a fondness for Kermit the Frog. At six years my senior, John was tremendously responsible.

Three years older than me, Greg was a quarterback and basketball jock but also artistic. He crafted beautiful gifts that moved us to tears with his talent. His gifted writing intimidated me like everything else, so I didn't pursue it in those years because I felt it wouldn't ever be as good as his. One summer, Greg got fitness crazy and also taught himself to juggle. *Is there anything he can't do?* More importantly, he finally grew to appreciate the virtues of tomatoes.

From early on, I occupied the shadows of my brothers with resentment, feeling I couldn't measure up to either of them or match their skills or popularity. My manliness resembled an embroidered doily whenever I compared myself to them. They were gods, and I was something else altogether.

A vivid memory from boyhood endures: the three of us getting ready for bath time. I could easily see that some parts of my brothers looked different to me. They noticed it too and made fun of my four-year-old penis, which made me cry. That incident held more significance than anyone would ever know, planting sinister seeds of insecurity and feeling not enough. It underscored the physical differences between me and my brothers, and later, all the other boys.

Feelings of being an unusual boy compounded because my dad was more into football and baseball, while I was interested in reading, computers, and the television series *Mr. Rogers' Neighborhood*. I knew in my heart Dad loved me unconditionally, but I still worried my inability to match his masculinity would come between us.

Spending time with Mum made me feel more secure and comfortable, highlighting my different nature. As a young boy, I often fell asleep curled up behind Mum's legs as she read on the couch.

My parents had hoped for a daughter to fill the second spot after giving birth to John, but they ended up with Greg. When they discovered they were pregnant again—with yet another boy—they adjusted for their real-life *My Three Sons* upon my arrival, which was an efficient scheduled delivery.

Finally, they had a girl, Tessa, named after her doctor. Spoiling our baby sister became a hobby for the entire family, quite justified. At fifteen months my junior, versus the large age gaps between me my brothers, Tessa and I bonded well.

However, I couldn't escape the "forgotten middle child" syndrome, often vying for attention. One successful trick was taking my sweet time to order from a menu at a restaurant forcing everyone else to wait. But they figured that out in no time flat and sending me in early became the new normal. This made matters worse because instead of feeling valued or important, my desires became an isolated task to be checked off.

Tessa grew up with great security with Mum's devoted care supported by four males at home. Her sense of family and its importance are probably the strongest of the siblings, evidenced to this day through frequent gatherings and celebrations. One also can't ignore myriad family photos that take up every square inch of wall space in her home.

Laughter defines our Ringness family nearly as much as love. The active goal of making each other laugh is the strongest between Tess and me. We hit a rough patch as I craved her approval when I was a struggling Grade 12 senior. In the end, our shared adventures reinforced our unbreakable bond. *I would do anything for my sister.*

\*\*\*

Concerned about Calgary's rapid population growth, Mum and Dad determined the time was right to move and raise their young family in a smaller and safer locale. So right after my precious baby sister splashed onto the scene, job hunting began in British Columbia, one province over.

On the road during the job search, they'd camped near picturesque Kelowna with my two older brothers while Tessa and I remained with godparents in Calgary. Legend has it Dad leaned out of the tent to pick a fresh peach from an adjacent tree. Convenient juicy fruit was an obvious sign from above, so he registered at the downtown employment office and soon accepted a job with a boat manufacturer. Dad's new job prompted a speedy return home to make the move west.

In Kelowna, our exciting new life began in a rustic lakefront rental house, a rare find. Within a year, a newly constructed home beckoned us to plant our familial tree in the fertile soil of a growing Kelowna suburb. Nan and Granch had also moved from Calgary to be closer to their young grandkids and in such a desirable location.

Dad was ever a hard worker, and Paul, his boss and mentor, duly noticed Dad's four years of dedicated service at the thriving plant. Paul was planning an exciting new venture on the other side of the country and needed help. A momentous new career opportunity resulted for Dad, impossible to resist.

Uprooting a family guarantees all kinds of risks and rewards. Gratitude emerges in my heart for many lessons learned, including my learned ability to be at ease with new faces in strange places. However, concerns linger about the lack of social stability resulting from multiple displacements and how that may have affected my identity struggles.

And so it was, right before my debut as a first grader, our family of six packed luggage and boxes in Kelowna, British Columbia and touched down three thousand one hundred miles to the east in Woodstock, New Brunswick. Our belongings included one crate shared by our lovable St. Bernard named Lad and our feisty cat named Snowball; before and after photos suggest they may not have enjoyed their bonding time. Our epic journey required multiple plane transfers and an overnight stay in Calgary, along with the courage to leave behind our doting grandparents through many tears. *Why can't they come with us?*

Dad's start-up managerial position at a manufacturing plant owned by Paul came with reduced pay to support the survival of the grand undertaking through lean times. Our maritime adventure ported us into a small basement suite, the only available rental in the area. It was modest for sure, and my young mother had her hands full caring for us growing kids in a cramped space. As fortune favored the bold, our successive dwellings soon scaled up with the growing business—first a two-story bungalow, then a sprawling historic mansion overlooking the river.

The towering white manor was extraordinary boasting hardwood floors, spacious living and dining areas, and an entryway with a beautiful hand-carved staircase. Greg and I shared one of the three bedrooms on the second floor, and John claimed a three-room private suite on the third floor. The back staircase designed for the help and an expansive dirt-floor basement with an octopus-like oil-burning furnace made for rewarding games of hide and seek. For a six-year-old and his siblings, it was a surprising adventure land well suited for all kinds of fun. Attached to the back of the house was a second part-time home for Dad's boss Paul and his wife, Ava, with a secret basement through-door aiding occasional surprise visits by their son Jerry, when he visited home from school.

Resourcefulness reigned in our home with six hungry mouths and a single income. The ever-present, bright blue plastic jug filled with powdered milk often yielded an intriguing crusty layer as the liquid level lowered in the jug. But overall, we wanted not, and it was unquestionable our parents adored each other and us—we had many happy times together. Our East Coast adventures included annual summer camping on Prince Edward Island and an American bicentennial short road trip to New York City.

Those early days were peppered with many special moments with family, and Dad was often the driving force. I can't remember us ever roughhousing or wrestling, but he had an airplane game he'd play with us when we were small. Lying on his back, he'd lock his feet together, and we'd climb onto his makeshift plane, gripping his hands. The adventure began as he straightened his legs, launching us into the air above him. Our laughter and the occasional "turbulence" made us scream with delight.

One week when I asked for my allowance, Dad sent me to fetch it from his jeans in the bedroom. To my amazement, I found a fortune in quarters stuffed in his pockets. I started to fish out my allotment when temptation struck. I figured he wouldn't miss a few extra quarters. So, I snuck more—way more—hiding them above the door frame in the bedroom I shared with Greg. Then I coolly thanked Dad for my supplemented allowance, unbeknownst to him.

Weeks later, during a family road trip, I was on Dad's lap as he drove, a common occurrence for young children once upon a time. The dashboard's soft glow lit our faces while everyone else snoozed to the hum of the highway passing beneath us. Dad shared a tale with me about a father, some apples and a barrel. The family sold apples they stored in large barrels.

One day, the father asked his son to fetch himself one apple from the barrel as a reward for his help. But the boy liked the fruit so much that he took several of them, thinking his father wouldn't notice. Dad's story struck paydirt in my six-year-old heart. I knew full well it was wrong to take those extra quarters, and I broke out in tears on his shoulder, blurting out my regret. Feeling his comforting embrace in return meant everything. *I'm lucky to have a good dad.*

\*\*\*

Our elementary school offered a few conveniences, including door-to-door transportation via Mr. Parkinson's bus and a free school lunch program. We sang "O Canada" and recited the Lord's Prayer every morning. It was a good school with great teachers, and I felt happy there.

Primary school was a positive experience because I was a lover of books, numbers, and people too! However, unexplained migraines led to an IQ test, resulting only in a verdict of "superior intelligence." Potential lonely nerdiness loomed, save for a few good pals like Tony, Angus, and sweetheart Tina, all eight years old.

Down the way from our family home lived an elderly man named Grinny, whom I would visit often to hear him play his upright piano. An ever-present hanky wiped away most of the frequent drips from his nose, the piano keys or the old wooden floor catching what the hanky didn't. One of his favorite songs to play was "The Bear Went Over the Mountain"; I can still sing the words.

Grinny was a great storyteller, and he seemed to know a lot about much, including how the tattered curtains in the old window can conceal oneself while peering out. An old wood-burning stove in the kitchen was scorching hot, and the campfire-like smell made Grinny's home even cozier. I liked watching my spittle sizzle away on the black iron top. I can only recall enjoyable memories of my visits with Grinny. *I like how he pays attention to me.*

Nearby lived Jenny (aka Boo), who joined me on various adventures in our neighborhood. Her dad worked for a commercial bakery, and she liked sugar sandwiches. John and Greg both believed Boo was my sugar, though to me, she was simply my friend Boo. I can still remember her phone number, so that's saying something.

Next door, on the other side of a waist-height stone wall, lived a sweet widow named Mrs. Maudie Dibble in a large yellow manor. I took an instant liking to her and enjoyed our chats. She'd often send me to the corner store which I would have done even if she didn't let me buy something for myself. I can't explain how or why she gave me the nickname Toddford, but it stuck and still gets used by family from time to time.

At ten, I felt settled in my home and school with true friendships. Angus hosted a few sleepovers, and we had great fun playing games like *Risk* and *Pit*. Tina and I were smitten with each other and often enjoyed recess together, though it remained innocent. It appeared I influenced culture and style with a peculiar predilection for buttoning up my shirt collar all the way. It caught on with others but also earned me the handle "preacher boy" from my brothers. *It makes me feel more secure.*

My elementary school experience seemed standard and included considerable anticipation for my sixth-grade swan song before heading down the block to middle school, where my brothers were making their mark. Alas, upheaval loomed, ready with a surprise attack to catapult a stable life into a storm of unforeseen trials. Turmoil's wicked winds howled slightly beyond the horizon. *No, not again.*

# Get Your Free Audio Book Sample

Receive as a gift the first three chapters of this book as an **audio file**, narrated in the author's own voice. Enter your email address below and instructions will be emailed back to you.

Please visit this website:

**gift.nlatob.com**

Included in the **free downloadable MP3 audio file**:
- *Introduction (Spoiler Alert)*
- *Roots and Wings*
- *Danny's Lessons*

By providing your email address, you'll also **receive author updates about the book and the upcoming sequel**.

*Your email address will be kept strictly confidential and you may cancel at any time.*

## PLEASE STAY IN TOUCH!

**gift.nlatob.com**

# Danny's Lessons

After four struggling years, Paul, the owner of Dad's plant, threw in the towel. Termination letters went out, and Dad began a local job search. However, the absence of opportunities caused horizons to broaden. He soon secured a promising management position at a construction-related manufacturing plant four provinces away.

The decision was made to skedaddle during the Christmas break, offering a rebirth in a new home in a new year. We crammed our worldly belongings into a massive moving truck, and our bustling brood of six prepared for the journey.

No series of fancy flights for us that time around, however. It would be an epic road trip expedition for the ages, spanning almost two thousand five hundred miles due west across a frozen chunk of Canada in the most bitter month of the year.

Our dog Lad's aggressive behavior had increased over time, so he had been sent to live with a new family on a farm. This made way for Vesla, a collie-mix received as a puppy from dear family friends, now a cherished family member who would also make the trip. The expedition would be even more exciting as Snowball huddled in her cage in the back of our roomy old Suburban, retrofitted with an auxiliary floor heater to combat the expected arctic onslaught.

We bade farewell to our itsy-bitsy New Brunswick town (pop: a cozy five thousand), setting our sights on bustling Saskatoon, Saskatchewan (pop: a rather intimidating one hundred and twenty thousand). Culture shock, here we come!

One immortal tale from our frosty adventure was my ailing brother John's impassioned plea for an abrupt stop. His request was at odds with Dad's concern for our safety in the remote setting, alongside his strong determination to stay on schedule. John, ever the considerate soul, at least managed to roll down the window... and let it fly. It turned out that minus thirty degrees and rapid highway velocity were no friend to the liquid-based evacuation, which quickly presented itself as colorful, chunky graffiti on our rear port-side window. A gas station pitstop for Dad's less-than-pleasant de-icing session followed as the rest of us snickered at the poetic justice.

\* \* \*

Music beckoned during my formative years with stirring persistence, though no one else in my family embraced its call except for Mum. She often serenaded our home with her beautiful singing voice, which I adored. Our school morning routine sometimes included her singing me awake with my personalized rendition:

> *Good morning to you.*
>
> *Good morning to you.*
>
> *Good morning, dear Toddford.*
>
> *Good morning to you.*

However, unlike Snow White, animated birds rarely encircled Mum, and she wasn't flitting about in a pretty blue house dress as she warbled us awake. Another round of shouts echoing from downstairs was often required.

Our home often resonated with music, even more so when my parents hosted weekend gatherings of coworkers and friends. Despite their parties stretching late into the night, I enjoyed the variety of tunes my dad played on his turntable, with country music the clear favorite over the years. Some albums were so well enjoyed that he needed to weigh down the needle with quarters to reduce skipping.

His favorites often required at least a dollar's worth to produce their melodies, each one known by heart.

On occasion, Tessa and I would be invited (aka strongly encouraged) to break away from the TV downstairs to join their festivities as semi-reluctant performers but not as singers. You see, a disco craze had prompted school officials to include disco dancing lessons in our Phys. Ed. classes. My sister and I had learned the steps of the New York Hustle, delighting Mum and Dad's guests with our synchronized dance moves as the Bee Gees song "Staying Alive" reached every corner of our house. Cheers and applause trailed us as we returned to the basement and whatever we were watching. *Not sure that's normal, but it's still fun.* Decades later, when the circumstances are right, Tess and I can prove we've still got the boogie.

My first experience hearing a live orchestra occurred during an assembly at a neighboring school. Sitting on the gym floor front and center, musicians in their places on the stage in front of me, the sounds of dozens of mysterious instruments flooded my ears with wonder making my heart soar. The ensemble performed several selections, but the most memorable was the theme from the TV series *Hogan's Heroes*. It was as if my black-and-white world burst into a kaleidoscope of living colorized sound.

Also piquing my musical interest was a unique hybrid piano-organ instrument gifted by my favorite auntie, who recognized my fascination with keyboards beyond computers. A delightful compact and portable melodic apparatus featured a narrow keyboard with push-button chords. I spent countless hours on it in our basement playroom. However, in striving to figure myself out, musical interests didn't help me be any more like my brothers, father, or any other men in my life. In fact, my yearning for melodious expression made me feel even less masculine. Perhaps tickling the ivories should have been traded for slam-jamming on an electric guitar?

In Grade 6, Mrs. Gold, an elegant, older teacher with stylish blonde hair and classy taste, led our mandatory choir with grace. I liked everything about the new experience, including several religious songs, foreign not only to me. Mrs. Gold's heart was on display every time we participated in what seemed to be a project of passion.

I don't know why, but at one rehearsal, she asked me to conduct and showed me how to move my hands to make a rhythmic air triangle in time with the music. At first, I enjoyed leading the others. But as practice continued, I felt the heat of everyone's eyes focused on me pretending to be a choir director. Embarrassment lurked, ready to tackle. So, after only one song, I told Mrs. Gold leading wasn't for me and returned to the safety of the masses, increasing my enjoyment immensely. Some songs we sang together remain imprinted within me.

* * *

Many of the other boys in my class were experiencing body changes, and their frequent sexual references stirred up curiosity within me. As a recess break was winding down one day, a popular, attractive guy named Mark was snickering with other boys near his desk. He called me over, still chuckling, drawing me in close to talk.

"Todd, do you have hair on your goink?" Mark half-whispered as the others listened in.

"On my doink?" I clarified, considering my uneasy response with care, unwilling to reveal I was a little behind in my maturity.

"No, your goink. Do you have hair on it?" he again asked as the sniggering increased around me.

"S-s-sure I do," I stammered, not telling the truth. Full-out howling ensued as Mark revealed his "goink" was the part of his finger above the knuckles and below the first joint. And sure enough, upon close examination, there were small, fine hairs on ours. *Okay, hilarious, but why does talking about hairy goinks feel kinda funny?* It seemed all the other boys knew what was going on, and I was on the front lawn looking through the window seeing everyone else at the party.

It was around this point in life that The Incident occurred with Patrick, as I shared earlier. The combination of shame and embarrassment mixed with the realization of not fitting in would come at a high cost. I was miles away from the acceptance I longed for from my peers. If this continued, it would be a downward spiral to who knows where. *Perhaps it's time to expand my horizons.*

\* \* \*

In the bustling hallways of my Saskatoon school, a spunky and unassuming girl named Laura with short, dark hair caught my attention, and I began to connect with her. However, I soon discovered those city girls left me even more insecure in the uncharted realm of elementary romance.

My school's safety patrol program for volunteer students assisted with crosswalk supervision in the neighborhood before and after school. I eagerly joined and reveled in the training and its quasi-military environment, allowing me to indulge my ambitions and rise in the ranks.

As a year-end reward for our dedicated service, the school organized an exciting excursion—a three-hour bus ride south to Regina to attend a Saturday afternoon CFL game. While the sport held no interest for me, having fun with my classmates was irresistible, especially given that Laura would be joining us as a fellow safety patroller. The bus trip down was uneventful, but at the game, I found myself seated next to Laura, and she was interested and playful.

However, my jitters hindered my ability to reciprocate in a meaningful way.

Frustrated and disappointed in myself, I sat beside a good-natured older student named Danny on the return bus ride. Feathered blond hair and a gleaming front tooth drew the attention of anyone looking at Danny. Despite some reservations, I confided in him about my interest in Laura and my lack of kissing know-how. Danny startled me with his casual offer to help, suggesting he could teach me the knack of kissing. Intrigued and aware of rising nervous excitement, I accepted his offer. *Guys teach guys how to kiss?*

To ensure privacy, Danny told the two guys in the back to switch seats with us, creating a secluded space under the dim lighting. Many others seated in front of us were already drifting off as the bus hummed down the highway. As Danny imparted his wisdom on the intricacies of necking, his shiny tooth would catch the overhead reading light, adding a magical sparkle to an unexpected scene. His enthusiastic instructions faded into the background as I fixated on his mouth. A whirlwind of conflicting questions mud-wrestled in my mind compelling me to see my tutor in a different light.

> *What would kissing him feel like?*
>
> *Wait, that's not good, what about Laura?*
>
> *Seriously, what's wrong with you?*
>
> *But what if?*

A hands-on necking demo with Danny didn't seem *that* farfetched. It's not as if we were discussing the intricacies of nuclear fission. So, there we were. Privacy? *Check.* Romantic mood lighting with added twinkle? *Check.* Curiosity and enthusiasm? *Double check.* But alas, Danny stopped short of a mouth-on-mouth display, and with a sigh, I believe I concealed my disappointment and thanked him for his lessons. *What was I thinking?*

Then, even more unthinkable, Danny insisted on inviting Laura to join us, given that he'd equipped me with brand-new intimacy skills. *Ha!* Oh, what a brain-twisting predicament it all spiraled into. Talk about changing gears.

Upon Danny's invitation, Laura squeezed into our row and settled on the floor in front of us while explaining he wanted me to practice on her. She was into it, so I believed I could at least try, but Danny seemed intent on being a focused onlooker. Cue the arrival of extreme self-consciousness! As a result, it was a couple of timid pecks with an abundance of mutual tense laughter before I bowed out. I thanked Laura for her willingness to take part, guiding her back to her seat to sort out her own feelings about what happened.

Little did I know the outcome of Danny's impromptu smooching school would extend far beyond my initial contemplations, bordering on baffling. Instead of feeling prepared to tackle Laura with newfound confidence and desire-filled kisses, I found myself sideswiped by an unexpected curiosity about Danny and soon, all the other boys. As a result, my budding relationship with Laura came to a halt, leaving me reluctant and cautious to navigate new curiosities and complex desires.

\* \* \*

During a warm prairie summer before crossing the threshold into the sixth grade, my eyes fell upon our family 8mm camera, stirring a creative impulse. Gathering some of my new friends together, the gadget beckoned us into storytelling.

We envisioned simple horror movie concepts with help from forgotten Halloween costumes to feed a haphazard storyline. I was the director, but instead of a script, we improvised each scene as they unfolded. The camera didn't have sound, so we used a cassette recorder to record audio, thinking we could synchronize them later. Persistence prevailed, allowing us to shoot a couple of reels after much merriment and kidding around. As was the common practice then, I packaged the exposed film and sent it off to the processing lab, requiring great patience and a few weeks.

My impassioned plea to Mrs. Gold allowed us to project our final production to the class, but we discovered the audio workaround didn't quite work out. However, student reactions were positive and encouraging. An inkling of awareness sparked within me that I could impact school activities, an enticing prospect for a boy struggling to find his social footing.

Emboldened by the realization, I soon discovered a fun educational game, involving a silly chicken theme. Again, I was eager to introduce it at school and was delighted to get the nod, serving as the event host. For a couple of weeks, lunch hours became my domain of amusement and imaginative learning, where I presided over my peers as they partook in playful competition. *I want more of this!*

Discovering influence over friends and classmates tickled my senses with delight, revealing the joy of giving people a good time while being in charge. At eleven years old, I began to flourish as my budding leadership skills came to the foreground, pushing contradictory insecurities into the background.

Dad coached baseball, and both John and Greg played in their younger years, but it held little interest for me. I first played ball during an elementary school Phys. Ed. class and discovered I didn't mind it so much, so I joined a league where I often ended up in right field—the position often conceded to less skilled players. However, something in the art of umpiring ignited curiosity within me, more so when I realized it was paid work. With some encouragement, I took the leap, ignoring the lingering shadow of doubt about my preparedness for such a responsibility.

It's difficult to forget the first pitch of my maiden umpiring outing as eyes, a collective entity, focused on me in silence, anticipating my verdict. "Strike?" I uttered in hesitancy. Probably not a good guess, from the murmuring and booing, but it got better from there. While authority proved to be delicious nourishment for my ego, it also bore a daunting weight of judgmental pressure to test my tolerance, culminating in a single-season performance.

I came to comprehend, much to my elation and amusement, that channeling my self-confidence into leadership resulted in great rewards. Inspired by Dad and modeled by my brothers, I grew as a leader and gained communal approval from everyone, most notably, all the other boys. *Seems like a win-win!*

\* \* \*

All I had ever known or heard about male-male relationships was beyond negative. The men and boys around me were ceaseless in their ridicule of anyone suspected of being that way. A common insult or putdown was the accusation of being gay or attracted to other guys, regardless of what may or may not be true.

Fitting in with my peers was already an arduous challenge, and their elusive acceptance of me as one of them was paramount. As a result, curiosities and newfound same-sex longings were unwelcome and unworthy of distraction. Therefore, I retreated deeper into my insecurity, determined to keep my feelings a secret. *Damn you, Danny.*

Random same-sex attractions increased even more with guys who had everything I felt I lacked—strength, muscular physiques, attention from girls, good looks, and lots of friends. Compared to all the other boys, I perceived myself as downright lacking in masculinity, which only amplified my desire for their acceptance.

During my early years in Saskatoon, I had endured some minor bullying before The Incident with Patrick. Some saw me as a bit of an egghead because of my good grades and love for books, and I began to wonder if those academic pursuits were too important to someone desperate to fit in. Moreover, my increasing non-masculine behavior, which mirrored my insecurities, made me stand out even more from the other boys. That unfortunate distinction painted a target on my back and plagued me for years.

In Woodstock, I had thrived as a young, natural leader, settling into social circles with ease. However, a world away, I felt like a mere nobody and grappling with the discomfort and awkwardness of puberty. The worlds of reading and electronics became my jam, and my disinterest in sports was clear, a stark contrast to the athletic prowess of my brothers. Fear shackled me, preventing me from even attempting sports unless mandated in physical education programs. In those classes, I vividly recall forced long distance runs. Instead of envisioning the victorious thrill of the finish line, I wondered in abundant exasperation every hundred yards or so: *But whyyyyyyy?*

As the boys lined up in the gym during one such class, we awaited instructions for the impending drill. I relaxed and clasped my hands behind my waist. A sudden jolt of electricity shot through my body as my fingers accidentally brushed against the crotch of a classmate named Bob standing behind me. It was quick, and nobody saw what happened. The surprising result was a sensation that awakened something with an immediate yearning to feel it again.

Capitalizing on the opportune moment, I replicated the pose in feigned nonchalance, locking eyes with Bob for a split second before averting my glance to maintain plausible innocence. My mind imagined him replicating the accidental scenario. However, he did not. But it didn't change the stirring and curiosity within me. *Why do I want it again even though it feels so wrong?*

After Laura, pursuing girl romance in real life felt like a closed chapter, but it didn't mean I steered clear of girls altogether. At one school dance, I spotted a group of quiet girls keeping to themselves. Feeling a bit gallant and somewhat sympathetic, I decided to ask one to dance. The first dance led to another, and before I knew it, I had danced with all those girls, enjoying it all. Their genuine smiles and thank-yous were my unexpected reward. That night, I realized we're all pretty similar deep down, only with different wrappers.

Life continued, but the unexpected happened in Grade 8: I ended up on the boys volleyball team. It was almost entirely the fault of an enthusiastic guy named Robin, who affirmed a rather extraordinary play I had made during a Phys. Ed. class. Reflecting upon what happened (for days), I shocked myself as I considered trying out for the team, representing a first-ever attempt at anything athletic beyond the involuntary exceptions. And it scared me spitless. But another voice in my head had a thought. *What's the worst that could happen?* Perhaps the coach had considered my brother's abilities from three years earlier because, before I knew it, I was on the team. *Wait, me? On a team, as one of the boys?*

Practices fit with ease into my open, uncommitted schedule. I worked hard, showed up early, and stayed late, like my dad taught me. My actual volleyball skills may or may not have improved over time, but it didn't matter because I was grateful to be there. What I lacked in ability, I made up with enthusiasm. The boys on our team were skilled, and within a few months, we made our way to the provincial championships.

The final game occurred on a Saturday in December. My dad, who traveled a lot for work, was there for the remarkable event that coincided with my birthday. We were dominating, and as the big win neared, it was as if something from the great beyond let me know the coach might put me in. So, I did what any eager and ambitious

Grade 8 athlete would do. Not. I high tailed it to the empty changeroom, overcome by careening anxiety and visions of the loss being blamed on me right there in front of my embarrassed dad. Such was the cost of pretending to be a normal athletic boy.

Coach figured it out and sent a teammate to retrieve me, but despite my stall tactics, he put me into play—my first actual competitive appearance since joining the team. *Is he freaking nuts?* The gym walls reverberated with my speeding heartbeat. As luck would have it, my teammates wanted to win way more than I did. They covered most of the shots that came my way, except for two saves that also surprised me. We won the game and the tournament. So yes, I was a provincial champion—a strange and encouraging outcome!

Indeed, there was something significant about being on a team, appearing more normal on the outside, disregarding what I was feeling inside. But no, the triumph did not launch further athletic pursuits because I still felt out of league with all of them. In no way could I ever match the skill and confidence displayed by the others who all seemed to be like my brothers. Matters were made worse with the uncomfortable realization I was more attentive to other boys in their snug shorts or the shirtless physiques of those who worked out. *Try not to stare, or someone will see.*

All through those years, the selection process for the two team captains invariably closed with me being chosen near last, as anxiety teed up for the home run of humiliation. Playing shirts versus skins was also an automatic trauma trigger because of my body insecurities and the cruelty that forced me into half-nakedness. The onset of puberty filled me out some, which helped a little. However, I still preferred to keep my shirt on in public, even if it made matters worse.

\* \* \*

In anticipation of puberty, it was a promise that new hair was going to appear in new places, and I wished for a hairy chest so I could feel more manly. I don't recall the dreaded birds and bees talk (except for Mum's casual overview one day, which was awkward). The discovery of masturbation and ejaculation was quite accidental. I soon determined I enjoyed frequent trips to my tingly new wonderland and often found private time in my busy house to explore a stimulating new frontier.

While the initial excitement and ongoing pleasure of getting busy with myself were enough to maintain its own momentum, some same-sex thoughts and memories, such as Danny's kissing lesson and the Bob touch, found their way into those private intimate moments. Tessa's teen magazines were filled with images of cute boys who gripped me as well. Irony abounded as I fantasized about those boys with strength and courage while staring all-too-familiar weakness and fear straight in the eye, even though all of it was only in my mind.

The dreamlike illusion of being naked with another boy who sees and accepts all of me as a boy—in a sexual way—became powerful and alluring. It was a fantasy fuel that didn't burn out. But afterward, double doses of shame had their way as the fear goblin circled again and again for the attack. *What if someone finds out?*

Before puberty, many of my insecurities stemmed from my perception of my body. I still grappled with early self-doubt about my proportions, carrying excess weight around my waist based on poor eating habits and low activity levels. Puberty brought a hormonal growth spurt that helped me slim out. However, acne soon emerged, soliciting unwanted attention to ugly blemishes on my skin mirroring the stigmas and scars of my inner self. The condition added to my negative self-perception with more fear of ridicule and rejection, which had a significant impact on my behavior in the years to come.

The severity of my acne—more so, my reaction to it—prompted my doctor to recommend a new drug called Accutane, which provided some relief along with some risky side effects; the cost to change my feelings couldn't be too high.

Nail biting became an ingrained habit in my life, with occasional vigorous sessions that resulted in bleeding and persistent sores. It wasn't really intentional behavior; rather, a mindless response to pacify my uncontrolled thoughts and feelings. Frequent reminders from my parents were ineffective, and even apprehension toward others noticing my nasty fingertips failed to deter me. My anxious habit carried on for years, finally resolving as my angst lessened.

Amidst various body insecurities—including height issues, at only five feet, eight inches tall—I found comfort in certain aspects of my appearance, especially my thick, dark brown hair. Feathering was a popular style, requiring various products and considerable time with a blow-dryer in front of a mirror. You could count on my hair to look fabulous in a quest to gain approval and acceptance from others.

Despite generous compliments on my appearance, I had difficulties accepting them during my younger years. The inner turmoil and self-rejection rooted in my body issues and masculine insecurity created a chasm between what was real and what I *felt* was real. And at thirteen years old, more than anything, I wanted my peers to see me and be drawn to me. *Tell me I'm like you.*

During Grade 8, I discovered my passion to bring more fun to school came to life within student government initiatives. So, instead of finding and keeping friends (and being known), my focus shifted to becoming a leader. Despite my internal struggles, I had no trouble getting involved in school government, accomplishing much, and telling others what to do.

I still yearned for the camaraderie of male friendship, so for a short time, I made the rash decision to hang out with a bad-ass character named Al. His rebellious streak drew me in, and I found myself more than once helping him disrespect our new teacher, Mr. Sanders. Once, when Mr. Sanders stepped out of the room, Al started chanting his first name followed by sexuality slurs. He nudged me to join in, and I did, swept up in the rush of defiance and the exhilaration of rebelling right there in front of everyone.

We had begun our second round of taunts when the classroom door burst open, revealing an enraged Mr. Sanders.

"Who said that?" he bellowed, his grimaced face hot and red. The room fell dead silent. He again demanded an answer. I glanced at Al, whose eyes warned me with a cold, threatening look. Despite his cautioning, my hand started to rise as my gaze dropped to the floor in guilt.

"Only you?" Mr. Sanders pressed as silence encased everything, including me. Finally, Al owned up, and we both found ourselves facing the music in the hallway. Mr. Sanders launched into a tirade, throwing around words like disrespect and disbelief. It felt surreal, like I was an outsider looking in, witnessing the chewing out. I couldn't believe I had done such a thing, all for Al's approval. Both of us got slapped with two weeks of detention, which, in my opinion, didn't seem too harsh. But making eye contact with Mr. Sanders remained difficult for weeks. *Smell you later, Al.*

The school year climaxed with my graduation from Grade 8, when I received a citizenship award. I was immensely proud of the accolade, viewing it as a solid steppingstone to a new school and chapter. Getting involved in school leadership had shown itself as an unexpected yet effective means of maintaining a safe emotional distance from my peers (and my profound fear of rejection). However, I still longed for approval from my peers. *Why is it so important to me?*

Two other boys also received citizenship awards, bringing us closer together. Doug and Harry were friends and part of the "in group" of guys. Determined to maintain a connection, I made ample effort to spend time with them during the summer break between Grade 8 and 9. Our favorite pursuit was a card game called *Rummoli* for pennies. It didn't bother me that I often lost or thought I saw Harry cheat more than once. He showed up once with a game and told us it enabled communication with the dead. But I suspect Harry again inclined the outcome more than we realized, and I decided it wasn't for me. Nonetheless, their friendship was a healthy boost to my struggling self-esteem, even though it all was a bit of a mystery. *Seriously, making friends is as simple as this?*

However, my exciting three-way friendship came at a price. It soon became obvious the social dynamics were off kilter, with me being the sole initiator of most of our interactions. In time, the deficit further exacerbated my insecurities. By the end of the summer, I was ready to move on, eager to discover the challenges of high school, forge new friendships, and encounter new possibilities. The only hitch was the enormous weight of my unresolved identity issues dragging behind me like a forgotten anchor on a ship with a drunken captain. Arrgh... thar be dragons!

# Tightrope Walking

As I launched on my Grade 9 journey, I went for it. It was my third school, a sprawling secondary school with multiple levels, various wings, and a bustling student population of over fifteen hundred—equal to about one-third of tiny Woodstock's population. A big transition, to say the least! Amidst a sea of unfamiliar faces, I found solace in my innate organizational and promotional abilities which allowed me to engage in student life and channel my insecurities into productive political undertakings.

All students were organized into four "houses" based on our last names. Each house had a male and female leader from each of the four grades, and those leaders represented the interests of their classmates. Within weeks, they honored me with an appointment as a Grade 9 house representative, perhaps influenced by the reputations of both Greg and John. Being in leadership opened the door to help create and organize school activities; I was pre-wired to serve and loved to help make school life more fun.

My moralistic upbringing instilled in me a responsibility to be a help not a hindrance, rather than a mere critic. Because of my dad's guidance, I enjoyed being part of creative solutions and fixing problems, which brought many opportunities and earned me much appreciation in volunteer settings throughout my school years and beyond. Those efforts came easy to me regardless of ongoing internal struggles and concealed social angst. *I'm bringin' the awesome, which makes me awesome, right?*

While my Grade 9 adventure unfolded well, a lingering awareness of detachment from my peers still troubled me. Nonetheless, I had come to terms with the cost of avoiding humiliation and rejection if they found out. The AV and computer clubs provided safe havens where my valued electronics skills and political status elevated me to the highest status possible. It resulted in a unique opportunity for safe connections with my peers without risk.

It was fortuitous that while I was a Grade 9 freshman, Greg was a Grade 12 senior, and even with our limited closeness, he took his freshie brother under his wing. Greg, known by his peers as "Ringo," joined student government, holding the admired position of Social Director. His kind nature led him and his friends to often have lunch with special needs students, fostering an inclusive and heartwarming environment around their table. Early in the school year, Greg invited me to join their table in the spacious cafeteria, and I jumped at the chance. Greg's friends, many of whom were also influential school leaders, offered a sense of belonging and acceptance that had previously eluded me.

Interacting with those special needs students was an enriching experience. Their diverse abilities presented a spectrum of social challenges, yet they all shared a genuine appreciation for our friendship. It was a privilege knowing them, and some left an indelible mark on my heart evoking a lasting warmth whenever I recall those times with my brother.

The daily lunch hour habit with Grade 12 students and the special needs gang became an integral routine in my new school, shielding me from the need to interact with my Grade 9 peers. *Safe again.* A little extra maturity on my part made the arrangement even more suitable, and I reveled in the perceived status that accompanied my association with such a noteworthy group.

The moment Greg invited me to announce their basketball games, I was all in. Public speaking? *Yes, please.* Yet I harkened back to my short-lived stint as an umpire—because, once more, there was zero training, and my grasp on the game was, well, shaky at best.

But the guy in charge of the digital scoreboard was awesome. He made it easier, telling me to simply announce the names of players and the points they scored, letting go of everything else until I became more confident. Sure, there were moments when I wasn't sure who scored what, but I kept at it. Even with a few slip ups, I did pretty well. Watching Greg play was a bonus, making the experience more enjoyable and bringing me closer to him and his circle, all while supporting our school team.

My social safety shield fizzled out as I entered Grade 10 after Greg and all his friends had graduated. *Do I really need to eat lunch?* However, fate had a plan in store. During an extra busy lunch hour in the cafeteria, on impulse, I offered to help at the cash register. It grew into a regular service opportunity, where I was glad to trade about twenty minutes of handling money for a free lunch special.

It was a worthwhile exchange because it was another effective way to avoid being known. By the time my brief shift ended, most students had already finished their meals and were on their way out, leaving me to savor my hot lunch in solitude. Even though it meant I couldn't socialize with the special students, I was safe once more.

It became apparent during Grade 10 that my early commitment to school life and sharing a last name with Ringo had boosted my social capital. As a result, I was elected president of the Pep Club, a position normally held by a Grade 12 senior who would be entrusted with organizing the school's pep rallies. At one memorable rally, we blasted the music theme from "2001: A Space Odyssey" while dramatic lighting heralded our guest speakers from outer space: Canadian astronauts!

Pep Club volunteers also ran the snack bar for home team games, requiring volunteer organization, inventory, and cash management. I also headed the casual Pep Booster Band for away football games. Our "instruments" consisted of kazoos and me on a big bass drum, adding a touch of lighthearted fun for fans and players alike. After all, as Eve Arden said in *Grease*, "If you can't be an athlete, be an athletic supporter!"[1]

The Pep Club also took on the creative task of designing and hand-painting all school event promotion posters using watercolors on huge rolls of brown butcher paper placed throughout the school. We were a small but mighty group of active volunteers making a substantial impact on student life.

It was as if the role had been custom designed for me, and with joy, I embraced every aspect of my Pep Club involvement. Sure, the demands on my time and attention were heavy. But it kept me involved in school activities as a leader, content with my ability to contribute without the burden of excessive social interaction. All the while, affirmation from staff and students who appreciated our hard work was heaped upon me and others in the club. *Good things equal good Todd, got it.*

My do-gooder motivation was tested when I met Trevor, a Campus Life representative. Campus Life was a team of religious people who visited our school and held special events to tell people about God. My brief chat with Trevor helped him understand my motivation to serve others was based on the moral influence of my parents versus any religious beliefs. He offered me more information, but I politely declined, though I appreciated his kindness at the time.

\*\*\*

Right before the midpoint of Grade 10, a new Phys. Ed. teacher arrived at the school, and at first glance, nothing seemed ominous at all. Mr. Kowalski, a man in his mid-thirties, commanded attention with his striking appearance—silver, feathered-back hair, trimmed-neat beard, dark-rimmed glasses perched on his nose. On that fateful first day, he sat us down on the polished gym floor, explained his approach to teaching, and began to outline his expectations of Grade 10 boys. *Uh-oh, this doesn't look good.*

My silent struggle with not feeling equal with all the other boys was about to be magnified. Our previous teacher, consumed by his passion for football coaching, often turned a blind eye to our class. The freedom had allowed me to navigate unscathed through the treacherous waters of high school physical education… until now.

After a quizzical overview of the "exciting" body changes all of us boys were experiencing, he landed on the actual subject of his disdain: body odor. Mr. Kowalski felt such unpleasantry shouldn't be imposed upon our classmates, especially the female kind. So, to minimize such a hazardous occurrence, he issued his bold decree. In that moment, I swear I could smell an intensifying odor from everyone's body, mostly mine.

"From now on, everyone will take a shower after class," Mr. Kowalski announced.

Ten simple words echoed through the cavernous gym with authority and conviction, then struck me like a thunderbolt. My heart plummeted into an arctic void. *A shower, as in naked? In front of all the other boys? Oh, not safe.*

You see, up until that calamitous moment in my young and fearful life, I had avoided showering with other boys at school or anywhere. Anxieties tossed my mind around their circle like a poisoned hot potato, and they were legion.

> *What if they mock me like when I was young?*
>
> *Will someone notice my curiosity?*
>
> *What if I like what I see?*

*If I get excited, will someone notice?*

In that moment, every fiber of my being screamed with a single, horrifying certainty: I was on a collision course to repeat the humiliating calamity of shop class, but this time exposed in the very fullness of the word. Shame, shunning, and a shitstorm of problems would end my civil service career, forcing feared detachment and isolation to front and center. But until then, everything had been going so well and was under my control. So, frankly, opening myself up to that kind of shattering risk was inconceivable.

Returning to reality on the icy cold gymnasium floor, Mr. Kowalski loomed over us, my heart double-stepping toward panic. Could I devise a strategy to evade the dreaded group shower scene and preserve a crafted facade of innocence? In an instant, I resolved that whatever it took, the shower situation was not going to happen. *Not ever.*

However, the cunning and crafty Mr. Kowalski tested my resolve. I couldn't have imagined how attentive he'd be in carrying out his mission—or that such a thing could ever become someone's mission. When the class ended, he transformed into a hypervigilant sentinel, overseeing the locker room to ensure every boy complied with his overreaching mandate. It was a scene that defied belief, bordering on sadistic and surreal. After class, Mr. Kowalski observed several boys were unclear—or uncomfortable—about the new policy and announced it would take full effect next class. *So, now what?*

The brief grace period allowed me to concoct some survival schemes before returning to the steamy gallows. By the next class, I was equipped to employ mission-impossible avoidance tactics with careful precision and heroic creativity. As the class ended, I darted into the changeroom before the others and peeled down to my underwear, a comfortable enough posture for me, thanks to a thin concealing layer of cotton. Towel over my shoulder, I proceeded to the bathroom stalls adjacent to the showers.

Once inside the stall, I pretended to have a bathroom break while sitting on the toilet for a few minutes, my heart racing. After a conclusive flush, I emerged from the stall with contrived casualness, dabbing myself with the towel as a prop. Gaze fixed straight ahead, I coolly strolled past the showers and returned to the bench in front of my locker. By then, most other boys had their showers and had also returned. *I think it's working!*

Class by class, new maneuvers made their debut. I sometimes rubbed my towel over my body to simulate drying off. Occasionally, I needed to dry my hair after an emergency credibility countermeasure forced me to wet my head at the bathroom sink before appearing back in front of my locker.

One unfortunate time, as I was executing my plan as usual, I spotted a critical oversight while in the stall—I'd forgotten to remove my socks. The perilous error prompted me to conceal the socks in my towel until I could create the impression of retrieving them from my locker. *How could you miss those?*

Week after week, the inventive and tenacious strategies seemed to be successful in that not once was I forced to expose myself in any way while concealing non-compliance with Mr. Kowalski's edict. At least, that's how it seemed to me. In retrospect, it's doubtful I was misleading everyone or even anyone. No one ever uttered a word about it to me, fostering the fantasy I was pulling off my desperate no-shower charade.

As the school year progressed, maintaining the mirage required constant originality and fresh ideas. Thus, on occasion, I would succumb to a mysterious malaise right around the same time as gym class. But I still adhered to school policies, securing my release from class with proper authorization and combatting new pressures to maintain believability.

Several more occasions involved claims that—while Mr. Kowalski was barking orders in the showers—I coincidentally had *very* important school government business to address. *No, it can't wait.*

Judy, the affable attendance secretary, became my unwavering ally, not questioning myriad excuses I concocted to evade countless "Phys. Dread" classes. *Safe again.* I remain utterly perplexed by how I achieved a passing grade in Mr. Kowolski's physical—and hygienic—education class. Perhaps he gave extra marks for effective strategizing.

As the school year ended, I had come face to face with naked boys exactly zero times. Regrettably, there was no achievement award or certificate for my incredible feat. Nevertheless, I had accomplished my protective ambition: shielding myself from confronting my burgeoning curiosity and attraction toward other boys and all the anticipated pain and suffering. It felt as though I had forever eluded the daunting dragon. *Am I actually safe again?*

\* \* \*

Amid my internal struggles, concealed vulnerabilities, covert manipulations, and absence of genuine peer connections, I harbored a grander, long standing, and lofty political aspiration: to become school president in Grade 12. However, the role was shared between a male and a female student. To be clear, I was gunning for the male office; I was not wrestling with any desire to be a girl. Almost every action I took—or refrained from—was orchestrated to achieve one enduring political goal.

As Grade 11 began, they appointed me as an assistant leader for my house. Instead of resuming my Pep Club presidency, I rested on my laurels, choosing to allocate more time for political posturing and campaigning for the big prize. I did manage to squeeze in tennis and guitar lessons by then, and I preferred making music over serving aces, though it would be some time before I took music seriously.

Tennis was okay, but by happenstance, I discovered an unexpected athletic alternative to avoid trauma in the changeroom: Intramural curling. It was a little like the computer club but in a larger, even colder room, with brooms, big round rocks, and occasional outbursts of "Sweeeeeeeeep!" *Now, here's a sport I can handle.*

Needless to say, my extensive extracurricular activities relegated my academic pursuits to the lowest rung on my priority ladder. After achieving the Principal's Honor Roll in Grade 9 (reflecting an overall average of 90-100%), my good grades sacrificed themselves for what my yearning heart deemed much more significant: total peer acceptance through the highest level of leadership. At least my governance endeavors *felt* like acceptance from the throngs of other teenage boys who saw me everywhere doing everything at school, even though they didn't *know* me.

But none of it mattered. I was on the cusp of becoming *their* leader—all of them. From my exalted position as the highest-ranked student official, I would compel them to like and accept me, and they would do as I say. *Won't they?*

Not so fast.

## Your Opinion Matters

Please consider the gift of **an honest rating** of this book (1 to 5 stars) that you can submit quickly and anonymously. ALL RATINGS are welcome and needed to help keep this book in front of those who may be encouraged by this story.

Please visit this website to **give your star rating**:

rating.nlatob.com

Also, below are some simple suggestions for your **optional review**:

*"It's a good book!"*

*"I couldn't put it down... so honest and insightful. Oh, and Todd's humor cracks me up."*

*"I was uncomfortable reading this book."*

*"I don't recommend this book for anyone looking for a light summer read."*

*"I'm glad I read this book."*

## THANK YOU FOR YOUR FEEDBACK!

rating.nlatob.com

# The Great Escape

Early in Grade 11, my parents dropped a bombshell that detonated in my crafted realm like an atomic blast. Tessa and I learned a promotion for Dad meant we were moving—again—to somewhere exotic: Madison, Wisconsin. The shocking news struck me with an intensity that left me reeling. *This can't be happening.*

The revelation was nothing short of devastating. Not only did it annihilate my political plan, but it also threatened the fragile peace I had manufactured with diligence by suppressing and concealing my same-sex curiosities and attractions.

John and Greg had graduated and would remain in Saskatoon and their independent lives. The monstrous life detour would involve just the four of us, and Tessa and I were destined to attend our fourth school at the beginning of the second semester, like before.

Perhaps I deceived myself, thinking I had been successful in concealing my insecurity and anxieties from the prying eyes of unsafe outsiders—which was everyone. I kept my struggles locked away, never daring to confide in anyone. In retrospect, however, I cannot fathom how my lack of pursuits—not even a single date—from the time Laura and I parted ways in Grade 5 until halfway through Grade 11 could have gone unnoticed.

As the after-effects of the harsh news diminished, a glimmer of enthusiasm began to emerge with the expectation of a new chapter in an American high school. My theatrical mind envisioned every bustling corridor festooned with vibrant school colors and booster posters. After all, it was America who put the "pep" in a club in the first place, wasn't it? *Oh, I can see it now!*

Fade in on a spacious, modern cafeteria transforming into a full-scale musical set where everyone burst into song with fancy choreography under colorful stage lighting. *That almost never happens in Canada.* So yes, the allure of moving to the U.S.A. held some intrigue. After all, we could be moving somewhere way worse—like northern Manitoba. *Or northern anywhere.*

And so, another giant moving truck was filled again with everything we know and love, except, of course, my abandoned political ambitions and things that belonged to my brothers. The movers drove on ahead of us while the four of us took to the skies, bound for the Badger State, ready as we could be to embrace another new chapter together.

\* \* \*

After settling into our spacious and comfortable American house, Tess and I had little time to relax before diving headfirst into school life. She rarely had any trouble making fast friends, and her attractiveness also ensured a line of suitors. My priorities, on the other hand, lay elsewhere.

Without delay, I learned the student leadership structure stood in stark contrast to what I had known in Canada. There, candidates for various offices seemed predetermined, meaning no open elections. *How is it even possible?* Perhaps we had taken a wrong turn and landed in the Soviet Union. But even more problematic for a determined representative such as myself was the harsh reality that no one had the slightest clue who I was. Who would even be so brazen as to try such a thing? Well, perhaps me, but it was impossible.

Even though the American experience held some anticipation, my initial concerns reigned. Without any involvement in school leadership, I sank into a pit of melancholy. Once again, I felt isolated still encumbered by my insecurities and unsettled same-sex attractions.

In a harsh twist of destiny, school athletics were an even bigger deal there boasting multiple track fields, a stadium-like football field, and an indoor pool. Regular physical education was mandatory for all students throughout their entire four-year tenure. *Yes, this must be the USSR.* I thought I might collapse under the pressure, confronting my body insecurities and the horror of humiliation in a hyper-athletic environment where nothing could remain hidden.

Amidst quiet, daunting despair, there were a few flickers of light. I forged early connections with Rob and Jason, neighbors up on the hill near our home. We were fortunate enough to ride the bus to school, and those friendly fellows soon invited me to join them at the back. No canoodling classes on that bus, but as a foreigner in more ways than one, their acceptance meant the world to me. Later, I discovered they granted only seniors and honored students the right to occupy those rear seats—it was an unspoken code, and I was grateful to have somehow cracked it. *At least they think I'm normal.*

In a well-timed gift of generosity and love, Mum and Dad treated Tessa and me to a spring break vacation to Grand Cayman Island. Aside from an unforgettable family trip to California during the tenth grade, the opportunity for non-relocating travel was rare, making it a truly special event.

On the island, Tessa soon captivated the attention of various beach boys near our hotel with her natural beauty. I also found some of those boys quite alluring and intriguing. It occurred to me a remote tropical paradise presented a unique opportunity to attract some special attention of my own, hidden away from the prying eyes of familiarity. *No one will ever know.*

One late afternoon as others delighted in various activities, I was curious to see if I could be noticed, so I positioned myself near the pool. Despite the high humidity, my hair maintained most of its splendor as I attempted a sultry come-hither expression to passersby, open to any reciprocation from a suitable admirer. Alas, all of them appeared to be otherwise focused, perhaps on their way to charm Tessa down in the sand. My short-lived experiment yielded nothing but an intensifying sense of inadequacy. Nevertheless, the holiday fulfilled its purpose, providing restful time and cherished family memories despite my failed hush-hush mission.

Back on the mainland, reality crashed back in on me at school, and I realized it would be smart to try and fit in as best I could. The much-anticipated junior prom drew near, and I somehow charmed a young lady to be my date. Rose was a pretty girl with long brown hair, a graceful figure, and a kind, principled nature. She reminded me of my Grade 5 sweetheart Tina, so I liked her right away. I hadn't even heard of a prom, so it would be a foreign experience times two for this backwoods Canuck.

Taking Rose to the prom involved the family station wagon, renting a white and black tuxedo and getting a corsage to match her peach dress. Our prom's anthem? "Almost Paradise" from the movie *Footloose*. I wouldn't call the evening a fairy tale, but it was fun dancing with Rose and learning how an American prom worked.

We ventured out a few more times, even tagging along on a double date with my parents to a nearby tourist attraction. But when the moment came for my first romantic kiss, it was a complete flop. You'd think Danny's crash course in the back of the bus years earlier could've helped seal the deal. But perhaps the troubled years since and my increasing attraction to boys got the best of me. Rose didn't hide her disappointment.

"You kiss like a fish," she declared, and all I could do was try to shrug it off with a laugh. *I'm doomed.* Recounting the evening later with Mum, she got a bit riled up, expressing anger toward Rose and a thoughtless comment made to her sensitive son. We talked it through, and after she calmed down, she tried to spin it light-heartedly.

"Well, don't worry, there's plenty more fish in the sea!" she jested, getting a kick out of the irony. "Oh honey, you'll find the right one when you're ready." *One what, exactly?*

\* \* \*

I made out fairly well during my Phys. Ed. classes in this foreign land, blending in with my peers due to the large class sizes. I was also relieved by the noticeable absence of a misguided, militant teacher hell-bent on forcing all the boys to shower together. Another difference was structuring classes into units of similar activity lasting several weeks versus more variety week by week. But catastrophe struck near the end of the basketball unit when our teacher announced the upcoming concentration: Swimming.

A sonic *kaboom* struck my mind with an aftershock of awareness that slapped my senses. Several weeks of swimsuits meant it would be near impossible to avoid seeing or being seen in front of all the other boys. My brain clicked and kicked into warp drive, rerouting all available power to devise a rescue plan. *Perhaps I could wear my swimsuit under my regular clothes, go swimming, then simply put my clothes back on. Nope, pretty stupid.*

I wish I could say clever tactical and evasive maneuvers presented themselves as they had before. But with only two weeks to implement a scheme to conceal my highly classified material, stress and anxiety compounded. The thought of materializing stark-naked in the boys locker room remained unimaginable. There, light years away from the original battlefield, yet another titanic threat surfaced to attack my shielded dread. It panicked me to think I would soon be forced into the full frontal facing of my overwhelming anxiety of being laughed at and rejected. *I'd rather be vaporized.* And yet, the seed of a getaway plan began to germinate that very moment.

Day after day, the threat and fear of humiliation lurked as a grisly goblin under a tumbledown bed. My same-sex attractions loomed, as did the terrifying possibility of an identity as a gay teenager. The undeniable result of which was the very shame, ridicule, and ostracism sworn by my troll of terror all those years. It was a prison of my own making, and I was the jailkeeper. *Does anybody even have a clue?*

Being gay clashed with my family's traditional and conservative morals. It was unfathomable to imagine one day bringing a boyfriend home for a family Christmas, anticipating the hurtful comments and judgment I had witnessed all throughout my childhood, or worse. Beyond my family's reaction, I still held a strong desire for a wife and children. I ached for my own family life to mirror my childhood, except for all the ways I would do it better, of course.

As I've said, I felt enormously loved by my parents and my siblings, a core gift to boost my faux confidence in the midst of my identity struggles. *At least I know I belong to them.* Perhaps something within my depths was afraid the anchoring gift of parental love could be taken back if I traveled down that road. Any risk of losing their acceptance felt like death.

In high school, I didn't want to be any *more* different than I already believed I was. I craved acceptance, not rejection. Discovering or confirming my deepest dread became the terror I would do nearly anything to prevent. As a result, I was a young man on what truly felt like a life-or-death mission to save himself.

My gracious English Literature teacher, Mrs. Alrep, was a kind and supportive woman. She once told my parents I could do whatever I wanted with my life. One class assignment was to write a personal poem. I didn't consider myself a beatnik nor a bard, so it was daunting. However, I followed Mrs. Alrep's instructions to delve down into my feelings, and write in truth exploring the full depths of my sixteen-year-old self. The result was a creative expression of my impasse, illuminating open-heart rawness and unrepentant honesty for the very first time.

**Depression**
Everything is wrong.
Things not right,
All is confusing.
Don't know which way to go,
Feeling aging chicken egg rotten.
Thinking too much,
Everything looks bad.
People can't understand,
But try and tell them.
How?
Should make the decision.
Afraid it won't be right.
How to escape dreaded depression?
Feel like a fly, crazily buzzing its wings,
Trying to get past the window.
Make the decision.
Nothing is left confusing.
Escape the giant sheet of glass at last.
Who knows if right decision?
Who would know if it were wrong?
Only me.

Instead of handing it in, I decided to take it home with me and tuck it away for safekeeping—*not quite ready to share this with anyone.*

On the exterior, I appeared to be a well-adjusted sixteen-year-old adept at navigating normal to medium difficulties in life. However, beneath the facade, I was facing a personal crisis of epic proportions. I'd resolved I wasn't okay with being gay; in fact, I was dreadfully fearful of it. And I would do everything to avoid coming to that conclusion. And I mean everything.

* * *

It was a challenging conversation at home with my parents on that momentous April evening. However, I had already decided what needed to transpire, so the discussion felt more like a courtesy than anything else. Even so, I knew my conclusion would cause them great distress with far-reaching consequences. Instead of blurting it out, I presented my case with logic so perhaps they might also reach the same difficult decision. *Keep going. They're buying it.*

"So, the primary reason everyone attends school is to get a good job and end up in a successful career, right?" I initiated, observing a muddle of concern and confusion on Mum and Dad's faces. "Therefore, if the objective is achieved sooner, then there's no need to continue in school," I concluded, settling the argument before it began.

"What are you saying, Todd?" asked Dad as he hunted through my unexpected words for a trophy of understanding.

"I've been in touch with my old bosses at the computer store, and they've offered me a full-time job. I want to quit school and accept the position," I declared with conviction and sincerity.

Their faces delivered prompt disbelief, which was understandable. My loving parents were downright unaware of the depths of my struggles at school and my desperate search for alternatives. They didn't know I was driven by an overwhelming desire to escape the trap that threatened to expose (and confirm) veiled attractions pointing to a gay identity. They attempted to seek clarification, but I deflected each point and returned to my foundational and irrefutable argument about the primary goal of one's education.

Forcing my parents into such a difficult situation strained our relationship. Compounding the complexities was the unsettling prospect of their youngest son dropping out of high school to leave home and return to Saskatoon, about twelve hundred miles north. Furthermore, this audacious proposal originated from the same son who most often toed the line, displaying "superior intelligence" and bright career potential over the years. *So it's true, I will be the disappointing child, but it's not going to stop me.*

My unwavering determination to execute an overconfident exit was so intense I hadn't even paused to consider the possibility they might not allow it. They later described their emotional turmoil as unparalleled as they pondered their options.

In the end, Mum and Dad permitted me to drop out because they had witnessed my resolve when I set my mind on something all through my childhood. And I shudder to contemplate the consequences had they denied my escape—and avoiding or achieving everything connected to it. I'm convinced I would have given in to substance abuse and addiction, or worse, given the profound depths of my anguish.

The great escape from all the tumultuousness and stress by quitting school would finally allow me to vanquish years of fear-induced anxiety stemming from not aligning with societal norms of masculinity. Fear of humiliation. Fear of rejection. Fear of isolation. Fear of being gay. Fear of a life plagued by fear. With a single decision, all were obliterated.

It's an understatement of biblical proportions to say I was euphoric and impatient to begin my journey to freedom. Therefore, I wasted no time preparing for this sensational new quest into assured tranquility and joy.

# Salesman and Soulmate

Before our family moved to Wisconsin, I had chanced upon an innovative downtown computer store. Globally, the personal computer's arrival triggered a stampede of renowned manufacturers vying for market share. Apple Computer unveiled the Apple II in the late seventies, targeting the education sector. The early eighties witnessed entries from Radio Shack/Tandy, Commodore, Texas Instruments, Atari, and even Timex joined the frenzy. It was the golden era for computer retailers.

The shop boasted a modest showroom displaying various demo models to aid customers in selecting their ideal models and accessories. They were not an authorized Apple dealer due to the proximity of another dealer and disdain for Apple's exorbitant pricing. Despite high sticker prices, Apple's popularity soared.

In response, the owners decided to import dubious Apple-compatible computers from Taiwan, retailing them at about half the cost of a genuine model. They stocked other brands and models but championed those Apple compatibles, which ran the same software and yielded a lucrative profit due to offshore manufacturing savings.

My first stint working at the computer store came after my work as a janitor, dishwasher, and busboy—none of which qualified me for computer sales. However, the store co-owners took a quick shine to me, and I began part-time while still in high school.

The rare opportunity aligned with my contentment to serve the public in an established role, and I was delighted to be paid for "playing" with computers and selling them while still in high school. When news had surfaced of my impending move to the States, having that job only intensified my bitterness. Fortunately, I departed amicably.

* * *

Two weeks after permission from my parents to quit school, I left them and Tessa behind in Wisconsin as I descended upon Saskatoon, where my brother John had offered me the couch in his apartment. Meanwhile, Greg was busy preparing for his upcoming nuptials, establishing a new home with his high school sweetheart.

After about a month of cohabitating with John, he nudged me to start building my own life and suggested I find my own place. Initially, his suggestion was difficult to hear but as I envisioned newfound freedom and opportunities, it began to make perfect sense. It didn't take long at all to find the perfect place.

My new abode was a cozy apartment building comprising three floors and eighteen units in the heart of downtown Saskatoon. Ever the resourceful entrepreneur, I soon negotiated with the property manager to entrust me with the keys to the recreation area. In exchange for opening and securing the exercise area on weekends, I received a reduction in my already affordable rent, bringing it down to less than a third of my modest salary.

The privilege also gave me anytime access to the hot tub, which I often enjoyed on my own with showtunes cranked on my boombox. To this day, I remain perplexed about the legality of such arrangements with a sixteen-year-old. Perhaps my newfound boldness overcame them as I was finally thriving in freedom from the shackles of school-related anxieties!

The store owners were true to their word and welcomed me back as a full-time employee. Within weeks, they appointed me manager with the responsibility of opening and closing the shop. I loved the privilege of coming and going as I pleased after store hours. It was a pretty sweet setup, made even more delightful given that my one-bedroom apartment was located only a stone's throw away. *Was this really happening?*

As tangible symbols of my newfound independence, I abandoned the mundane day-to-day tasks of making my bed and brushing my teeth. A handy doughnut shop sandwiched between home and work enticed me into a new breakfast habit of a quadruple-sweetened coffee with a delectable dutchie. I counted the sugar-covered raisins embedded in the deep-fried dough as credit toward my recommended daily intake of fruits and vegetables. Chewing gum became my indispensable ally, aiding my image of a smooth-talking salesman brimming with enthusiasm... and plaque.

One sunny day off found me appreciating the beauty of Saskatoon's riverfront park near the grand historic hotel. After a lot of walking, I settled on a stone bench, absorbing the sights and sounds. An older man, emerging from the path in front of the bench, sat down to my left. He was friendly, and we engaged in light conversation without much effort. I was clad in light-brown corduroys, and as usual, my hair looked great.

However, I was utterly unprepared for what happened next. Without forewarning, the man's right hand rested on my left thigh. In an instant, my body and words froze in disbelief. My gaze remained fixed straight ahead. *Nope, not for me.* Rising to my feet, his hand slid off me as I turned away to hasten my departure while muttering some sort of reason to leave. I was left quite shaken by the encounter.

> *Was I that obvious?*
>
> *How could a stranger think I was attracted to men?*
>
> *Was it something I said or how I said it?*

The unsettling incident shattered my no-school freedom fantasy. It turned out I wasn't free at all. *Maybe it's got nothing to do with all the other boys.*

\*\*\*

After a few months at the store, I met Dale, a nice guy only a year younger than me, at fifteen. Good looks, thick blond hair, a winsome smile, and a great sense of humor—I found him attractive from day one. Dale brightened my day whenever he popped in on his way to or from school and almost every Saturday. A fellow computer nerd, he took full advantage of our store demos as I tried to serve actual customers.

We both enjoyed the perks of my job, and we spent more and more time together. After hours, we played video games and computer games and often enjoyed the store's VCR and comfy loveseat to watch rented movies together. In short order, Dale became the friend I had dreamed about, and I couldn't have been happier.

Still living at home with his single mom, Dale's fuzzy lip and body odor signaled puberty ringing the bell at his door, yet unanswered. Helping him learn how to shave and sort out deodorant and other rites of passage was rewarding, making me feel even closer to him. His mom said she appreciated my positive influence on his life.

Soon, almost all my free time was spent with Dale. I loved being with him, sitting beside him, and making him laugh. I often tried to take him down in video games or occasional mock wrestling bouts. My feelings and attractions intensified, unearthing a romantic sexualized energy whenever I was with him. But I discovered that finding freedom from all I'd fled had been a phony fantasy. Many of the old, fear-based emotions and concerns returned and became stronger than ever before.

There is no way to overstate the importance of Dale's friendship in that season of life. He embodied the male peer acceptance I had yearned for the past five years. However, having fun together and sharing similar interests soon merged with the undercurrent of my romantic attraction to him. It became an irresistible combination that engulfed me, insisting on its self-protection. Consequently, risking our thrilling companionship with any rejectable words or actions was unthinkable. *So, the ball's in his court.*

The evolving nature of my true and growing feelings for Dale remained submerged. It rendered me alone with my racing thoughts and raging hormones as I once again became intimate with my fear goblin, not Dale. *No one can ever know.*

Greg's wedding was that summer at a local hotel, and my new young friend Dale was my plus-one. An open bar and a cooperative bartender meant we minors had no trouble getting way too much booze. I ended up nursing a puking Dale in the public restroom.

In my vulnerable state, I couldn't help wanting to feel even closer to him. So, I talked him into taking his shirt off so he wouldn't puke on it as we sat on the floor in one of the stalls. An intoxicated version of Dale was much more intimate with the toilet than he was with me, much to my chagrin. The same goes for us sharing one of the beds in John's room that night: nothing happened except for the familiar round of my mental what-ifs. *What if he made a move?*

Having my family all together at the wedding was a real joy with my parents and sister making the journey after I had left them about three months earlier. Mum and I managed to catch some quality time together. She was keen to check in on how I was adjusting to my new life. I spent most of the conversation highlighting all the positives about being back in Saskatoon like my fantastic job and meeting my new friend Dale. She might not have been sold on my assurances, but I can't blame her for worrying about her youngest son—the high school dropout.

I later learned Dad and my brothers had their own chat over drinks at a pub where my sexuality was a topic. Dad was cautious, stressing the importance of not jumping to conclusions and advising my brothers to tread lightly on the topic. It seems probable they had similar talks over the years, but no one ever approached me about any of it. In a way, the void might have been a blessing giving me the space and time to sort myself out.

\* \* \*

One holiday weekend, I conceived the idea of borrowing the car from Dale's mom for a spontaneous road trip to Regina about three hours away. Even though we didn't know a soul there, I proposed we stay overnight instead of coming back home the same day. However, securing a hotel room without a credit card—and posing as adults—seemed like a formidable challenge. Consequently, I needed a simple alternative.

My long-standing intrigue with sleepovers bordered on compulsive. I wonder how many friends over the years were concerned with my incessant refrain, "Hey, how about a sleepover?" To my delight, Dale agreed, and after dinner, we found a remote street where we parked and settled in for the night in our reclined bucket seats.

The morning summer sun was baking our black car as we awoke, not well-rested. Once again, the hope of something a little more physical had dried up like my throat. After an early breakfast, we returned to Saskatoon where everything was as it was before we left. *Perhaps a bench seat could've made a difference.*

On another Sunday, Dale and I made our way down to the river to explore in the warm sun. It was a welcome change of scenery, and we had fun together with lots of laughs. After a while, we perched ourselves side by side on a pebbly sandbar as the cool, clear waters of the South Saskatchewan River rushed by. To be more comfortable, I suggested we sit back-to-back for better support, and he agreed. Our shared posture engendered a welcome sense of closeness to Dale; I could have relaxed in the moment for ages.

Perhaps the opportune moment had arrived to broach the risky subject burdening my heart and mind. My pulse accelerated as I steered our conversation toward touchy-feely issues. I still harbored a hint of optimism Dale felt something for me, and yet, I found myself impeded by the steadfast fear of rejection. Our dialogue was stilted for sure, and to my dismay, it wasn't going where my heart wanted. In a moment of resignation, I expressed my frustration.

"I just wish, uh, I was…" I stammered, unsure of my heading.

"A girl?" he interjected, his voice tinged with melancholy. "Yeah, too bad you're not."

His candid words stuck me with surprise before hanging in the summer air like a lone kite on a gentle breeze of sincerity. There was no need to add any punctuation. He had expressed definitive feelings matching some of my own, but my hopes were thwarted by a convincing disclosure of his sexual preference. The immediate result was sorrow mixed with incongruous relief; The Question had finally been answered without actually asking. *Well, shit.*

In truth, Dale had concluded my sentence with a notion that had never crossed my mind until that precise moment. An intriguing idea, considering how dynamics could change between us if I were a girl. But my struggles weren't so much about not wanting to *be* a boy —I simply wasn't very good at it.

It was undeniable Dale and I shared profound affection and care for each other. However, it was also clear his orientation barred any possibility of a romantic sexual relationship between us. It was a resounding signal to slam the forbidden door and embrace the reality we were destined to remain close, but platonic, friends.

Dale arose from the beach, and we brushed ourselves off, acknowledging in silence the weight of all that remained unsaid. Nothing of the like was uttered again—until about eight years later when we rekindled our connection.

*  *  *

That autumn, Dale and I saw a hit movie called *Risky Business*. I was captivated by Joel Goodsen's entrepreneurial spirit, which was well-portrayed by Tom Cruise. Joel's creative endeavor to raise the money needed to repair his father's expensive car after it took an unexpected plunge in Lake Michigan was noteworthy.

One specific thing from the film struck a profound chord within me, resonating long after the credits rolled. If you're familiar with the movie, you might be surprised by the scene that altered the trajectory of my life.

Joel had an obvious special connection with two of his school friends. Beholding their natural camaraderie, which seemed effortless and secure without any hint of hidden attractions, stirred something within my depths. I recognized I hadn't experienced such genuine friendships during my high school years. Our frequent family moves along with my issues conspired to prevent me from forming true and lasting connections. The awareness struck me with the force of revelation, and I knew I had to make drastic changes to seize an authentic friendship experience before it was too late. My heart ached for such an innocent friendship.

Driven by a newfound determination, I reached out to my parents in Wisconsin. I shared my thoughts about returning to school, a decision helped by the news that Dad was considering a job relocation to Denver, Colorado. The potential move presented another opportunity for a fresh start, another new school with favorable conditions that might finally banish my masculine insecurities into exile forever. I held onto the chance that a more grounded and sensible Denver school would be a stark contrast to the hyper-athletic Wisconsin school, allowing me once again to mask my fears of being humiliated and rejected by my peers.

I contacted Gloria, my guidance counselor in Wisconsin, to explain my sudden change of heart without exposing too many details. Her response was overwhelming and positive assuring me she would handle everything for my return. Until the move to Denver came about, I would be placed in classes with my former classmates who all had advanced to the next grade in my absence.

Perhaps the unresolvable tension and bleak outlook with Dale contributed to what might have appeared to be an impulsive and reckless decision to quit my good job and leave him behind, along with my brothers, and my hometown. It was sudden news for John and Greg but they couldn't deny my returning home—and resuming high school—was more important.

Dale was surprised and seemed to understand my motivation though a part of me hoped he would stand in firm opposition and finally declare his shrouded desire for me. Perhaps our talk by the river helped him recognize the unique dynamics in our friendship that might be better left alone. While mutual sadness lingered, a more potent force compelled me forward: the appeal of a new plot to get true guy friends and connections without deterrents.

With a sense of finality, I gave my notice and vacated my apartment. Laden with all my worldly possessions, I returned to my eager family in Wisconsin before we would all set off for Denver. Accompanying me on my flight south was a renewed sense of optimism, believing I could forge healthy male friendships untainted by my masculine insecurity, awkward male attractions, or nomadic lifestyle. *This time, it's going to be different!*

# Coming Home to Change

While the proposed move to Denver held significance in my decision to return home, it didn't materialize because of a change in plans for Dad's employer. Instead, I would stay at the same Wisconsin high school. Given the time lapse since my departure, it was effectively a new academic year at my fifth school.

Thanks to the diligent efforts of my counselor, I was granted privileges allowing me to advance to twelfth grade Phys. Ed. Unlike previous years, the fourth year was similar to an elective class, devoid of structure or mandatory units. The shift enabled me to meet graduation requirements and avoid swimming classes or any other athletic activities that could spar with my masculine insecurities.

One positive aspect of being barred from American school government was the noticeable improvement in my grades. I once again found joy in academic challenges, after the razzle-dazzle of public life had diverted my attention. Coupled with a less consuming fear of rejection, I held greater openness to the characteristic risks of forming friendships.

One such new friend was Jerry, a tall, amiable fellow with a radiant smile and curly dark blond hair. Jerry was a senior, and in a twist of irony, we became acquainted through our shared Phys. Ed. class. Once again, I found myself drawn to my new, attractive friend. He worked out, was more muscular than me and exuded an air of masculine confidence. *But dammit, this time, it's going to be different.*

As with my feelings for Dale, I valued the acceptance I experienced between Jerry and me. But something else was needed to achieve the aspiration of a true friendship without the cloudiness of attractions and desires. I'm unsure if it was my new resolve or the recurring fear of rejection that helped me hold the line, but it was also helpful that he unlikely felt anything similar.

One weekend, Jerry and I headed to the drive-in theater. Before you run anywhere with that, let me assure you it was an activity many other classmates also enjoyed as friends. Jerry indulged in Old Milwaukee beer while I opted for Pepsi. Beer tasted nasty to me, and I wouldn't have anything to do with it or any recreational drugs. If Jerry had encouraged me to join him, I may have succumbed (and who knows what regretful consequences my liquid courage may have prompted). Fortunately, he found my Pepsi-drinking amusing. Jerry's easygoing nature provided a treasured source of comfort and support, and he indeed became a true friend when I needed it most.

In all seriousness, had anyone introduced me to illicit drugs during that period, I am sure the escapism and relief would have wooed me like a bewitching temptress. I am so grateful it didn't happen; perhaps someone was watching over me.

Despite the pleasure of reuniting with my parents and sister in Wisconsin and the improved situation at school, a sense of unease lingered. My astute parents noticed my unusual, depressed mood. Much to their credit, they wanted to figure out what was behind my unusual behavior.

I'd protected my secrets all along, never uttering a single word about my same-sex struggles to another person. Many others may claim they "knew it all along" based on their observations of my behavior, such as an abnormal dating life, lack of interest in sports, and great hair. However, as far as I was concerned, finding other teenage boys attractive had remained my heavily fortified private battle.

Imagine my astonishment when my parents suggested I call Dale. They didn't elaborate or insist on "a talk" or anything of the sort. It felt like a loving and compassionate invitation to reach out to connect again with my special Saskatoon friend. *Maybe I miss him more than I know.*

At first, our phone call started a little awkward, but hearing his voice—and his laughter—affected me like a healing balm for my soul. Mum and Dad's thoughtful act of kindness touched my heart as a potent reminder of their unwavering love for me. The heartwarming chat with Dale ended with an agreement to do it again.

My continuous focus on ignoring my struggles and escaping dread resulted in blissful unawareness of the costs involved. The absence of emotional processing was a tall price to pay, more so during such a heightened period of internal and external change. Not talking with anyone about my struggles prevented much, including objective understanding that may have helped prevent or ease some of the heartache and suffering.

In retrospect, I believe I fell in love with Dale during our short season together. While he held obvious physical attractiveness, our emotional connection never resulted in physical intimacy for reasons I've shared. Nevertheless, my vulnerable heart was moved by his interest and desire to spend time together. While it frustrated me that we couldn't be more intimate, my feelings for him still intensified during those months. It wasn't until my move separated us for several weeks when the depth of my emotions surfaced.

Dale and I maintained contact, but that was long before the advent of email. Letter writing didn't happen between teenage boys. Occasional phone calls became more infrequent, yielding to the absence in each other's lives. Nonetheless, my feelings for Dale persisted, retreating into a lower, more concealed recess of my heart made easier by the distance between us. *Maybe one day, or maybe not.*

\* \* \*

To keep it interesting, my acne erupted on occasion—quite unhelpful for someone already self-conscious about appearances and fearful of humiliation. One morning before school, a significant facial blemish taunted me in the mirror. Inspired by the makeup Tessa used to enhance her natural beauty, I hatched a harebrained scheme to use her concealer to camouflage my zits. Tessa found it odd and funny agreeing to be my accomplice. After the makeover, we examined the results and determined it might work if I didn't get too close to anyone. *Oh, not a problem!*

The school cafeteria prices were reasonable and their menu was diverse, so I ate there often. My unique status as a trans-junior Canadian refugee had granted me a few acquaintances other than Jerry and we all often shared a lunch table.

Across from me sat Lance. As we chatted and savored lunch together, I noticed Lance studying my face more closely than usual.

"Hey, are you wearing makeup?" he blurted, loud enough for all the other boys to hear. *I'm going to throw up.*

Like a ripe zit popping, his query instantly transported me back to the worktable in my Saskatoon shop class. However, unlike Arnold's avarice-laced bellow, Lance's words held more innocence and curiosity. Yet the impact was similar and startling.

My chest rose and fell with rapid breaths. Every boy's head seemed to swivel toward me as I snapped back to present reality. Their gazes were a composition of curiosity and speculation, perhaps wondering if Canadian boys indulged in such ladylike practices.

Again, like in the shop class, an urgent and illuminating response was imperative to dispel any notions and convince my classmates of my 100 percent boyness and disinterest in anything resembling feminine behavior. My heart raced; time slowed. They awaited my response.

"No, as if!" fell out of my mouth as I snatched up my tray, discreetly retreating to the most remote restroom available to cleanse my hot, beet-red face from all traces of Tessa's incriminating makeup. *How could I be so stupid?*

No further inquiries came my way, and I never again resorted to makeup to blend in. However, the damage was done. The wound of peer humiliation reopened, prompting deeper emotional retreat into privacy and safety. So much for being convinced no one had the slightest inkling of my inner turmoil.

\* \* \*

To celebrate Tessa's birthday in March, we packed our bags and escaped to Milwaukee. The festivities began with a memorable dinner out, then overnight in a hotel with an indoor pool—a long revered special treat for the Ringness family.

Awaiting our arrival was the Public Natatorium, a concept restaurant housed in a restored public bathhouse dating back to 1894. In the vibrant atmosphere of the bustling restaurant, two well-trained dolphins named Scotch & Soda entertained the audience with their dazzling acrobatics. Without effort, they navigated the clear waters of the confined pool, casting a mesmerizing spell on every enchanted diner.

As a guest of honor, Tessa received the unique privilege of rewarding the talent with delectable raw fish. However, the lingering scent of the fish on her hands dampened her enjoyment of her special dinner. Nonetheless, it remained an unforgettable birthday party for all. But it paled in comparison to the rest of the night.

The celebrations continued upon our return to the hotel to enjoy its amenities. Tessa and I escaped into the warm chlorine-scented air to make our way to the pool, only to discover a group of children huddled near the deep end. Their gazes fixed on the water's surface. Curiosity piqued, I asked about their focused attention.

"He's still down there," one girl uttered with a solemn sigh.

"How long?" I asked, my mind conjuring images of a playful game of breath-holding, an activity we often enjoyed.

"Quite a while," she responded, in a concerned tone.

Compelled by a growing sense of unease, our eyes joined the search, scanning the depths of the pool plunging to ten feet. The carefree splashes of other children echoed in the shallows, all oblivious to the unfolding drama. Less than a minute passed, and with each passing second, my unease grew stronger. Finally, unable to bear the uncertainty, I plunged into the water with a determined resolve.

My eyes strained through the stinging chlorine and searched in desperation for any sign of movement. There, right above the pool floor, I spotted a motionless figure, a young boy suspended in a state of eerie stillness. Convinced he was holding his breath, I reached out and tapped his arm. No response. Without hesitation, I grasped his hand and propelled myself upward with his limp body in tow, breaking through the water's surface. I guided him to the poolside, where I beckoned the others to support him as I swiftly exited the pool and hoisted his body up out of the water. His head hit the tiles with an unexpected thud.

The boy, about nine years of age, lay unconscious on the pool deck. His lifeless condition left me bewildered and uncertain how to proceed. We called out for help. Within moments, a hotel guest and doctor by profession rushed to our aid, immediately starting CPR. We all stared and held our breath as the doctor fought to restore life to the boy's body. The heroic efforts were rewarded as the boy sputtered and coughed, expelling the pool water that had invaded his lungs. *Oh man, that was scary!*

Later the same night, hotel management requested a meeting with me and my parents to discuss the event. As I recounted the details of what I'd witnessed, a torrent of pent-up emotions burst forth, overwhelming me with uncontrolled sobs. Mum held me close, for there was little anyone could do to halt the tide of my emotional release. Dad wore a perplexed expression, perhaps unable to comprehend why I was so affected, considering the boy had survived. I didn't understand it either. The hotel staff, initially concerned about me, concluded they had gathered sufficient information and excused themselves. The three of us were left to process the aftermath of the traumatic experience before heading back to the room and Tessa.

To this day, the intense impression of that incident remains etched in my memory as an enigma to be fully deciphered. Perhaps the scene assaulted my heart with the realization that I, too, was drowning in the emotional depths of overwhelming anxiety. Like the kids at the pool, everyone was watching from the edge as the boy's life drained from his body. *Will someone come and rescue me?*

The ordeal didn't come up again until we received a congratulations card from our bank accompanied by a newspaper clipping recounting my heroic actions on that significant day. Mum and Dad mailed out copies of the article, and my brother John later told me he admired my courage and was so proud of me. *Wow!*

\* \* \*

Wisconsin living continued, I celebrated my seventeenth birthday with family at home and an angel food cake with strawberries, my favorite. I'd been enjoying Jerry as my friend, and school was on track. Anxiety decreased, and my fears became manageable as I was anticipating my final year of high school.

However, our world was rocked when we received word that my Aunty Evy, Dad's second oldest sister, was battling terminal cancer back in Canada. The awful news was unsettling for us all, especially considering the vast distance separating us. The heartbreaking situation compelled Dad to reevaluate priorities and values.

After much deliberation, my parents decided Dad would give his notice at work. But his employer didn't want to lose him, so they offered to relocate him. However, the proposed locations were still too far away from his ailing sister and other extended family. Ultimately, they agreed to let Dad decide what he wanted to do for the company and where he wanted to live.

Dad proposed a home-based sales position in Kelowna, British Columbia, our former hometown. Kelowna was already familiar and close to relatives in western Canada. It also boasted an international airport allowing Dad to travel easier to his clients as needed. His unconventional request was granted, and the wheels spun into motion. The colossal moving truck arrived in June ready to pack up our entire lives for yet another adventure.

Another move meant I would soon begin my sixth school—during my final year—and from scratch. *Seriously, one more move, now?* It seemed interesting that this time, the school change felt less disruptive, perhaps because I no longer harbored the same political aspirations as before. I'd finally established a comfortable rhythm allowing me to focus more on my relationships and studies. As a result, my feelings about another family move were more mixed compared to the emotional devastation of one prior.

But saying goodbye to Jerry wasn't going to be easy. My parents included him in our family hotel farewell event before we left. He was graduating the same year, and I didn't know if we'd stay in touch or if I'd find such a decent friend again. Turns out, Jerry and I would reconnect nearly forty years later thanks to social media. My heart was deeply touched when he surprised me by sharing the photo of the two of us together at my farewell party. *Wow, a true friend.*

And so it was, another massive life shift dawned on the horizon. The move would propel me into a new life and school for Grade 12. And once again, I was reminded of all my deep, dark fears locked away in a steel chest on the bottom of a sea of bogus tranquility. *I'll drown to protect it.*

# Fitting In or Stand Out

Our relocation from Wisconsin back to Canada presented an enticing opportunity for an epic road trip. All our possessions traveled ahead in the moving truck, we began our adventure in our trusted family car traversing about two thousand miles across six western states. Mount Rushmore was the most awe-inspiring view along the way, leaving even us Canadians in wonder. It served as a grand prelude to our new adventure back in our beloved homeland.

Our grandparents, having remained in Kelowna after our eastward migration about twelve years prior, secured us a welcoming rental house ready upon our arrival. Its best feature was an inviting swimming pool, a much-appreciated respite from the encroaching toasty summer.

My school's scenic location served as a picturesque backdrop for a new and final schooling chapter. After discovering the school's leadership structure would yield open elections, the allure proved too great. With some encouragement from Mum and Dad, I decided it was an ideal stage to reignite my political aspirations even though I was a complete unknown and had a single year to make my mark. *It's now or never!*

\* \* \*

With hundreds of classmates (aka voters) who would need swaying, dramatic assimilation measures were imperative. I resorted to relying on alcohol, which appeared to be common for many in my class. The tactic proved effective, and the electorate embraced both me and my booze at many social gatherings.

I developed a fondness for vodka and tonic—with an obligatory lemon wedge—which made me stand out (perhaps *not* in a favorable way). One bizarre scene was a party out in the woods (also known as a "bush party") where most people drank beer from cans or wine coolers from bottles. There I was, fastidious in slicing lemons for garnish and mixing my cocktails. *No, nothing queer to see here at all.*

Finally, achieving acceptance meant I was imbibing with frequency in social situations. Absorbing what felt like personal validation in Grade 12 was all that mattered to me. I was acutely aware of the political costs if they continued to perceive me as an outsider, any more than any new kid already is.

In my relentless pursuit of peer approval, I hosted a house party when my parents were out of town. *Maybe this will help me feel accepted.* It may or may not sound somewhat normal to you, but for me, it was an exceptional act of defiance.

My reputation as the "good boy" in my family (except for the hiccup of dropping out, of course) meant the risky effort for acceptance was even more surprising—especially since the party transformed into quite a raucous event with the wrong crowd. Making my rounds, I passed through the kitchen and noticed a couple of unfamiliar guys hovering over my mom's stove, engaged in suspicious activity; it wasn't until later I learned they were using drugs. *Yikes!*

Despite my valiant clean-up efforts and attempts to conceal all evidence the next day, I couldn't camouflage all the party's impact on our family home, including several missing items. From a pair of astounded parents, there were consequences for my actions. No worries, I convinced myself being grounded for a month was a small price to pay for what felt like a legendary house party that helped me feel like I truly belonged.

\*\*\*

During all the efforts to knit myself into the school's social fabric, I experienced another difficult round of bullying driven by a popular jock named Roger. If I were to identify the most intimidating and masculine high school sport, rugby would claim the title. Roger, of course, was a rugby player. Consequently, whenever a rugby game or practice arose—or even a semblance of rugby-like activity—I positioned myself at the opposite end of the school grounds. My aversion encompassed all sports offered at the school, not only rugby. Obviously, I was no longer an *athletic* supporter.

Roger must have possessed a sixth sense about me for I can't recall flouncing up and down the hallways with flowing scarves nor —even more absurd—flirting with him at a party. The actual catalyst for his animosity remained a mystery; perhaps I merely looked at him the wrong way. Out of the blue, while walking down the hallway, a word from his mouth struck me like a hard slap to the face.

"Fag," Roger muttered, almost contained beneath his breath, his eyes saturated with contempt as we passed each other. But it could have been far worse. He could have bellowed the insult, letting the entire world bear witness to his accusation. But even in its non-boisterous delivery, the sting of humiliation was undeniable.

My initial shock blocked a response, and I pretended to not hear him the first time and every subsequent time, week after week. I'd see Roger in the distance, and when diversion wasn't possible, I'd brace for impact. It was awful, but it didn't escalate into something physical or threatening, nor did it become more public. Nonetheless, a schism developed within me. On the outside, I appeared confident and outgoing… the full opposite of a victim persona. And yet, I didn't fight back, which was also surprising. Perhaps Roger was on to the truth. *Nope, still not ready.*

By Grade 12, most high school students were solidified into different cliques and social groupings (including groupings of one) and were gliding through to graduation. But my circumstances had prevented it. Perhaps I was too desperate to fit in—and in a rather lofty way, given my full immersion in student government—painting a bedazzled bullseye on my forehead that couldn't be resisted by the likes of Roger.

As I wrestled with my sexuality, the possibility of being gay loomed regardless of my intense apprehension. It wasn't as if Roger was accusing me of being something laughable, like a marine biologist or an impressionist painter. In truth, he wasn't all wrong. But his shame-laden approach with mean-spiritedness injured my well-being in several ways. The bottom line was I simply wasn't ready to come face-to-face with a pronouncement.

Finally, I mustered immense fortitude to seek help from Mr. Reynolds, the guidance counselor. The initiative opened a first-time possibility of uncomfortable conversation about my well-guarded secret attractions to men. He was immeasurably kind and sensitive, navigating through sensitive discussion with wisdom and awareness.

In a roundabout way, I confessed I was struggling with my sexuality and not prepared to accept a gay identity. I still needed more time to process it all. Mr. Reynolds was understanding and supportive, and we ended our talk with a warm hug making me feel everything would be okay. He invited me to return and talk again anytime I wanted. I was so thankful for his gift of a transformative opportunity to finally air the anxieties that had held me in captivity for so long. *Wow, just wow.*

I left my session with Mr. Reynolds feeling an extraordinary sense of freedom that had only taunted me until then. He encouraged me to share it with my parents, something that would require almost four more years of courage-building.

By some miracle, the bullying ceased the very next day, as if someone had thrown a switch. Each passing day brought increasing joy as I believed it was over. However, it would take years to work through my anger and face Roger.

The remainder of the school year was devoid of similar incidents, except for a random event at another bush party. I don't know who started the rumor I'd been a cheerleader in America, but perhaps it was a trigger for a partier named Dean, who wound up and walloped me out of nowhere. Fortunately, excessive alcohol numbed the pain of the impact that caused me to tip over in slow motion off the bench I was perched upon. Others rushed to my aid, cleaning me up and yelling at Dean for his drunker-than-me actions. I simply carried on as if nothing had transpired, fitting in like all the other boys. *Hold on here, maybe they all know.*

\* \* \*

My political aspirations had switched into frenetic overdrive, ignoring my status as a capable yet unknown candidate from Wisconsin, of all places! Even after the arduous campaigning, I fell short in my cheeky (okay, delusional) bid for class president; they bestowed the honor upon the heir apparent, a charming young lady who would become a friend despite our brief political contention.

Within the first month, I ascended to the position of senator and became president of the computer club. The yearbook committee welcomed my passion for photography, and I secured a seat on the grad council. Yes, it cannot be disputed. I had overextended myself, and as a result, my grades took a big hit. It led to my first-ever failing grade in a subject of questionable relevance: chemistry. Since

I had no plans for further education, I saw no reason to be too concerned about my academic showing. And let me tell you, all those so-called distractions led to the most fun I'd had since the Pep Club days! *Well, I'm almost in charge again.*

Our esteemed faculty advisor, Ms. Halliburton, gave me the moniker "The Fixer." I reveled in every opportunity to effect positive change and introduce creative ideas, drawing upon successful strategies at previous schools.

At one point, I had become so familiar with the friendly office staff that I could bypass the formalities and head straight in to make public address announcements to the student body. It all seemed so normal to me at the time, but in retrospect, I realized I'd gained an extraordinary level of trust and enjoyed many privileges in a remarkably short time.

Such a high level of involvement and authority starkly contrasted with the deep-seated insecurities still lingering within me. I had become adept at concealing my duplicitous mindset—a habit with residency in my psyche that would remain for years to come. I convinced myself I was successful at keeping my fears hidden. Yet I acknowledge the probability that others knew—or at least suspected—foreign waters ran through the young man from Wisconsin.

\*\*\*

At eighteen, cystic acne was ravaging my skin. Most of the unsightly zits plagued my upper back making me hyper-vigilant in situations needful of a shirt removal. While unconcerned about my increasing weight, those purplish cysts were ready to rupture at any moment and it repulsed me. A friendly slap on the back could cause a mortifying stain on my shirt, along with physical pain.

A bunch of us school leaders were gifted with an outing and a swim at a hotel pool. *Oh, wait, ack!* However, the idea of a swimming jaunt with my classmates sounded okay because I was confident I could find a private bathroom stall for changing. My resolve was firm to not be seen with my shirt off in all my zitty glory.

So, there I was, splashing around in the pool with my fellow leaders, the only one clad in a T-shirt. Sure, a few teasing comments came my way, but I was more worried about them seeing my naked, scarred back. After all, it would prove I wasn't who I appeared to be. *Keep the shirt on and be safe.*

In retrospect, I recognize the irony of keeping my shirt on in the pool, creating a subtle form of separateness. But at the time, nothing mattered more than avoiding humiliation, even if it meant looking ridiculous.

\* \* \*

The contradictory confidence instilled by my loving parents came to life when I pitched a business idea to Apple Computer. Dad said he needed to travel on business to California and invited me to join him, a unique opportunity for father-son bonding.

As an ardent Apple Computer enthusiast in 1985, I discovered *The Apple Collection*, a mail-order catalog packed with high-end clothing and gift items emblazoned with the distinctive Apple logo. The problem, identified by yours truly aka The Fixer, was their high-quality, expensive items became much more costly when shipped over the border. That was attributed to international shipping fees, currency exchange rates, and the agonizing delays associated with international shipping and customs brokering. Many other Apple-loving Canadians like me found it all too complicated and way too pricey, which likely affected Canadian sales. Remember, all of this occurred decades before anyone offered free and fast global shipping.

I conceived the ripe idea they needed a Canadian distributor who could import the items in bulk, reduce shipping costs within Canada, and sell in CAD. After Dad offered our trip to California, I contacted Apple and secured a meeting with a lovely woman responsible for marketing The Apple Collection.

We convened in her office at Apple near San Jose, California, while Dad attended his business calls. The meeting went as well as it could, but she informed me they contracted out operations for The Apple Collection to a third party, and they couldn't alter their long-term agreement. I don't understand why she agreed to meet with me in the first place, but it was a thrilling experience for an eighteen-year-old Apple fan to receive his visitor badge and wander unescorted through their headquarters. As I passed offices with empty desks, I imagined myself accomplishing much while working there. *What a life that would be!*

The actualization of my innate entrepreneurial spirit in such a manner aptly demonstrates my internal conflict. Indeed, only a self-assured and secure teenager could conceive and pursue such a bold business proposition. *Right?* On one hand, I had all I needed to execute such an undertaking. On the other, my sexuality struggles, and masculine insecurity plagued my mind, affecting my behavior. But I had learned to compartmentalize myself and function quite well despite mounting fears of what might be inevitable.

After the Apple meeting, Dad and I ventured to Las Vegas and attended the Consumer Electronics Show, one of the biggest events of its kind anywhere. Visiting the Apple Computer display area held even more special significance to me after my recent meeting with their marketing department. We also spent part of a day at a Six

Flags park where I tried out a karaoke singing booth and recorded "We Are the World." It was so much fun!

The trip was a perfect opportunity to bond with Dad, helping me to comprehend how much he loved and supported me and what interested me, even when it wasn't sports related. It was a pivotal event in our relationship to usher us into a new phase and it allowed me to embrace my unique interests, knowing they were acceptable to him. After years of uncertainty, I finally believed that I—his special third son—was worthy of his approval. *But there's this other thing.*

# Longing and Love

For the past two years, a paralyzing panic of being naked with my peers dominated my anxious thoughts and behavior. It was welcome news to learn Phys. Ed. wasn't mandated for Grade 12 seniors at my final school, heralding the victorious conclusion of a long and vexing period in my journey. Despite some close calls, I had accomplished my desperate mission to evade the menacing locker room tradition of open nudity. However, the triumph did little to quell my increasing curiosities and same-sex attractions.

Enter an intriguing and handsome classmate named Derek. He had dark hair, dark eyes, a moderate build, and an impish grin hinting at rebelliousness. He exuded a charming air of indifference, a trait that captivated my rule-following temperament.

Derek was a night owl who indulged in late evenings during the school week, resulting in frequent absences the following day. In my world, the burden of too many public service commitments made it difficult to entertain such an irresponsible notion as skipping school. Nevertheless, I was undeterred from pursuing a friendship with Derek. In addition to hanging out after school, we often immersed ourselves in lengthy evening phone conversations extending into the wee hours of the morning.

The presence of a landline in my bedroom—a coveted luxury in the era preceding cell phones—paved the way for our nocturnal telephone socializing. The privilege allowed me to recline in my bed during hours of captivating conversation with Derek, unbeknownst to the outside world. *Is this real?*

Our talks revolved around his thoughts and opinions on various subjects, including everyone we knew at school and all that was wrong in the world. However, what enthralled me most was the consistent attention Derek gave to me; at least, it felt that way, even when my attention was given to him. Our relationship was unparalleled and intoxicating because I'd never known such a friend. Fatigue and bleary eyes didn't matter the day after another late-night discourse. Derek quickly became a cherished friend, seeding a novel sense of belonging to another who was also different from all the other boys.

* * *

In alignment with his rebellious persona, Derek rode a cool black street bike. It struck a glaring contrast to my humbler mode of transport: an orange and white moped, gifted to me by Nan & Granch, complete with a gleaming white helmet. I had some initial concerns about how it might affect my cool factor… puttering into the busy school parking lot straddling my mechanical creamsicle (imagine a slow zoom in on me dismounting, slowly removing my snow-white helmet, tossing back my thick dark hair with a flourish). No doubt, Derek had superior street cred with his bike, and he often took pity on me by inviting me to ride with him instead. *Sounds so good to me!*

Sitting behind Derek on his motorbike while figuring out how to hold on was intriguing. I wanted to wrap my arms tight around his waist, for safety reasons, of course. So, after some awkward maneuvering, I mustered the courage and did it. There were two ways that could have gone. But instead of humiliation or something similar, I was elated to see he didn't mind at all. His openness to what felt like a public pseudo-display of affection made him even more alluring. I chalked it up to his unconcerned disregard for the opinions of others. *Or just maybe?*

The way Derek could disregard what others thought flummoxed me as much as it spellbound me. I'd forever been more concerned about what others would think or prefer versus what I wanted. It was an embedded pattern operating on autopilot for most of my life, and it seemed impossible to switch off. Spending time with Derek and attempting to attain a similar state of carefree abandon seemed a worthy goal.

\* \* \*

As I bid farewell to Derek late one night in his driveway, I mustered the courage to ask for a hug, and he obliged with a brief but connecting squeeze. Then, without warning, he wound up and punched me—hard—in my right shoulder. Caught off guard, I doubled over in pain. Derek's ensuing laughter echoed like that of a maniacal carnival clown. Confusion clouded my mind as I attempted to comprehend his actions. The distant memory of Patrick's attack rushed forward in my mind.

"Why did you do that?" exasperation dripped from my shaky voice. He kept laughing.

"I have to go to bed," his monotoned reply.

Bewildered, I uttered a feeble suggestion to discuss it later and sped away in an orange-and-white blur, emotions and questions racing me all the way home. The affront replayed itself over and over in my thoughts, unable to shake off the emotional turmoil stirred within me. Sleep eluded me that night.

The following day at school, I began a discreet mission to gather intel to help me better understand my friend. Whispers and murmurs revealed a disconcerting truth—several others were familiar with Derek's erratic behavior and his ongoing plight with mental wellness. Learning he battled suicidal thoughts and relied on medication to manage his condition was an epiphany, explaining his solitary nature and the suffering he carried.

My discovery fanned the embers of empathy within me, increasing my desire to offer support and understanding of his needs. Perhaps, in some small way, I could make a difference in his life. I could possibly be the one to help him navigate the challenges he faced and save him from more anguish. I felt certain the result for me would be the diminishment of all my petty tribulations that paled in comparison. *I think he needs me.*

*\*\*\**

During all my chummy interactions with Derek, there wasn't any explicit acknowledgment to suggest our relationship could be different. Once again, I resolved to settle for being a close friend who suppressed his deeper feelings in exchange for protecting the irreplaceable friendship itself. *I know he cares about me.*

I still maintained a desire to seem "normal," and despite my hectic student life responsibilities, I started dating a girl named Bianca, who worked with me part-time at a pizza restaurant. She was pretty, with long, curly blonde hair and a cheerful personality, and she seemed to be interested in me (very helpful)!

After two dates, we found ourselves in my car parked outside her house, and it appeared to be the pivotal moment when I was supposed to kiss her. A pit formed in my stomach while a flashback emerged of kissing Rose, followed by her insensitive words. So, like any uneasy person, I tensed up, and my clumsy efforts failed to impress Bianca. Given my lack of experience, I would have welcomed even a passing grade. To her credit, Bianca responded with utmost kindness and attempted to provide some guidance. But the situation teetered into embarrassment, compelling me to depart with haste. *What the freak is wrong with me?*

The aftermath only intensified my confusion and masculine self-doubt, ending the short-lived Bianca footnote in my life. Continuing to work with her became awkward, compounded by the fact her family owned the restaurant. I soon resigned in more ways than one. *I think I'm doomed.*

As graduation approached months later, a radiant girl named Valerie captured my attention as a potential grad date. She was petite, attractive with long, dark hair, flashed a great smile, and loved to laugh. To my surprise, she said yes. We shared an enjoyable time together, but I sensed her motivation was innocent or perhaps concern about missing out on grad. There was an absence of mutual sparks between us, but who knows, perhaps my pining for Derek stifled potential for other romance.

Felina was an attractive Grade 11 junior and friends with Tessa. Her big smile, vivacious personality, and charm made her even more appealing to me. Felina and I expended many, many hours of deep conversations. We'd talk about anything, including some of her dating escapades. *Could it be me one day?*

Connecting with Felina was enjoyable and meaningful. I valued our freedom to not worry about initiating (or perceiving) any romantic cues, even though I was open to exploring more with her. I also believed our relational dynamic created safety and space to open her heart in trust. Sensing her need, I prioritized and protected our connection over my own hopes—not unlike what happened with Jerry and, even more so, Dale.

Without an expressed mutual desire, a greater romantic connection remained elusive. I was extremely grateful for her ongoing kindness and support that helped me feel a little normal. A school photo with her touching inscription touched my heart.

> *"You're one of the few caring guys around, and I am massively glad we met. I want to thank you for being there to talk to. Here's to talking in driveways for HOURS and not realizing it. Love and hugs, Felina."*

It's impossible to guess what could have happened if my girl interactions had gone in different directions or if I only had more confidence in them. More perplexing is the question of feasibility, given my dominating attraction to guys. Front and center: the abiding romantic sentiments I harbored for Derek.

\* \* \*

Much of my social time with Derek involved booze. An unforgettable example found us sprawled face up on the thick carpet of my family's rumpus room when I had the house to myself. Sambuca was our boozy temptress, and she had her merciless way.

I can't explain how or why the stereo was blasting my dad's Charlie Pride LP, but I was delightfully stunned by Derek's flawless recollection of every word from "Behind Closed Doors," which the two of us belted out at the ceiling in unison. Sure, it was a song about the benefits of privacy between a man and a woman, and we'll look past the lyric proclaiming no one knows what goes on behind doors that are closed. *Hmm.*

Our unintended bonding event drew me even closer to my ragamuffin renegade that night, but there was still no way I'd even attempt to open *that* door. However, our fun was interrupted by the aftereffects of far too much of the licorice-flavored liqueur. A taste of copious vomiting yielded a persistent aversion four decades on.

One Saturday afternoon, Derek invited me to smoke pot with him. I would have expected my homegrown moral compass to steer me toward a hard no response. However, the idea of strengthening our bond proved irresistible, so I relented. We retreated in his car to a secluded area behind a fast-food restaurant, where I gave it a go. I was apprehensive about how I might react or what I might say. *What if I confess my feelings for him?* I was surprised the pot elicited almost no discernible effect, leaving me disappointed. Nonetheless, Derek appreciated my willingness to walk a little further on the wild side. *Oh, you have no idea... or do you?*

A couple of months later, Derek invited me to do it again. By then, I'd heard pot possessed the power to sway some guys toward amorousness or the exploration of unchartered territories. Despite the lackluster outcome of my first attempt, I was keen to try again. I hoped we might get behind the forbidden closed doors without the dreaded risk of devastating rejection or humiliating exposure.

That time, we found ourselves settled in his bedroom—how convenient! Yet, once again, the marijuana effects seemed to bypass me without a smidgen of influence. Furthermore, there was no discernible door, inviting window, nor even a minuscule crack hinting at something sensual from either of us. I settled again for solace in the simple joy of having a mutual friend who enjoyed my company despite the inner turmoil and unresolved tension simmering beneath my surface. *Here we are again.*

\* \* \*

While riding the gusts of whirlwind escapades alongside Derek, another poignant but current song by Foreigner caught my attention. "I Want to Know What Love Is" came to have weighty importance, representing my intensifying romantic sentiments for Derek. The soulful ballad delved into the depths of loneliness, heartache, and pain, with desire for someone to reveal what love truly is. It made me grapple with incessant questions, pondering whether my feelings for Derek were, in fact, genuine love or if I even knew what love was. *Can it be real if it's just one way?*

Either way, exploring romantic gay love remained as impossible as me coming out with my own hit record. Yet within the private playground of my thoughts, Derek was the beguiling merry-go-round I eagerly clambered upon. Our wild ride demanded and acknowledged my unrelenting grip, hurling me off only a few times into the hard-hearted dirt.

Despite the rocky difficulties and the internal turmoil clamoring for more, Derek's friendship intensely shaped my final year of high school. I am confident I surrendered to the allure of love for this troubled teen, yet it remained unspoken and one-sided. The future was uncertain for Derek and me, with some promise it would unfold beyond the margins of high school. Little did I know that it would and only two years later, his heart-breaking choices would unleash a devastating and enduring impact, forever altering the course of my life. *How could you?*

# Outlasting the First Time

Dale and I had maintained our connection across two provinces, and as graduation neared for us both, we hatched a plan to share an apartment in Saskatoon. I was delighted, despite all that happened (or didn't happen) between us. Dale still held a place in my heart reserved only for him, which seemed to broaden after my highs and lows with Derek. Even if nothing romantic or sexual ever happened, I wanted to be part of Dale's life again, especially if he wanted the same thing. However, my immediate priority was graduating.

Hampered by a failing grade in chemistry and a dismal 53% in algebra (once my forte), I escaped with my diploma by the hair on my chinny-chin-chin. I maintain no regrets about my decision to sacrifice academic achievement over public service. As a Grad Council member, I got approval to borrow some TV lights for some extra brilliance at the ceremony. Having Mum and Dad there, along with Nan, Granch, and Tessa, made the celebration much sweeter.

I opted to remain in Kelowna through the summer, working and saving for the move, aided by living at home. Derek didn't seem too concerned about me moving away, which stung in a familiar way. But no matter, I'd be returning to Saskatoon soon with funds and enthusiasm to establish a new home with Dale. *I wonder if we'll go and pick out curtains together.*

Did I indulge fantasies of our friendship blossoming into something even more? Indeed, I did, even after he told me he wished I were a girl. However, the long-entrenched fear of rejection and shame from an unwanted advance would be sure to muzzle any expression of my true desires. *Perhaps it'll be gone by then.*

* * *

After saving enough, I was ready to move as September arrived. Dale was enthusiastic about getting an apartment—eager to embark on his journey of independence from his mom. I packed up my trusty Dodge Arrow, my first car after three payments of $300, and set off on my eastward road trip.

We ended up in a modest two-bedroom apartment in a second-floor corner of a walk-up in a Saskatoon suburb. In no time, Dale secured a job at an Esso station while my experience as a dishwasher and busboy at a fancy French restaurant opened the door at a Greek restaurant. However, seeking a change of pace—and an escape from the addictive baklava—I left there to join a home renovation company. My new work was scheduling appointments for their sales agent, a role that required me to go door-to-door.

Every morning, Marcel and Andrew picked me up to join our sales agent for breakfast. Our daily ritual cultivated a unique sense of connection I'd not known in workplaces or social settings, and for a time, I felt like all the other boys. The job was interesting because it was fun with occasions of frustration, such as doors being slammed in my face or facing harsh words from rude homeowners. But there were also times of co-worker camaraderie. Marcel was French-Canadian and introduced me to a colorful array of foreign swear words, though I didn't keep any of them. The pay was okay, with added cash bonuses for booking appointments that led to sales.

Despite my initial apprehension, I quite enjoyed my foray into the manly home improvement industry, a field I knew almost nothing about. I reveled in fast learning and the opportunity to portray myself as a "normal" guy... who happened to have a very attractive roommate who got abnormal attention.

Dale and I spent a substantial amount of our free time together, appreciating each other's company and humor. However, our relationship became marred by frequent arguments over trivial matters, such as the proper way to wash dishes. I was headstrong and not easily moved off my position on most everything. Tension often simmered beneath the surface of our interaction.

In retrospect, I believe my suppressed desire for our interaction to mirror my romantic sentiments contributed to those conflicts. As far as I knew, Dale remained oblivious to my inner turmoil, and thus, my struggles remained hidden. *What's it going to take to change things?*

\* \* \*

As a sexually primed eighteen-year-old, my same-sex curiosity and internal strife soon propelled me toward the classified section of the newspaper, where I'd heard about personal ads of interest. Even in the quaint city of Saskatoon during the eighties, a few of them identified men seeking men.

My heart pulsated as I bought a paper in haste and sought a private corner in a coffee shop. Three ads were posted; one drew all my attention. One night when Dale was out, my unsteady fingers dialed the number. No answer, so I left a cryptic message, attempting to project coolness while flustered from the inside out.

A few nights after my anxious outreach, our home phone rang while Dale and I were engrossed in a TV show. Dale answered, and to my astonishment, the caller was the young man from the ad. My instant dry mouth and clammy hands implied concern of Dale's discovery, yet I focused on appearing nonchalant. I concluded the call with haste, desperate to avoid arousing suspicion.

"Who was that?" Dale inquired with casual curiosity.

Summoning acting skills from nowhere, I mustered a casual response as the words wrestled past my carpeted tongue. "Oh, just a guy I met through work."

Dale seemed satisfied with my explanation and returned his attention to the TV. I exhaled a sigh of immense relief he wasn't more curious. *Why does it feel like I'm cheating on him?*

It wasn't until the following week when I finally gathered the courage to return the call when Dale wasn't home. The advertiser introduced himself as Stephen, and after a brief exchange, his words and excitement piqued my curiosity enough to meet him for a late coffee at a downtown restaurant called The Bird Cage. Yes, its actual name, and yes, I recognize the irony, considering the movie of the same title would be released a decade later, starring the versatile Robin Williams and the campy Nathan Lane as gay cabaret owners.

As was my habit, I arrived early then eased into a booth, my nerves buzzing like a live wire. It was a risky gamble, the likes of which had been avoided at great cost for years, now energized by heightened emotions and unresolved curiosity. However, the nature of the rendezvous had lowered my fear of rejection, primarily because of Stephen's courage to post an ad to find romance.

Someone near the entrance looked like it could be him, about my age, with dark, wavy hair and a pleasant smile. Stephen radiated friendliness and animated verbosity. However, anticipated sparks didn't fire up, perhaps because the oh-so-oblivious one who made my motor run was back at home. Even so, like an insect to a zapper, I found myself drawn to the mischievous possibility of being intimate with a stranger who could embrace raging desires within me.

My curiosity prevailed when he bashfully invited me back to his place. As a student, Stephen resided in a small apartment near campus, conveniently near the restaurant. The proximity allowed us to escape the Cage like two little enamored birdies who would become better acquainted along the way. Stephen's brisk walking pace reduced our available time for hypothetical familiarization. *Is this really going to happen?*

Upon entering his apartment, a large black-and-white poster featured the pouty-faced Corey Hart in his ripped 501s quickly drew my attention. *Is that gay-normal?* Furnishings were sparse, reflecting typical living conditions for most starving students. Stephen offered me a Coke, which I was happy to accept while wondering if something stronger might help calm my prancing nerves.

We settled on his couch and engaged in brief conversation when it became abundantly clear Stephen had only one thing on his mind: Me. Despite his limited physical appeal, the combination of his directness, enthusiasm, and evident inclination toward me was sufficient… even without the stimulation of alcohol. And so, we found ourselves in his bed. *Now what?*

It was then I realized I hadn't watched any instructional videos or completed a home study course on how intimacy was supposed to work. But things did work for Stephen, so to speak, and in his dark bedroom, we became familiar with each other.

It was as if a long-sealed door had perilously burst open, unleashing undeniable exhilaration within me. But Stephen appeared to be about as clueless in the sack as I was. Even so, he was much more charged than me, and in under four minutes, it was over. *Seriously, that was sex?*

The subsequent cuddling was nice, and I accepted his invitation to stay the night convinced there must be something more fun than what had happened. But still, as I lay there in the buff beside an affectionate young man named Stephen, an utterly foreign sense of tranquility enveloped me. After what seemed like an existence of consuming anxiety, relentless strategic maneuvering, and avoidance, there I was. Baring my soul and every last inch of my naked self with another naked self. In a welcome state of serenity, I imagined the fun we might have in the morning and drifted off to sleep.

I jolted awake to find myself uncovered and entirely alone. Stephen had vanished without a trace. On the kitchen table, a handwritten note.

> *I'm so sorry, but I have a class this morning.*
> *I really hope you'll be here when I get home around 11.*
> *—Stephen*

Intense emotions swirled within me as I re-read his note a few times to make sure I got it. *How could he abandon me like this?* A familiar bash of rejection hit my heart almost as hard as Derek hit my shoulder. Granted, Stephen had a class and perhaps it was important. But I couldn't fathom how he could simply get up and go to school, assuming I'd wait for him or perhaps enjoy some idle chit chat with the brooding and unresponsive Corey Hart. So no, there wasn't more fun in the morning, not by a long shot. I didn't want to be there when he got home and couldn't get out of there fast enough.

Quite madly, my thoughts shifted to a plausible explanation for Dale about not coming home last night. There was no way I'd allow him to discover the truth: *Oh, I spent the night with a strange man, doing strange things.* The ruse must be convincing, or everything would crash in around me. It so happened John lived nearby, so I concocted a tale of running into my brother and then spending the night at his place —not too weird and quite believable. To my relief, my cover-up proved successful with Dale. *But why do I feel so dirty?*

The lingering bitter aftertaste of my first sexual encounter left me seriously unsatisfied. In an unforeseen turn of the tides, the underwhelming experience doused some of my burning desires and sowed seeds of doubt. Perhaps I'd been mistaken all along, and a potential gay identity was a freaky illusion. As a result, I retreated further into my secret space, now adorned with a fresh coat of paint in the lovely color of confusion.

* * *

Perhaps it was hundreds of childhood hours spent escaping through our rumpus room TV that kindled my love for all things boob tube, and not only Mr. Rogers. In addition to hit shows and miniseries (we had made *Roots* a family event), I enjoyed the energy of live newscasts and specials. The annual Jerry Lewis telethon was a must for me, transfixed by more than twenty continuous hours of live television production challenges. I often imagined what it would be like to work on those shows, or just be part of it somehow.

Like most cities, Saskatoon boasted a community-access television station, so in eagerness, I sought a volunteer opportunity there. Their facility dwarfed Kelowna's, where I had cut my teeth, flaunting a more spacious studio and an impressive array of equipment. Imagine me there, resembling a child let loose in a candy store or, in my case, a pie shop. So, I jumped at the chance to volunteer again, and my prior training in Kelowna opened the door without delay.

During one studio production, I was operating camera two when a friendly woman on camera one struck up a conversation during our break.

"Hi, I'm Linda. Is your hair color natural?" A surprising opener for sure, but justified, and enough to intrigue me. *It's harder to fool people than I think.*

It's true my inclination toward fair-haired gents caused me to begin a series of experiments, using various lemon juice concoctions to lighten my hair without resorting to overpriced chemicals or treatments. Although my stubborn dark brown hair remained quite distant from blond, my efforts yielded a noticeable enhancement of natural-looking highlights. Those reddish accents came alive under the hot lighting conditions prevalent in a TV studio. Evidently, my self-styling hadn't escaped Linda's notice, and I was a little sheepish about confessing my vain pursuit.

Upon completing our shift, Linda was kind enough to invite me to her place for coffee, a gesture I accepted with gratitude. *It's what men are supposed to do!* Linda's long dark hair complemented her soft features, appearing to be a woman about four or five years older than me. We ended up at her cozy and rustic apartment, in flowing conversation as we sipped on cups of tea and indulged in flavorful cookies. Linda seemed lonesome, appreciating the opportunity to connect with someone. As the evening wore on, I realized I needed to catch the last bus back to my place. I soon thanked her for a nice time and said goodbye.

A few days later, I described the encounter to Greg, who couldn't get over how clueless I was. He insisted her interest in me was unmistakable and I'd squandered an opportunity to make a romantic advance with a good chance of receptivity. Of course, in my mind, I'd already made my move: I found myself in a strange woman's house!

I'd never told Greg about my sexuality struggles, but perhaps the occasion tipped my hand a little more than intended. The truth was, I felt no physical attraction toward Linda despite her forthright behavior. As a young man alone there with her at night, I suppose I should be thankful she wasn't an axe murderer. Or an aggressive pole dancer. *Wait, maybe that could be a good thing.*

\* \* \*

Unidentified and unresolved tension escalated between Dale and me, and within only three months, we conceded we couldn't live together anymore. The harsh reality of unreciprocated romantic feelings caused strain, affecting my emotional well-being and our friendship. As painful as it was, Dale and I needed to break up.

He needed space and freedom to pursue his own intimate relationships, which were problematic with me around. I soon secured my own place and moved using a taxi while Dale retreated to his mom's. We intended to maintain contact, but even that would prove to be frustrating and unfulfilling alongside the ache of his absence in my day-to-day life.

My affordable new suite on the main floor of an old house was decidedly dodgy. After three long sleepless nights with a butter knife at the ready near the door, it was another call to the taxi company. I midnight-moved out of there (and forfeited my security deposit) and used what little money I had left to move into a high-rise apartment with security.

I landed a new job at RadioShack, and I loved it, in spite of the long bus ride to get to the mall in the suburbs. It was a good fit for me with my computer experience, quick learning abilities, and social ease with customers and fellow staff. But I either misinterpreted the pay structure, or they were exploiting my eighteen-year-old naivety. In less than a month, I found myself unable to pay my rent. I was desperate, lonely, heartbroken, and penniless, so I did what any normal son would do: I pleaded for help from my parents, which brought my dad out from Kelowna to bring me home, again.

# Flickering Lights

Within weeks, I snagged a part-time retail job in Kelowna. The store was an authorized Apple dealer—the nirvana of workplaces, a dream come true. We also sold copiers, typewriters, and related items also of interest to me. Tackling the challenge of becoming familiar with all the office equipment was something I delighted in. My co-worker was a handsome young surfer dude named Jimmy, and training with him was easy. Within a few weeks, Jimmy tendered his notice to move with his girlfriend to Vancouver Island, and they promoted me full-time. It was welcome news and it allowed me to squirrel away even more money.

Television still tempted me, so I returned to volunteer at the station and produced and hosted the computer training series called *User Friendly* and the local events talk show *Local Motion*. Every aspect of television production intrigued me, and I easily transitioned between the various disciplines. The creative solitude of editing a video segment for *Local Motion* was as equally enjoyable as gathering diverse public opinions on the upcoming Expo 86 in Vancouver.

My computer job continued to be gratifying, more so after we moved to a much larger location with a dedicated computer department. The marketplace debut of Apple's Macintosh computer was huge, as was being part of its launch in Kelowna. The department was my responsibility, and I received sales commissions on top of my salary. I couldn't have been more content in life, until an unexpected revelation put an end to that.

The more television volunteering I did, the clearer it became my passion was bubbling up and over. My desire to sell computers decreased, fueled by the greener grass of limitless creativity in a technically advanced media environment, impacting thousands of people. The seeds planted during childhood sprouted into opportunity and passion, converging to reveal my calling.

Further confirmation from trusted loved ones triggered me to pursue a television career, and vigorous research into technical school options helped me determine Calgary was the place to be. Southern Alberta Institute of Technology (SAIT) had a strong reputation for its media programs, but Alberta residents received priority admission for the oversubscribed program. Nonetheless, I submitted my application from Kelowna while living at Mum and Dad's. Several anxious weeks passed before I received my rejection letter, dealing a blow to my enthusiasm while forcing a reckoning. *I've never liked this feeling.* Mum noticed depression come over me, an uncommon occurrence.

Determined, I decided to better the odds of my acceptance by becoming an Alberta resident. So, at nineteen, I prepared for another move, to the bustling city of my birth and home to over six hundred and fifty thousand people, more than ten times the size of Kelowna. The new chapter would open either Pandora's box or Zeus's treasure chest, I'll let you be the judge.

\* \* \*

After arriving in Calgary, I accepted the invitation to move in with my cousin Lola and her roommates for a few weeks before I got a place, which worked out great. Big city living took some adjusting. Downtown was so huge and overwhelming that I lost my car the first time I parked on the street, requiring almost an hour to find it. Lola assisted me with adapting in those early days with her casual, relaxed approach and showed me the ropes as we shared laughter over almost everything.

Finally, SAIT reopened applications for the upcoming year, and I submitted mine right away. Within a few weeks, I received a delightful letter telling me my application was accepted, but I was fifth on the waiting list for enrollment in their two-year cinema, television, stage, and radio arts (CTSR) program. *Is this a dream come true?*

They assured me my chances of gaining admission for the upcoming school year were promising because there were often cancellations. I wished I could start right away, but I had to look for work and build up my savings before I jumped in with both feet and began my television career.

I stumbled upon an ad for a marketing representative to recruit people for credit card signups at The Bay, a Canadian retail icon with a monumental downtown department store boasting seven stories encompassing half a million square feet. My employer was the marketing company The Bay contracted for the service.

Within my first week, I observed many customers who wandered into the store on the main floor and became disoriented. It seemed like an opportunity to present store management with a problem and a solution; after all, I am The Fixer! I landed a meeting with a vice president and pitched my idea for a main floor information kiosk. She embraced my idea and believed I could excel beyond peddling credit cards, so she extended a rare full-time job offer in their jewelry department—on the main floor. *Didn't see that coming!* It helped that I'd gained enough related experience back in Kelowna the summer before school began. I was overjoyed and loved being part of the exciting retail environment, earning a full-time wage to help me save up faster.

One ordinary day in the watch department, a rather colorful Bay promotions employee named Reg, ornamented in the full regalia of a character called "Captain Hudson," intrepidly introduced himself to me on the bustling store floor. In short order, Reg came by to see me quite often, instilling both fascination and apprehension within me because he was clearly not like all the other boys. His charm and dry humor were beyond doubt, but it was his palpable curiosity in me that beckoned. *Just what is going on here?*

One evening, Reg talked me into drinks after work. His charismatic demeanor and a few adult beverages coaxed me into comfort to share some of my story with him. Not surprisingly, it turned out he also harbored same-sex attractions, and he shared some of his story with me.

Reg became the second person ever to bear witness to the full depths of my insecurities and struggles. It felt liberating to finally unveil so much in such a casual setting with another man who accepted me and seemed to care about me without other motives. We engaged in hours of absorbed conversation that memorable night in a dark lounge that felt empty except for us.

Life took an unexpected turn when I was laid off without warning after less than three months. Reg later explained the company's decision to let go of many full-time employees to reduce benefit-related expenses. Even though my dismissal was sudden—I was wiping away tears on the bus ride home—it was okay with me because I'd already planned to begin school within a few weeks and intended to resign soon.

\*\*\*

My two-year diploma program began in September, and I decided to major as a broadcast news anchor. My ambition was to become an entertainment reporter, perhaps ascending to anchor on a specialty program similar to *Entertainment Tonight*.

The CTSR program was extreme and required an abundance of extra work in the evenings and on weekends. However, I loved it all because I was fully immersed in broadcast training for television, radio, and film, as well as theatrical production and performance techniques. Like-minded people who shared my passion for the industry surrounded me all the time, creating an electrifying but exhausting environment.

Another nasty acne flare-up stirred up the old fears of humiliation and embarrassment. A troublesome scenario given that I was training to be an on-air personality. A visit with my doctor resulted in another round of the medication Accutane to ease the acne. Eventually, it made a difference. *At least I look okay on the outside.*

A television production student named Alan and I formed an instant connection. He was tall and slender, around my age, and possessed a contagious and somewhat sarcastic sense of humor. We spent a lot of time together at school but not so much outside of that. I found Alan disarmingly attractive, but there was no sign of anything reciprocal, and he often spoke of his girlfriend.

To cope with the program's grueling demands, we all resorted to consuming copious amounts of caffeine. One of the snack bars offered a unique concoction called a mocha around the time Starbucks popularized its expensive version. However, our mocha was a thrifty DIY original, combining a cup of drip coffee with a pouch of Carnation hot chocolate mix. Alan and I would frequently get mochas for each other, often exchanging jokes about being each other's "dealer."

Alan proved to be a steadfast friend, even assisting me once on a date (with a girl named Raven, whom I'll formally introduce later) by chauffeuring us on a night out at a dinner theater. Alan arrived wearing a jovial chauffeur cap and exuded an infectious energy elevating the entire evening, making me so thankful for his support.

Having a designated driver allowed Raven and I to indulge in the overpriced cocktails at the theater, but they had no apparent effect. When the date faded to black, so did the prospects of anything further with Raven. I was surprised to find myself even more drawn to Alan and his sweet kindness.

The situation had become sorely familiar to me: captivated by a close friend and entertaining fantasies, yet not summoning the courage to bring it out in the open. In retrospect, I realized much could have been resolved with an honest confession about my feelings. His disinterest expressed plainly could dissolve all my magical what-if scenarios in the blink of an eye. Oh, did I mention his girlfriend? *Maybe I could make him happier.* But I haven't said there was anything logical about my inner battle. Without a closed door with Alan, the invented what-if imaginations remained ever present, perhaps energizing the relationship even more on some level.

I also acknowledge the assured safety in concealing romantic attractions for a same-sex friend and that it could be somewhat fulfilling to entertain delusional fantasies in private. Otherwise, the only alternative would be to confront the harsh, cold, romantic rebuffing after a candid confession. Perhaps followed by possible offense and overall rejection as a friend that could lead to public shaming. All of it was simply too great of a risk.

And so, balancing the precarious conflict like a pro, life continued in its familiar trajectory with my dear school friend Alan. Our connection felt comparable to what I felt with Derek but without all the drama and unpredictable behavior. I was so grateful for Alan's friendship and would do whatever I could to protect it.

\* \* \*

# NOT LIKE ALL THE OTHER BOYS

At twenty years old, I'd been sheltered from many sexual influences and had never seen or used pornography. The first time I ever saw the word was in a word-guessing game I played with my former best friend Patrick and his brother in Grade 7. They both thought it was freaking hilarious I couldn't guess the word, with almost all the letters showing. I didn't even know what po*nograp*y meant, let alone spell it right. *Talk about embarrassing.*

My friend Reg was no stranger to smut, and he kindly shared his after arriving at my house one night. All kinds of men appeared throughout those glossy magazines, posing in sexual situations with other men, enticing me into their world. *They're really into it!*

Reg left one magazine behind, and over time, I became overly acquainted with its racy images. It was the beginning of a long battle against the addictive powers of sexual imagery. Yes, there were immense pleasures in the rewards of the hunt. However, there were often unpleasant feelings of regret and even shame afterward, though not enough to overcome the allure to rinse and repeat.

Reg also introduced me to gay porn videos that we watched together. Those sessions could have easily led to messing around if not for the lack of chemistry between us. Reg seemed more like my naughty, like-minded neighbor than a romantic prospect. Those adventures made it blatant that men could sexually arouse me, and the potency of the sexual images was strong. It was as if those attractive and athletic men had given me permission (acceptance) to view them altogether exposed and sexually active. From there, my imagination took over, envisioning myself in similar intimate situations. I wanted more and more and more, and soon, a regular habit of fantasy and self-pleasuring became my new normal.

\* \* \*

In the bustling northern Alberta city of Edmonton, the expansive West Edmonton Mall stood as a global beacon of shopping and entertainment. On several occasions, it was there the bond with my high school friend Derek endured despite the distance between us. He remained mostly a loner, but I would drive north about three hours to get together every month or so. The what-ifs still rose up occasionally in my mind, but our get-togethers were filled mostly with laughter and, you guessed it, booze. I was elated to still have any kind of connection with him.

Meeting his new partner, Angela, during one visit dredged up myriad emotions within me. It certainly put an exclamation point on my lingering, misguided, perhaps-one-day thoughts. But mostly, I was elated for Derek finding companionship, and I couldn't help but admire Angela's maturity and humor. She seemed like the perfect match for him, and I fervently hoped his newfound love would bring him the peace and contentment he so desperately sought.

*  *  *

Reaching Derek was becoming difficult, and two months had passed without hearing back from him, leading me to finally contact his father. The somber tone in his voice sent prickles down my spine.

"Oh, Todd. Haven't you heard?" his dad asked.

"No," I replied, hesitating. "What?"

A pause. My mind scrambled to anticipate. "Todd, I'm so sorry," he continued. "Derek passed away last week. He took his own life."

A black void opened in my heart as my entire world began crumbling around me in slow motion. I strained to hear him through the ringing in my ears. "The funeral is tomorrow afternoon here in

Edmonton. Todd, please come if you can. It would mean a lot to us, especially him."

"I'll be there," I squeaked, not knowing what to say to a grieving father who had lost his troubled son. My watering eyes released streams of salty tears down my fallen face.

Grief-stricken and guilt-ridden, I rushed to Edmonton the next day. Lost and late, I arrived at the funeral home, where the full weight of my emotions threatened to overwhelm me. Questions ran through my struggling mind like rats in a maze.

*Wasn't I supposed to be the one to help him?*

*Would he still be alive if I reached out more?*

*Was it my fault?*

*Why didn't he tell me how bad it truly was?*

The guilt of failing my cherished friend was crushing. I didn't know how life would go on.

Angela surprised me with an invitation to stay overnight. Perhaps sensing my distress, she also sought solace in companionship with her boyfriend's former schoolmate. The two of them lived together in her house, so when I got there, she dug up some of his clothes for me so I could escape my suit. At first, I didn't think I could do it. But with Angela's encouragement, I put on his favorite gray sweatpants and a baggy sweatshirt. She later insisted I take them home; for months, they helped me feel close to him.

Together, while enjoying what Derek had called my "damn vodka tonics," Angela and I delved into our memories, sharing stories that brought him closer in a new light. Angela revealed the nature of his mental health, tearfully recounting the events leading up to the horrible moment when she found him in his car.

She said Derek had been withdrawing and spending more time alone. Coming home from work one night, she noticed the garage door was closed, the light was on, and his car was inside. It was running. She opened the garage door and saw a dryer vent hose taped to the car's exhaust pipe, leading to the driver-side window. Inside the car was Derek. She ran and opened the door and screamed at him as she shook his body. She called 911 in a panic. The paramedics could not revive him. They were too late. We were all too late.

Angela knew Derek had attempted suicide before, and still, she wasn't able to stop him. The pain she endured was tangible, yet her strength in the face of tragedy was awe-inspiring. Being there for her that night not only eased her pain but also allowed me to be there for Derek in a way I never could've imagined.

The significance of Angela's warmhearted invitation and my participation was multifaceted. In my organized and controlled life (stay safe!), accepting any last-minute invitation was uncharacteristic of me. Plans were plans, and they were *not* for changing. As I departed the next day to drive back home, I was a transformed man in more ways than one. I couldn't have been more grateful for the tremendous reward of such meaningful time with Derek's girlfriend, let alone the extraordinary timing of my phone call to his dad.

One profound thing Angela said remains with me to this day, and I often share it with others who tragically lose someone.

"Life will go on. It's just different." There's such simple grace within those words, encouraging us to parallel the gift of a departed loved one's impact with the painful steps forward into continuing life.

And that it did, and yes, I was. *Different* for me meant I better get a move on and live the life I wanted. Derek's sudden departure served as a stark reminder of my limited time on Earth. I am forever grateful for his friendship and the unexpected prize of a new perspective on life. From then on, I became more open to embracing spontaneity, allowing unexpected outcomes to unfold without the burden of excessive planning and control. *Thanks, man. I miss you.*

The initial news of losing my special friend in such a sudden way scarred me for years. The trauma included longstanding hesitance to reach out to loved ones as fear crouched to shout they were no longer with us. Though I'll never know Derek's understanding of me and my feelings for him, losing him taught me the true meaning of love. As I reflect on our journey together, I realize love can take many forms, sometimes revealing itself in unexpected ways.

* * *

Calgary's thriving gay bar scene was screaming to get my attention, thanks to Reg's encouragement. My first visit was terrifying and thrilling at the same time. The entrance to the nightclub of choice wasn't on the street but in the back, appearing even more clandestine. I followed Reg through the door and into the dim, cramped entrance area. The booming dance music made my heart beat even faster. A cover charge was typical, but it turns out, if you're new, some rules fly right out the window. With great big smiles, they waved us right in.

Years of built-up anguish and suffering evaporated the instant I entered the crowded hallway behind the main dance floor. A powerful feeling of safety was immediate. In that place, nobody would threaten or hurt me or turn my haunting secrets into fodder for rejection or shaming. The awareness that all those men not only understood my struggles—but were expressing them with great abandon—affected me on a whole new level. As Reg guided me around the maze-like building, I remained in a trance-like state.

It was evident I was being noticed and drawing some attention. And I was *really* liking how it felt. Many attractive men were noticing and approving me (as one of them) with their eyes, a smile, a nod, or a friendly touch. My still-uncertain masculinity was being affirmed and it became more intoxicating than anything they served from behind the bar. In the shake of a donkey's tail, visiting gay nightclubs was a regular weekend experience.

Despite my longstanding insecurities around men, the attention I enjoyed soon became expected. I had gained a new magical power to choose whomever I found attractive to become better acquainted. Don't misunderstand; Hollywood's good looks weren't mine. Turns out they showered all their concentration upon anyone new. I soon discovered it was a game for regulars to compete to see who would win the new one. And I confess, I was *won* many times over the next few months.

Those sexual experiences were drastically better than what happened with personal ads Stephen two years earlier. Perhaps boys were simply more experienced in the big city. Most encounters involved a fair amount of booze, which gave me extra courage. In addition to exploring my sexuality with increasing freedom, there were often regretful choices and consequences.

Yet even with several fresh experiences of male affirmation and the thrills of being pursued as the new guy, I couldn't shake the longing and discontent within me. The gay bar scene became an unending quest for affirmation and acceptance with cycles of positive and negative experiences.

The sting of rejection snuck up on me on a school night when drinks were two-for-one. It was probably my eagerness to save money that intoxicated me to end up at a random stranger's house. The morning after, he declined my request for his name and number—a first. Then, with almost no sleep, I had to get straight to an 8:00 a.m. class. I felt dirty, embarrassed, and ashamed as I tried to focus on my training and pretend everything was normal. *What is wrong with me?*

Each negative experience set me back, causing me to stay away from the bars—and more rejection—for a few weeks. I grew a full beard for the first time to become a little more anonymous and a little less appealing.

Somewhere along the way, my heart had talked my body into wanting more than fleeting sexual gratification. But I was finding it difficult to meet others who also wanted something more. So, like always, everybody would take their places in their established roles. It's time once again for everyone to act out the script from a West End show that could never be abandoned, like *The Mousetrap.*

Nonetheless, my choices and growing familiarity continued to move me toward settling into the likelihood of accepting myself as gay. Of course, Reg was still cheering me on to make it official and come out like he had, adding some of his trademark snarkiness.

"You know you're not a breeder, Todd," he asserted, with a trademark snort.

Yet I was still terrified of my family's reaction and fearful of the social stigma, which was robust in the eighties. Most of all, it was my dad who represented the biggest risk for the rejection of a gay son and all it represented in his world. Even though we didn't connect man to man (whatever that means), I was convinced he loved me because he was that good as a father. But I couldn't imagine anything good if I came out to him.

Dad placed family above all else, and I was mindful he might have to endure a son as the gay, black-argyle sheep of the family—and not give him grandchildren. I already felt like I was a disappointment to him because I didn't connect with him about sports or his other masculine interests, such as home renovations. It felt to me hearing his son was gay would be the biggest possible disappointment to a proud, family-loving man. And so, I'd better be certain it *was* my truth before I opened a gigantic can of flesh-eating worms.

The truth is after all that time of discovery and affirmation—all within secrecy—restlessness and an absence of peace still prevailed.

So, I conclusively determined that when I finally did come out, elusive peace with myself and my life would be mine. It's what you heard all the time, from almost every angle. Many affirming sentiments are often shared by others like me, including, "I wish I would have come out sooner," or, "I don't know what I was so afraid of," and from others who knew them, "Oh, we've known all along," or "We love you for who you are, no matter what."

My inner battle raged on, with a senseless seesaw of desire and contempt for men in the foreground, while swelling pressure to declare and own my gay identity bubbled in the background.

# House of Mirrors

Living in Calgary presented a few unexpected benefits. My dad spent his childhood in east Calgary during the fifties and maintained friendships for decades with a few of his school chums. One friend had a daughter named Deborah who had taken over the family home and she caught wind I was ready to leave Lola's house. She offered to rent me her spare bedroom, located only a block away from my dad's family home in Inglewood.

Deborah was an attractive, spirited blonde who took great pleasure in talking. Besides the appealing rent, I treasured the familial connection, knowing it would mean a great deal to my dad. Living with a non-related woman was an adventure, but everything worked out. She extended grace for my share of the rent until I found a job, which took a few weeks. And after a surprise termination from there, she helped me again and I was hired at her workplace. Deb was kind to me, and living with an older woman helped my reputation!

But our cohabitation came to an end after Deb shared her plans to move in with her boyfriend. She asked if I was interested in assuming the lease for the entire house. I was eager to become a landlord, so I agreed to the deal knowing the low rent for the whole house presented an opportunity. An empty spare bedroom could generate income to reduce my share of the rent, a tempting option for a soon-to-be starving student.

My inaugural roommate entered my life while I was in my exciting new job as the assistant manager at a rare single-screen theater, part of a chain owned by Paramount Pictures. But soon, my first-ever management position faded to black when my overconfident pride triggered a staff revolt led by the older candy bar girl who had wanted my job. A Paramount vice president visited us once and told me if I remained in the industry for a mere three months, it would become my life. *I guess it's not meant to be.*

Ryan worked at a brand-new luxurious sister theater where we provided extra popcorn and staff when they were swamped. While he wasn't my type, his friend David presented an altogether different story. Dark-haired, strikingly handsome and athletic, David would sometimes crash on the sectional sofa bed in our living room. It would have been easy to interpret David's overly approachable demeanor as a curious open door, but I curbed myself out of respect for Ryan, compelling private thoughts to untangle themselves as usual. Nevertheless, it was enjoyable to wake up during the night and catch glimpses of an appealing Adonis sleeping on my couch.

Roommate escapades continued when Ryan was replaced by Donny, boasting blonde hair, a slender build, and a soft-spoken nature. I became fond of him, but our paths seldom crossed due to his odd work shifts. However, about a year after Donny moved out, we ran into each other at 318, my favorite gay bar, named after its street address. Our mutual surprise was unmistakable. After a few too many drinks, we ended up making out at his place, although I suspect it was a novelty reaction to our shared reality after being roommates for several months. It was the one time I ever hooked up with a roommate, though it wasn't until he was no longer a roommate.

There are a few similar stories when I ran into someone I knew at the bar but had no idea they were paddling the same canoe. Every time, there's initial shock and surprise or delight, then the penny drops while thinking about past interactions and telltale signs. *I always knew!* The last step was sizing him up as a romantic candidate (or more) i.e., target acquired, initiate come-on sequence. Sometimes, it goes elsewhere and sometimes not. Nonetheless, it was most often a welcome diversion unless he was a boss… or family member.

\*\*\*

Donny's exit meant yet another vacancy, so my search for a new roomie shifted into high gear under the final countdown to launch my full-time studies at SAIT. While working at The Bay downtown, I forged a connection with Jones, a young, easygoing security guard. He introduced me to his friend Lincoln, who was eager to leave home and live in his own place.

Lincoln worked as a cashier at Safeway at a time when employees earned a baffling amount of money courtesy of their union's collective bargaining, so his share of the rent wouldn't ever be a problem. Lincoln and I clicked right away. He exhibited maturity beyond his years which belied his boyish appeal, and I appreciated his unconventional sense of humor. He was of similar height to me, with light brown hair and an attractive smile. Indeed, I found him charming. However, as in similar situations, fear shackled me from discussing (or pursuing) anything further, contented to enjoy his companionship. *I think I could trust him one day.*

Our spacious kitchen transformed into a site for occasional poker games. Lincoln invited Jones, who brought his friend, another Safeway employee. As you might imagine, there was plenty of money on the table when playing cards with those lads. Although I was no shark, we sure had lots of fun… and booze. At last, I'd discovered a beer that didn't turn my mouth inside out, so Old Milwaukee became a habit that seemed a lot more manly than mixing garnished cocktails while hanging out with all the other boys. My beer of choice was also a fitting tribute to my Wisconsin friend Jerry who'd introduced me to the brand.

Those social times expanded and encompassed more people, leading to weekend get-togethers sometimes hosted at different houses. I soon met an enchanting young woman from their social circle named Raven, who knew how to wear her long, dark hair. Her energetic yet ordered personality resonated with me, and we forged a quick connection. Remarkably, there was some chemistry between us, which stunned me. At the time, I was active in the gay bar scene, with a handful of male sexual experiences under my belt. *So, wait, I'm not actually gay, or maybe bisexual?*

Amidst those rounds of persuasive same-sex escapades, Raven emerged as an enchanting temptress. Given my past girl-kissing ordeals, it was all the more surprising our first kiss was wonderful. Best characterized by its wonderful gentleness, our smooch symbolized Raven herself: soft and sweet. Our tender encounter stood out in stark contrast against my experiences with men—no five o'clock shadow face burn!

After dropping Raven off after a special evening out, I was on my way home when something like an invisible tractor beam snatched me up and dropped me back at the gay bar. While Raven was enamoring for sure, the greater affirmation and flagrant flattery from forbidden gay adventures flickered like a neon sign. I truly desired to explore more of the mysterious with Raven, but as they say, a bird in the hand is worth two in the bush!

In an attempt to explain to Lincoln where I was at with Raven, I mustered the courage to be candid and shared my story and struggles with him. To my relief, he embraced my vulnerability with unwavering acceptance. I felt a surge of gratitude when Lincoln gallantly offered to intervene and inform Raven of my circumstances. The news allowed her to join the ranks of those who can say their guy dumped them for another man, more or less. That kind of rejection hurts less, so I'm told. Yes, I was troubled that my decision could hurt Raven, but I was locked in and couldn't turn back.

\* \* \*

To improve my financial situation while juggling the demands of being a full-time student with a part-time job, I transformed the vacant basement rec room into a bedroom for one more roommate. The ad I posted attracted a friendly, tall, athletic figure with a radiant smile named Simon, who moved in within days. He confessed that my decorative mini blinds visible from the street provided some reassurance, as he'd thought the house looked a little sketchy.

Simon was a little older than me and enmeshed with a high-maintenance woman named Brenda, who buckled him into a relentless rollercoaster of anguish; I assumed the sex had to be great. I frequently provided him with emotional support, engaging in countless hours of heartfelt conversations and pseudo-counseling sessions.

Alcohol was the habit that served as Simon's refuge to numb his emotional pain. One memorable evening, I returned home late from school to find Simon a weepy wreck. It was obvious he'd imbibed big time, revealing through tears that Brenda had ended their relationship, a dread he'd harbored for some time.

Being generous with my hugs was standard practice, and my roommate Simon was in despair and needed consoling. We stood in the archway separating the living room from the hallway as Simon clung to me. He was leaning over me, sobbing nonstop as I held him close. Amidst his slurred speech and slobbering, Simon's affection began to intensify as we stood locked in an intimate embrace. *What is going on here?*

His arousing behavior flummoxed me. But I had a deeper desire to support him, so I rejected exploiting his vulnerability. Gently pulling back, I asked if he'd like a drink of water, which I fetched for him. Recognizing the high level of his booze intake, I suggested he needed to rest and sleep it off. He agreed, and I assisted him to bed, closing the door between us.

Our near-miss incident became one of those moments that replayed on repeat in my mind, reminiscent of a fantasy scene from one of Reg's videos. *What if I'd gone along with it?* The next day, Simon apologized, and I acknowledged both his pain and amorousness. We had a laugh about it, nothing more.

Soon, Lincoln bought a house, and I was unhappy to see him move out. His departure meant that Simon was upgraded to the spacious main-floor bedroom. The way was paved for a new basement occupant, which in turn led to a parade of rotating roommates seeking affordable rent and benefitting from my impatience and lack of selectivity. Simon ended up moving out to reunite with a remorseful Brenda, hoping to salvage their hopeless relationship, and the roommate rotations continued.

\* \* \*

Simon and Brenda had a friend named Aleah, an intriguing woman with a dark complexion, dark brunette hair, an infectious sense of humor, and relentless self-confidence. We hit it off upon meeting, and her assertiveness led to a few dates with some early romance. She once described my secret singing voice as "phenomenal" and flattery had long been my downfall. Aleah still lived at home and her parents were delightful company when we all enjoyed dinner together a few times.

Despite what happened with Raven, a part of me still wondered if I would be aroused by a woman whom I found attractive. *What if sex with a woman is even better?* Aleah was so bold it seemed apparent I would soon find out.

However, only a couple of weeks into knowing her, Simon informed me they suspected Aleah might be pregnant and seeking a baby daddy. That became a possible explanation for her boldness, perhaps to appease her traditional parents. *Well, that's something new!*

But unless her fetus could be explained by an immediate and immaculate conception, our relationship would have to hurry the hell up to support a plausible backstory. But the mere thought of instant fatherhood with Aleah freaked me out, so I ended it by disclosing my ongoing attractions to men, which was getting easier to do. She was surprised and disappointed, but we remained amicable and occasionally met for lunch downtown.

\* \* \*

Out for a stroll in the neighborhood one weekend, I stumbled upon an abandoned puppy and rescued him without hesitation. An adorable medium-sized shepherd mix captured my heart, and I called him Buddy. Growing up, I had a special connection with our family dog, who was a forever faithful friend ready to listen during some troubling times. Buddy's unforeseen arrival before I began school seemed well-timed because a dogged companion could ease the anticipated stress of the program.

Buddy appeared to be part kangaroo because he could leap over the towering six-foot fence in the backyard with the greatest of ease. He developed into an exceptional frisbee dog, wowing the summer Saturday crowds at Prince's Island Park in downtown Calgary with his awe-inspiring aerial agility.

After several months of raising Buddy and forging an unbreakable bond—perhaps too much of a bond—I discovered his given name by accident. Faintly inscribed in red pen on the underside of his leather collar was the word "Mickie" beside a local phone number. While it may have been selfish, I couldn't bear the thought of releasing him to his original family. We had become a devoted duo.

Buddy grew into the most incredible roommate of them all. He appreciated the company of my roommates when I stayed late to complete school projects or when I spent the night in someone else's bed instead of on my own with him. *I'm sorry Buddy.*

My revolving door of roommates was worth the trouble because it had reduced my share of the rent to only fifty dollars a month. Past that, all those young men stepping in and out of my home and life demonstrated significant acceptance of my new alternative lifestyle. With gratitude, they all inched me closer to self-acceptance.

\* \* \*

Tessa and a friend decided on a whim to leave Kelowna, and I was delighted to hear they selected Calgary as their new home. My little sister had no trouble finding work and love in short order. Even though we shared the same city, our busy lives still got in the way of spending much time together.

But one summer afternoon, Tessa and I decided to hang out downtown and enjoyed a heartfelt talk on a shady bench. As we chatted, I found myself reflecting on how much of my real life I had been keeping from her. I don't believe it had been intentional; she was simply a victim of my prevailing "keep safe, don't tell" policy. It seemed ironic I held a degree of confidence that disclosing my sexual struggles wasn't going to change her perspective of me. Perhaps I was apprehensive she couldn't hold anything back from Mum and Dad. *Can I really trust her with this?*

I hadn't planned on it, but it seemed like the right time to come clean. It began with the standard disclosure of my longstanding desire to share something personal with her. I'm pretty sure most people figure out where the conversation is going with the textbook opener. Tessa looked at me with love in her eyes, and I spilled my guts as she listened with her heart.

"I love you, Todd, no matter what," she declared. She wasn't surprised and appreciated it being out in the open, agreeing to not share the news with others. Curious about my current status, I brought her up to date and she encouraged me to keep searching for the right one.

In a few daring minutes, I had bridged the sacred family gap that long felt like it led off the edge of the world. My reward was full assurance that at least my dear sister would remain true to me on this perilous voyage. Her full and warm hug sealed the promise.

\*\*\*

One would think after years of hiding and pretending all was *this* way when actually all was *that* way, that the double-life mindset would be abandoned as one enters the gay lifestyle and bar scene. Not so much.

While it's true I felt a phenomenal new kind of acceptance when inside gay bars, life quickly resumed as fearful normal on the outside. Public conversations with Reg or other knowing friends required codewords and nicknames to avoid detection and remain safe.

Constant divided thinking and careful navigation became normal practice in my gay circles. For example, if a gay friend lives with his lover, they might refer to one another as a "roommate" when in public. At work, while exchanging tales of weekend pursuits, one might lie and name a popular straight bar instead of specifying one's gay bar of choice. When dating a man named Bob, he might become "Roberta" during a conversation when others may overhear you.

Secretive, veiled behavior became second nature, and it taxed my mind. Besides the obvious social benefits, that ever-present dilemma was another reason gay people preferred to be around each other: to help each other keep their thoughts straight! However, does anybody truly understand the long-lasting effect of constant self-inflicted duality? For me, it meant I was hyperaware of what I was saying to whom and who might be listening. Everything passed first through the who's-listening filter for one reason alone: to stay safe.

The great paradox was in my efforts to be my true self, I'm convinced the duality conditioning and forced compartmentalizing caused me to become even more at ease with hiding in front of anyone different from me. Consequently, instead of achieving acceptance and freedom to be myself, I became trapped in maintaining the illusion that I was someone else. Talk about irony!

# Breaking Olympic Fever

In February 1988, Calgary hosted the Olympic Winter Games with great anticipation and fanfare enjoyed by all. CTV, the designated host broadcaster, forged a partnership with SAIT to recruit student technicians to help fill hundreds of positions needed to televise the games. Most candidates from SAIT were second-year students who would gain an impressive practicum experience. I felt honored to be selected by instructors as one of a handful of first-year students who would join their ranks. They stationed me at the International Broadcast Centre on the Stampede Grounds, near downtown Calgary.

The Olympics offered a once-in-a-lifetime privilege for any broadcast technician, and many veterans would've jumped at the chance even without pay. As a starving student, I felt a jubilation like that of a lotto winner. CTV compensated us with union wages, including overtime and meal allowances, bringing in thousands of dollars in only three weeks. *Oh, Buddy, you're gonna eat well now!*

If the prestige and pay weren't reward enough, there was more. Sunice Apparel, an official sponsor, lavished all personnel with complete indoor and outdoor CTV Olympics wardrobes to be worn during shifts—or, in my case, almost every chance I got. Plundering through the generous booty of clothing gifts, I held back tears of gratitude like a kid on Christmas Day. Olympic fever permeated every corner of the city, and anyone adorned in official Olympic attire commanded celebrity-like status, short of signing autographs.

Imagine the scene: me strutting into 318, attired in my fancy CTV coat, eager to seek special attention and affirmation, especially now that I was no longer the new kid on the block. While absorbed in a conversation with an intriguing and somewhat smitten man named Bill, I glimpsed an attractive patron entering the bar, wearing the same jacket as mine. He seductively made his way toward me as if voodoo or some other magic magnetized our matching coats. As he glided into my personal space, undeniable chemistry occupied the air. *Well, what do I do now?*

Still enchanting Bill as I faced him, I leaned on the chair behind me. I could sense "Jacket's" compelling presence, yet I hesitated, not wanting to slight Bill. To my surprise, I felt Jacket gently brushing his knee against my hand on the chair, a subtle yet effective way of reflecting my exact thought: *Hey, sexy!*

In that electrifying moment, I couldn't help but visualize the scene from across the smoke-filled bar right in front of everyone else. There I was, straddling two bar stools, chatting with one suitor while another shamelessly made his intentions known right behind me. I didn't know my heart could pound that fast while I remained seated in the thrilling and somewhat naughty moment. The knee-brushing persisted, and Jacket mustered patience until I politely excused myself from Bill, allowing me to turn and reward him with the undivided attention of Buddy looking at a peanut butter treat.

Jacket, more formally known as Matt, tousled his dirty blond hair while standing at about the same height as me but with a strong and athletic physique. His smile, like his shoulders, was broad and substantial. Matt radiated uber-confidence, yet he also seemed kind and gentle. His intense brown eyes hinted at mischievous playfulness, and his voice was smooth and sincere. *How on earth could a guy like this be interested in me?* It seemed unreal.

The next hour yielded a deluge of similar stories of overcoming struggles and feeling like outsiders. But unlike me, Matt had somehow navigated through it all with resilient purposefulness, and (also unlike me) how he quickly came to terms with being gay. As difficult as it was to conceive, learning about Matt's liberated journey made him even *more* attractive, spellbinding me like no other.

As the clock struck the appointed hour of bar closure, Matt ushered me outside with an air of urgency. Without hesitation, he initiated an amorous encounter leaving me breathless. *I'm not even drunk!* I found myself surrendering to the tender advances of the veritable stranger, a realization that scared me a little, even as I tried to pay little attention to the sizzling sparks flying about.

Summoning some self-control—or perhaps *any* manner of control—I asked if he could slow it down, a request he graciously granted. After all, we *were* out in public!

With a suave charm impossible to resist, Matt asked for my phone number. If I could, I would've etched it onto his skin with permanent ink. With equal enthusiasm, I secured his as well. With the moment of parting upon us, we hugged once more with a simple but promising kiss. We agreed to talk again. *Just how fast can I get home and call him?*

\*\*\*

As a broadcast student from Mount Royal College, CTV had also recruited Matt and stationed him at the Olympics press center in Max Bell Arena. My assignment was as a video controller (a "shader" in TV tech jargon) in the booking studio control room within the International Broadcast Center on the Calgary Stampede grounds. The proximity meant we worked about fifteen minutes apart by car or light rail transit.

Under strict regulations of the International Olympic Committee, the host broadcaster must maintain a television studio accessible to any nation wishing to utilize it. Our booking studio regrettably remained underutilized, leaving my SAIT colleagues and me to spend hours in the staff lounge, eager to receive a booking that could materialize at any moment. While I longed for more action, I refrained from complaining, as the pay, perks, and prestige were plenty worthwhile for me.

However, our moment of glory arrived when Katarina Witt, the illustrious German Olympic Gold medalist in figure skating, graced our studio for a live interview on German television. Although I couldn't comprehend a single word, it was an elating experience to be responsible for controlling the quality of her video image that beamed through the studio cameras back to her homeland. The menacing words of my brash television instructor yelled at me in my head. *Now don't f\*\*k it up!*

Amidst the intensity of our initial period of orientation, training, and occasional school commitments, Matt and I managed to find numerous opportunities to connect. I was enamored. Our shared Olympic credentials granted us access to restricted areas, transforming ordinary back hallways and unused studios into covert, rousing rendezvous.

Matt would have also been a starving student except for living with his supportive and understanding parents. At first, I felt uneasy visiting them as his latest fling, despite his reassurances. The remarkable acceptance and affection his parents showed their son and his gay lifestyle amazed me; it was like stepping into the Twilight Zone. I had long imagined such a positive response was doubtful from my own parents. *Could I be wrong on this?*

As our connection deepened, Matt and I shared private time at my place one evening, talking and lying close together on the sectional. Without any forewarning, I found myself overcome with uncontrollable torrents of tears. Neither of us knew what was happening. I wept for about fifteen minutes while Matt simply held me close.

"Hmmm, that was really weird," I offered as calmness arrived. He laughed in agreement, and nothing more was said.

Reflecting upon the episode, I think perhaps years of accumulated pain, fears, and self-rejection were purging through my tears. Enveloped in the warm and caring embrace of a guy I esteemed, I felt wholly known and accepted—warts and all. The transforming moment became a watershed in my journey into masculine security and self-acceptance. *If he can love me this way, maybe I can too.*

As the Winter Olympics drew to a close, Matt initiated a pivotal conversation to probe the trajectory of our relationship. It was blatant he commanded widespread admiration because of his striking appearance and ultra-charming personality—oh, and the six-pack abs didn't hurt. Yet, considering countless opportunities and invitations from more worthy suitors, Matt still asked me to make a long-term commitment to him alone. An easy decision, right?

We stood at the very zenith of my sexual awakening. The attention I still received from admirers was irresistible, and the selfish allure proved too great. Everything pointed to one answer: it was simply too soon to settle down. In the middle of tears and loving hugs, we agreed to take a hiatus and go our separate ways.

Within days, Matt connected with another Olympic technician employed by ABC in New York. Upon completing his schooling, Matt emigrated to be with him. Meanwhile, I sought what I wanted with new-found confidence thanks to Matt's interest in me. However, upon returning to the bar scene, I found myself ensnared once again in a repetitive *Groundhog Day* cycle of everything-is-amazing/everything-sucks, questioning whether I'd made a huge mistake. *Oh what have I done?*

\* \* \*

During one of the many extended breaks from the booking studio, I found myself in the Media Center at one of the banks of computers reserved for reporters and Olympics personnel. On the other side facing me, an attractive blond man piqued my curiosity. His prominent credentials made it easy to see his name was Bryan. Lacking the courage to initiate a conversation on the spot, I covertly noted his name, intending to pursue contact later.

Email wasn't widespread then, but the host broadcaster offered an internal messaging system for all personnel. Determined, I tracked down Bryan's info and sent him a note. I said I noticed he was from out of town and offered to show him around. My brazen act was unchartered territory, a departure from my comfort zone and well beyond the inherent safety of a gay bar. Excitement surged within me, and I awaited his response, wondering how or if he would respond. Two days later, my heart raced as I opened his reply on the public computer.

"Thank you very much for reaching out to me. Yes, I am here in Calgary all alone and the nights are very cold, and I could use some company," wrote Bryan.

Bryan's response seemed positive, but an undertone made it feel a little blurry. I noted he refrained from providing a contact number or suggesting a meetup. Perhaps he was also exercising caution, mirroring my own. Nevertheless, his willingness to continue our electronic dialogue required an appropriate response soon enough.

A day or two passed before one of my classmates named Jennifer—also working at the Olympics—sought me out on an urgent matter. I held a soft spot for Jennifer—she possessed an undeniable charm with her petite stature, long dark hair, captivating eyes, and cheerful personality. Yet, her demeanor was serious when we met that morning.

"As a friend, I care about you and must tell you something," she expressed in a hushed, subdued tone that belonged to someone else.

"Oh, okay, Jennifer. What is it?" I inquired, my heart thumping faster as I sifted through a jumble of secrets, both old and new.

Until that moment, I was confident none of my classmates had an inkling of my struggles or undercover adventures. I was careful to maintain my psychological compartmentalization, keeping my personal life strictly separate from my school life.

Jennifer proceeded to reveal a conversation with Susan, another classmate, also employed during the Olympics. Unlike us, Susan had landed a position as a personal assistant and worked outside the International Broadcast Center. Nonetheless, all personnel utilized the computers in the Media Center and throughout the network to stay connected to the message service.

"Bryan is her boss, and Susan reads all the messages he receives. This is awkward," she stammered, her voice laced with unease.

My heart skipped another beat, and my breath caught in my throat. *Oh shit.*

"She saw your message, Todd. And she's posing as Bryan in the responses you've received. I think she might be planning to out you. So, please be careful," she warned, her eyes filled with concern.

Trying to play it cool, I mustered up a sincere thank you and gave her a hug of appreciation. There was no way to conceal any more from Jennifer, but my brain whirred with a plan to backpedal out of the situation to salvage my reputation, as the fear goblin began its taunting.

The following day, I returned to the media center, logged into my message account, and found "Bryan's" message still waiting for my response.

"Thanks for the reply, Bryan. It turns out that I'm swamped with shifts and classwork. But maybe I'll see you around. Hope you enjoy Calgary!"

Later that day, his response arrived, indicating puzzlement over my message. I deleted it without any further thought, grateful to Jennifer for her timely intervention. Our SAIT class was small and close-knit, and news of that nature would spread like wildfire. The thought of the possible reactions from my fellow students and instructors was nothing short of frightful. *Why wasn't I honest with any of them before now? Am I really fooling anyone?*

As far as I could tell, our class was devoid of gay people which was unexpected considering the program's creative arts nature. However, I couldn't help but worry about the potential hurt or anger my duplicity could evoke in dear school friends, especially given the close bonds we had forged throughout our intensive program. Concern about my friend Alan's reaction and his possible rejection loomed highest of all.

Twenty years later, at a class reunion, one classmate remarked to me, "We all thought you were gay!" I couldn't help but chuckle heartily at the ample irony, reflecting on the intricate web of secrets and unexpected twists that had shaped my SAIT and Olympic experience. *I guess I'm the fool now.*

# Embraced and Released

Reg's constant encouragement to come out caused me to wonder if going all in might finally overcome my doubts and double-mindedness about my sexuality. It'd been about a year since I broke up with Matt and a new suitor was looking quite promising.

I was twenty-two when my family gathered in snow-covered Calgary on the eve of my beloved Uncle's funeral. He was married to Auntie Dagney, my dad's older sister.

Mum and I were able to grab a moment together, so with a spontaneous leap, the words formed in my mouth. Perhaps grief over my uncle brought it on... or the steady flow of vodka tonics.

"Mum, I've wanted to tell you for a very long time. And I'm concerned about how you're going to take it. But I just can't keep it from you anymore," I squeaked out.

Mum's loving eyes widened, her toes tensed, bracing herself for impact. The hotel room crackled with tension as my sweat beaded where it normally doesn't.

"Yes, honey, what is it?" she asked, with the hesitancy of a seasoned parent.

My heart pounded against my ribcage while my wringing hands raced over one another.

"I'm gay. That's it."

The words rushed from my mouth like a Boxing Day shopper dashing into an electronics store for a half-price big-screen TV. They also held more conviction than I anticipated. *Uh, who was that?*

"Oh, honey, are you sure?" she clarified.

"Since arriving in Calgary, I've met many others, and I feel like I've finally found where I belong," I shared from my newfound posture.

"Well, we just want you to be happy and have a good life, Todd, that's all," she emphasized.

Through her caring eyes and the tone in her voice, I sensed my mother's great love for me—her third-born son, not quite like her older boys. My heart flooded with gratitude. Mum had a few more questions, but our time was shortened as I had to rejoin the others. She reiterated my happiness was all that mattered to her, and I believed her.

The strength of our unique closeness over the years caused me to believe with certainty that once I made my declaration, my mom wouldn't reject me. But our chat helped me gauge how my family would respond to the news. And we were off to a good start... well, from where I stood, at least.

After we parted, Mum remained in her hotel room alone and wept. Auntie Winnie stumbled upon her in a troubled state.

"What on earth is the matter, Wanda?" Auntie inquired with honest concern.

"My son just told me he is gay," she shared through her tears as her long held suspicion was cast into stone.

Auntie Winnie's response brimmed with affection and empathy. They delved into heartfelt conversations about other extended family members facing similar circumstances. Indeed, a remarkable phenomenon within my father's expansive clan yielded a disproportionate number of us who embraced diverse lifestyles and identities.

* * *

My dad's oldest sister and her husband (also my godparents) had a son, who tragically passed away in his late teens, and two daughters. Both daughters ventured into marriage, and all seemed ordinary to the rest of us. However, life took unexpected turns as both daughters eventually left their husbands for the love of women.

My dad's second oldest sister, Dagney, and her husband had a son, Harold, and a daughter, Jean. Harold lived his life mostly secluded from the rest of the family. Jean and her partner Mary forged a steadfast bond that has endured for more than thirty years.

My dad's third oldest sister and her husband had a son who married and had a daughter named Danielle, who has since transitioned to Dan.

My dad's only brother (tragically taken from us in an automobile accident), and his wife had two boys and a girl. One son, Glenn, married Cindy and fathered three girls. One of their girls remained in her committed partnership with a woman for over five years.

My dad's closest sister, Winnie, and her husband opted for adoption, joyously welcoming two girls into their family. So far, it's the only family line devoid of anyone living a queer lifestyle. I say, "so far" because their daughter Lola has married and divorced four times and jested about "taking up with a woman." You may recall I lived with my cousin Lola for a few weeks when I first moved to Calgary, and over the years I've discovered she might be too much woman for any one man.

The extraordinary pattern of queerness in my extended family has sparked discussions and debates, with some positing that genetics play a role, perhaps pointing to the so-called "gay gene," publicized in the early nineties by a gay genetic researcher.

I remain uncertain about such origins and lean toward a combination of nature and nurture influences, but I know our diverse family dynamics made for a welcoming environment for someone trying to figure himself out. We've had some awesome chats at family reunions over the years, and I'm so grateful for the accepting love of my extended family.

\* \* \*

Back at the hotel, Mum disclosed everything to Dad that same night. She said he was doing okay with the news, but I wondered what he wasn't saying. Dad resolved this was a weighty matter demanding immediate family discussion, conveniently possible because we were already gathered for my uncle's funeral. I expressed some apprehension and resistance, but Dad was adamant my siblings hear the news directly from me. It bothered me a little he was being so pushy about the timing, but after Mum's response, I had new hope all might be okay.

The day after the funeral, my family gathered at a charming downtown restaurant called the Green Room; the name wasn't lost on me, given my skirmish with a bit of stage fright. Despite my test run with Tessa, I'd long remained apprehensive about how my confession would be received by my stereotypically straight brothers. Yet, I rested in the unusually close bonds we shared and remained hopeful for their acceptance and heartened by Mum's report on Dad's response from the night before.

Surprisingly, there was no astonishment, though tears were shed as we sat together in the reality of the moment. Tessa rose and embraced me without hesitation. She pledged her abiding love and support, not letting on that she already knew as a loyal member of Team Todd. John and Greg also joined the hugs and expressed their love for me—along with their stated inability to understand the nature of homosexuality. *No problem, maybe I don't either.* Dad hugged me too, but I was left doubting he actually was okay. We agreed everyone needed more time to process my declaration. *But, hey I'm good... I've had all the time in the world.*

Overall, I suppose it transpired as well as it could have, and I was extremely grateful. If my life were a hit TV show, I would have scripted the night to be a much more poignant scene. You could say I wasted a lot of years worrying about nothing at all, and I wouldn't argue. I'm grateful for the resilient bond of love within my family. It's such an enduring gift.

That summer we all got together for our annual family reunion with our extended family and longtime friends, the first one since I'd come out. Mum was the same as ever, so happy to see me and ready to have a good time. Her warm hug whisked me back to my younger years when we were even closer. I loved how Tessa ran from the car when she first saw me. I only needed to see her face to know I was valued and important in her life. As we sat around the campfire that night, Greg and John looked different in its flickering light. They didn't seem as unreachable to me and their smiles and laughter at my jokes reminded me of what I'd known all along: They loved their little brother, gay or not.

I realize others like me in similar situations don't fare as well. My heart breaks when I hear accounts of parents shunning their gay children, often due to their perception of faith and religion. Under the guise of "tough love," they hope their child will turn from their ways in order to regain a relationship with loved ones and their idea of God.

I cannot tell you how thankful I am that dynamic wasn't part of my story. If this mirrors your experience, please know you are *not* alone, no matter how it feels. Please believe it can and will get better, especially after you reach out to the right person at the right time. It's the *only* way to experience first-hand an emotional embrace that's critical for moving into self-acceptance and personal transformation.

Yes, it's scary as hell, but it's not optional for anyone seeking to integrate all the compartments in their own life. Wholeness can only come when all our separated mental and emotional bits and pieces come together in harmony. Besides, you could discover you're not that much different than all the other boys.

In the face of complex family dynamics and confronting the paralyzing fear of rejection, I was ultimately able to share my struggles, casting aside the decade-long burden of secrecy and isolation that had weighed down my soul like gravity times ten.

Note it began with less threatening prospects, i.e., roommate, co-worker, and friends, which helped build confidence and enough trust to open up to my family. Even though it didn't begin as an intentional strategy, I know it was the right approach for me. The immediate and profound sense of relief that washed over me was a testament to the transformative power of disclosure, and the doorway to freedom to finally and fully be me.

*　*　*

A few months later, Dad visited again and we connected in an unforgettable way. He visited my home in his old neighborhood, and we walked together to a nearby school playground where we hung out and talked without misgivings. Dad unloaded all his concerns on me, and I also unburdened myself, pouring out all my feelings and memories of growing up under his rigid authority at home.

It's true Dad enforced strict rules at home, especially table manners. To this day, I am mindful of planting my elbows on the dinner table. As an older child, I was sitting beside him when he observed my wayward elbow perched where it ought not to be. He seized my hand, yanked it straight up, and slammed it down on the tabletop with a resounding crack. A searing pain shot through my arm.

Everyone else froze, all mouths agape, as silence saturated the kitchen. No words were needed, but my tears couldn't be stopped.

While his behavior may sound cruel, I didn't sense any malice or ill intent from Dad in the moment. Sure, surprise and pain were mine, but it was an effective teaching method he inherited from his father, and that's all it was to him. Incidents like those solidified Dad's unyielding authority at home. And as intended, my table manners accelerated, perhaps surpassing expectations in many social circles.

As I've shared many times, I didn't resonate with my dad's masculinity, but I knew without a doubt he loved me as his unique third son. Over the years, we've grown even closer, and it still warms my heart when he deliberately uses the word "son" when addressing me in our conversations. It's a small gesture that emanates his love and reinforces my identity, no matter where life takes me. *I love you, Dad.*

# PART THREE

# The Revelation

One warm summer night, I ventured out to meet a couple of my regular bar buddies, Curtis and Gary. We enjoyed a friendly chat alongside the pool tables on the upper level of a new gay bar. Our conversation took a sharp turn when my friends shared about a support group for people unhappy with being gay and wanted change. I thought they were joking, but their expressions said otherwise. *Huh? Your sexuality isn't fixed?* The disclosure struck me like a bolt of lightning. My mind inflated with possibilities, like a shiny mylar balloon emblazoned with large fluorescent letters: WTF?

I'd never encountered such a concept. *I don't have to be gay?* My attention span collapsed at the very thought. After all, it was believed a person's same-sex orientation was inborn, and the sooner one comes to terms with it, the better it is for them and everyone else in their life. This newfound data sideswiped me, setting my mind and heart racing each other toward an unknown finish line.

With courage, Curtis and Gary took turns sharing their opposite kind of "out" experiences with me. They spoke of their weekly support group, where a dozen people gathered for encouragement and accountability to overcome their addiction to same-sex contact and seeking God's will for their lives. *Wait, what? An addiction? God's will? What does that even mean?*

My friends delved into the root causes of same-sex attractions that were thought to later contribute to same-sex behavior. Often occurring during childhood, factors included the absence of same-sex emotional connections and physical or sexual abuse. Completely foreign possibilities began to swirl in my mind and anticipation bubbled within me, I wanted to tell my friends to speak faster.

It was suggested that unmet masculine affirmation needs during childhood could leave a lasting psychological impact. Legitimate developmental needs then collide with the biological forces of puberty's raging hormones, eroticizing a boy's natural need for masculine affirmation. From a clinical perspective, the healing journey to reduce and defuse same-sex attractions was primarily based on resolving those early psychological needs.

Upon hearing those concepts the first time, I couldn't deny the possibility of a new reality where not only had I *not* chosen my same-sex attractions, but there were suggested explanations for them, contrary to the belief that one's sexuality was innate.

As the astonishing conversation opened before me there in the bar, the form of a larger-than-life jigsaw puzzle appeared in my awareness. The contoured pieces of the mental construct became recognizable and fell into place one by one. Various memories from my life emerged as puzzle pieces, clicking together to form a surprising depiction.

It was true that as a boy, I had resisted masculine connections with my dad, so I didn't receive masculine affirmation of my identity. I also grappled with his authoritarian style of leadership and discipline, triggering a decision to withdraw emotionally because I felt insecure in my individuality, even though I felt deeply loved. In some, the result of that kind of withdrawal (or withholding from a parent) can lead to gender dysphoria, but I experienced gender self-rejection—I simply wasn't masculine enough to want to be masculine.

In my childhood, it was painfully obvious I wasn't at all like my hyper-masculine brothers, who had active dating lives and shared my dad's manly passions. I found solace in the company of my mom, but to be clear, we weren't fabric shopping or doing each other's nails. She understood me and appreciated our shared interests, such as reading, cooking, and singing. The maternal bond extended to my grandmother, who also held a special place in my heart. As a toddler, I'd often be on one of their laps, as reflected in many family photos from those days.

Given my bond with my mother and my unboyish practices, I didn't feel "man enough" for my father throughout my later childhood. References to gays or homosexuals from the men in my family were disparaging and derogative. To be fair, my antennae became hyper-tuned to such comments as my same-sex thoughts and struggles increased.

The reduced meaningful masculine relationship with my dad left a void within my being, prompting me to turn to the same sex to satisfy my valid needs. Upon reaching puberty, those authentic unmet needs fused with fluctuating hormones thereby initiating the exchange of typical same-sex curiosity for erotic same-sex attractions. The ill-fated incident I'd suffered in shop class shaped a root of humiliation and shame that compounded my same-sex curiosities and feelings.

Masculine images and standards became more captivating and erotic, imbued with a sexual energy not there before. I became interested in more than my sister's teen magazines, instead being drawn to sports magazines and other images of ultra-masculine athletes.

I believed my subsequent same-sex encounters became a paradox coupling the masculine hunt for male affirmation with sexual intimacy. The ironic attraction often hinged on specific attributes of the desired object that I often already possessed but couldn't acknowledge or accept.

They said it was called the "cannibal compulsion," because it was thought cannibals devour certain others because they believed they would inherit the consumed individual's traits. The analogy extends to sexual attraction for the same sex, characterized by an inherent pull toward attributes and qualities we admire but are blinded to—or detached from—in ourselves.[2]

There it was, a plausible explanation of why, for so very long, I found other men sexually attractive. Our conversation and the unexpected insights shared by my trusted friends took immediate root in the fertile soil of my long-unsettled psyche.

As our discussion continued in our dimly lit corner of the smoke-filled bar, an insatiable thirst for more understanding consumed me.

> *Aren't all gay boys happy to be queer?*
>
> *But some aren't?*
>
> *Aren't they supposed to be the ones still in the closet?*

They said it was a "Christian" group and that God was in favor of their efforts because being gay didn't align with his plans for creation. Their religious references triggered apprehension within me because it didn't resonate with my personal beliefs, though I held no reservations about the concept of religious faith for others. In the moment, I couldn't help but acknowledge the inherent irony of being in a gay bar with two friends who didn't want to be gay.

"So, why on earth would you even be here?" I exclaimed aloud, noticing a smirk flicker across Gary's face. "Aren't you trying to not do this anymore?"

"We *are* trying," he said, with a twinkle in his eye.

When I told them I wasn't a Christian, they were kind, assuring me I was welcome to attend their meeting and check it out. *Wow. Gotta think about this more.*

# PART FOUR

# The Impossible Dream

You might think after I received my family's loving support and validation—of me and my sexuality—there'd be nothing but smooth sailing on the sea of same-sex adventures. I expected to be full steam ahead on the U.S.S. Good Ship Lollipop, decked out in my colorful nautical-themed separates. Soon after, I had docked once again for shore leave at 318 with great anticipation. But in no time, I began listing portside as a sinking feeling sloshed in my lower deck.

After officially coming out to my family, my triumphant return to the bar initially seemed less sneaky and more exciting. But there wasn't a balloon drop, and nobody handed me a membership card or slapped a yellow "I'm Out!" happy-face button on my chest. In fact, as the night wore on, everybody and everything seemed the same. The bar, unchanged. The music, the same. Even the flirty glances and pick-up lines were like they'd always been. *Hold on here, am I still the same too? Double vodka tonic please.*

A month or two later, an unexpected hookup with a nice guy named Gavin included a sleepover. Morning broke upon us as someone in the next apartment cranked up Simon & Garfunkel louder than what ought to be allowed on a Sunday morning. But it was okay while "Cecilia" played. I hummed along as the stranger named Gavin slept soundly beside me. But the next song sucked me into a melancholic muddle lasting for days that stretched into weeks.

Like the others, Gavin was sweet and affectionate with a great sense of humor. But he wasn't my "Bridge Over Troubled Waters," and neither was anyone else I'd met over the past few months. *Well, there was Matt, but I let him go.* I was weary and hoping that someone—

*the* one—would be there to dry my tears. But after all the ups and downs, it seemed to be an impossible dream, the kind that brings you down.

So, I fell into disillusionment and swore off the bar scene once more to find solace in the daily demands of school and my part-time furniture store job. I'd grown accustomed to a depressing underground life while everyone else enjoyed their happy, well-adjusted lives above. I retreated into what looked an awful lot like a closet, and it was as easy as taking a walk.

Weeks passed before Reg charmed me to join him again at 318 during the Christmas break. In unreserved disinterest, I was determined to be a wallflower, awaiting Reg's rescue to get me out of there. In front of me, the oscillating party lights punctuated the heavy dance beat I knew well as all the others were having their fun.

After ten minutes, a young stranger passed through my imagined barrier and approached me with boldness, inviting me to dance. His smile dazzled, his eyes twinkled, features impossible to ignore even in the low light. Despite my initial reservations, his appealing qualities chipped away at my resistance like a silent jackhammer on a block of melting ice.

Charles oozed boundless energy and an infectious passion for dancing. We surrendered to the rhythm, our unacquainted bodies moving in agreement. The throbbing dance music reverberated in our ears, the bass pulsating through our veins. The colorful beams splashed their paint around us, occasionally illuminating Charles's handsome face and mesmerizing dance moves. Something about his carefree demeanor and uninhibited spirit drew me in like an innocent kitten under a spell. I was utterly enchanted. *Mew.*

When Reg reemerged, he was shocked to find me out on the dance floor with someone. Without skipping a beat, I shouted that he could head out without me.

Charles and I remained engrossed in each other's company for hours. His refreshing sense of humor made him even more delightful. Our connection had deepened as we helped bring the bar to a close—a remarkable feat given the pre-dawn hour. The epitome of a gentleman, Charles insisted we exchange only phone numbers before our paths separated for the night.

Three days passed before we reconnected, our anticipation in plain sight. He was indeed younger, a mere eighteen compared to my twenty-two years of age. As cliche as it sounds, I'd encountered no one quite like him. His self-confidence was remarkable, complemented by his magnetic nerve. Our mutual chemistry bubbled up like champagne, and the depths of my soul tangled with the implications and possibilities. *Wow, good one, Reg.*

\* \* \*

As the weeks unfolded, Charles and I spent more and more time together, and it brought whirlwind romance, heightened bravery, and comfort with intimacy. Besides Matt, previous hookups didn't progress much beyond the basics of intimacy for various reasons. But out of the blue, I was suddenly facing the potential of a genuine, enduring relationship with mutual openness and commitment.

We both had roommates, which forced us to finagle private moments together. Charles's roommate, Dinah, was aware and supportive of his gay lifestyle. My current roommates were okay with mine but less enthusiastic about my overnight guests. So, we spent more time at Charles's place, with occasional sleepovers. If someone had taught her the art of knocking, we could have avoided the bedroom intrusions, but a signal system solved that in short order.

As you've heard, alcohol influenced many of my previous same-sex encounters. But not so with Charles; in fact, we seldom indulged in alcohol together. Intimacy became more powerful between us, perhaps because of our mutual commitment, a stark contrast to the fleeting outcomes of my other misadventures. His adventurous spirit was both enticing and refreshing. I found our intimate life gratifying and fulfilling, and it truly felt like what I'd ached for my whole life.

Through our intimacy, Charles championed my masculinity and strengthened it, and I reciprocated. Comparing myself to Charles held great allure at the time, but its significance wouldn't become clear until years later.

Even though my parents had generously bankrolled my school tuition and textbooks, I still shouldered my rent and living expenses. My part-time job and rental income helped, but I still had the mentality of a typical "starving student." Pasta had become a staple in my diet, with only occasional indulgences in ground beef. Pro tip: a microwave can transform a frozen block of hamburger into ready-to-eat meatloaf in under fifteen minutes. *I wonder how many will follow me for more delicious, time-saving recipes.*

As a result, it was awe-inspiring to enjoy frequent trips with Charles to Costco for giant bags stuffed with frozen chicken breasts and other luxurious indulgences transcending my modest food budget. Charles surprised me with his adeptness in the kitchen, so we often savored delicious meals and new delicacies together. *I like this drink called "herbal tea".*

Thinking back to the Simon & Garfunkel song and the subsequent tailspin of despair and withdrawal. *How things change!* I couldn't help but consider myself to be the "silver girl" encouraged to sail on because her time to shine was coming, with all her dreams on their way. Surely, Charles was my bridge, and the waters would be troubled no longer.

\*\*\*

As I propelled into my second year of intensive television training at SAIT, my career aspirations underwent a dramatic shift—but by then, almost everything was dramatic to me! I'd witnessed the extreme creative guidance applied by personnel in the control room, and it was compelling. In contrast, I observed on-air personalities are best when they do what they're told with limited creative input. I wanted to be the creative force behind the scenes, the one calling the shots. Fueled by the revelation, I changed my major to television writer/producer. The shift allowed me to write and direct commercials, a pursuit that reignited my passion for everything television.

The budding relationship with Charles also ignited a passion which evolved into a formidable distraction from my studies. The challenges of completing my second and final year of broadcast school were already formidable. As I've mentioned, the program was an unrelenting gauntlet that imposed rigorous demands and expectations on students. A nonstop barrage of projects with merciless deadlines intended to simulate the unforgiving, cutthroat realm of the modern media landscape—aptly labeled "The Real World" by our instructors. My grades began to suffer, and given the program's condensed and intense duration, even a slight misstep could send me spiraling into an abyss of failure.

The escalating tension at school set off frequent quarrels between Charles and me as I attempted to shift the blame for my academic trials onto him. Instead of allowing the challenges to drive us apart, my generous and loving Charles offered his devoted support, determined to help me persevere and emerge victorious. He came through in the crunch, and I completed my studies with passing grades. I graduated in May, only five months after Charles first asked a disinterested stranger to dance the night away.

When we first began to get serious, Charles gifted me with a sweet photo of himself. The snapshot showed him sitting on a branch in a tall tree, flashing his impressive grin. A handwritten inscription written on the back was the Trojan horse that defeated my unsuspecting defenses.

> *Todd: I've never met anyone like you before. You have a great deal of understanding about the importance of life, love, and laughter, more than most. You understand why a sunrise is beautiful, not just recognize that it is. Never put out your fire, and never be afraid of it.*
>
> *Forever and ever,*
>
> *Charles*

\* \* \*

Our incessant privacy issues and traveling back-and-forth between homes prompted serious discussions about getting our own place. It was an enormous commitment, but we overflowed with excitement and decided to go for it. To leave my rental house in Inglewood, I needed to give notice to my tenants and Deb, the homeowner. Charles also gave his notice to Dinah. Irreversible wheels of change were now in motion, which culminated in Deb's decision to put her house up for sale.

The quest for an affordable home to share with Charles needed to include my beloved Buddy, which resulted in a herculean challenge. For weeks, we scoured every corner of Calgary for something—anything—pet-friendly within our budget. However, as my roommates exited and the unstoppable moving day approached, we were still without a home.

Fantasies of a home with a large yard for a frolicking Buddy seemed like a cruel delusion. We discovered most affordable apartments had adopted strict no-pet policies, and those that hadn't were way too expensive. Deb's house was about to be sold, and I had no choice but to vacate on time. No options remained... I was coming undone.

Amidst soulful anguish and copious tears, we made the agonizing decision to find Buddy a new home with a new family. It was an excruciating choice, but there was no other way. We found some solace in picturing Buddy loving a better life with a large family, much more attention, and a vast backyard to bounce around in.

Despite our diligent efforts to find a new home for Buddy, nobody was coming forward, and only ten days remained on the countdown clock. Another painful decision was to house Buddy in a boarding camp outside the city. Daily kennel costs burdened my heavy ladened credit card adding yet another layer of stress to our already turbulent state, on top of the newspaper ad costs.

The first separation from Buddy was unbearable. Charles came by to see me as I was packing, and I was in quite a state.

"It's like... he's dead," I sputtered through my sobs. Even though he was receiving excellent care at the camp, it felt as if a part of me had also died. Charles said nothing as he held me close while I continued to pour out my tears.

Charles and I found our new place at the right price, except it was only the two of us who moved into a two-bedroom high-rise apartment in downtown Calgary. Buddy remained at the camp, but I couldn't bear to visit him there, which added even more guilt.

About two weeks later, a kind couple (who owned a house) finally responded to my ad. Preliminary feelings of gladness and reprieve were bitter-sweetened as we recovered the unsuspecting Buddy from the camp for a meeting outside our new apartment. My sweet kangaroo puppy won them over in an instant. In a moment of pure joy and relief, I voided the advertised price to the couple's amazement. They took him to their truck, and with a broken heart, I waved goodbye to my beloved Buddy, driving away with his new family—me left behind.

Another torrent of emotions ripped through me—gut-wrenching heartache intertwined with relief from mounting financial pressures. I clung tight to Charles with no regard for onlookers, sobbing nonstop, a part of my heart falling right there onto the street. *I can't even imagine going through all this without Charles.*

Even with our tight budget, I insisted on the extra bedroom in our new place. My covert plan was to maintain same-sex secrecy, telling visitors we each had our own bedroom. And, of course, that I slept on the sofa bed in my room—the same massive sectional from my old house that hardly squeezed into the small bedroom of our new place. Not once did I sleep on it.

The elaborate charade served as a poignant illustration of my ongoing struggle to accept—and openly acknowledge—my same-sex attractions. Even with an actual boyfriend in my bed, I wasn't ready to embrace any kind of gay identity in public. It became a persistent source of tension between Charles and me, as he was open and proud about his sexuality. He longed for open displays of affection, such as holding hands, while I resisted such exposed expressions with vehemence. However, I did enjoy holding his hand as we drove around in his little blue truck where prying eyes couldn't see us.

One warm Sunday, as we strolled through a remote park miles away from the presence of other humans, he attempted to take my hand. I yanked it away from him without hesitation.

"Someone might see us," I exclaimed, my voice oscillating with panic.

"You've got problems, Todd," Charles responded, his tone sullen with exasperation. There was no argument from me.

*　*　*

Living on the twenty-sixth floor in a downtown Calgary highrise offered many benefits, such as a lovely view of the Rocky Mountains and convenient access to transit. However, one drawback was the long, slow decent down whenever the fire alarm sounded, which happened more often than one might expect. I followed the same routine whenever the nasty clanging bell would wake us up in the middle of the night. False alarms were so frequent, that instead of evacuating, I'd simply check the stairwells for smoke or evidence of others evacuating. If there was no sign of a real emergency, then it was back to bed where Charles remained asleep and unconcerned almost every time.

We were enjoying pasta for lunch the day after yet another nighttime fire alarm when we were surprised by a knock on our apartment door. It was the police and they wanted to question us about the night before. They confirmed we were home sleeping when the alarm went off, like everybody else.

"Yes, I was in my room sleeping on the sectional and Charles was in his room," I explained, perhaps a little too emphatically. Specific questions about our presence outside of the apartment puzzled me, and I explained I'd carried out my usual routine and checked the stairwells before returning to bed. I guess they saw through me and asked for clarification about the nature of our relationship and our history together. *Okay fine, but I wonder what the hell this is all about.*

"We're investigating a suspicious fire. It appears someone forced burning papers under the door of an elderly woman a few floors below you," one officer explained as his eyes darted between Charles and me.

"Wow, that's terrible," I replied, as gears in my brain started to spin. "So how can we help?"

"We need to take your fingerprints so we can rule you out as a suspect," answered the other officer, who was looking around our apartment. "And we'd like to ask you both some more questions."

My pulse quickened, and I caught myself surprised by nervousness, given the certainty of innocence. But the matter wasn't up for debate, so we changed gears and got ready to go with them down to the station. *Well, this is a first!*

It felt like we were in a movie, but instead of a surly chain-smoking cop, a kind middle-aged lady took our fingerprints. The officers put each of us into separate rooms for "interviews" that felt a lot like interrogation. What followed was an incredible barrage of questions about Charles and my familiarity with him, how much I trusted him, if he could have done such a thing, and so forth. It might've been comical if rage wasn't rising within me. And for a split second, I did pause to reconsider my convictions. *He's manipulating me to blame Charles!*

The threats to disclose my interest in men and get my family involved didn't work either. I called his bluff and shouted at him to call my family and bring in whomever they wanted. I was done talking. It worked, and our interview ended. I waited until they'd finished with Charles. He said the same thing had happened in his interview, trying to get him to think I'd started the fire. *I know they're just doing their jobs, but I'm livid!*

In reflection, the scenario had all the potential to detonate our young relationship, forcing us apart in a cloud of suspicion and doubt. But it wasn't meant to be, and it made us stronger and more resolved to stand by each other no matter what anyone threw at us.

\* \* \*

In addition to the jubilant achievement of a communications diploma from SAIT, they honored me as one of two class speakers like a valedictorian. I attributed the accolade to my active involvement as a senator in the student association, a responsibility I had taken seriously enough to merge it with the harsh demands of my program. Delivering the graduation speech still stands as one of my proudest life achievements, a moment etched in my memory forever.

The Jubilee Auditorium buzzed with a crowd of over three thousand attendees, all eager to celebrate the momentous occasion for their loved ones. Amidst the sea of faces in the audience, I spotted my parents, grandparents, my beloved aunt, and one special guest named Charles. Even though I had come out to my family about three months prior, I still openly referred to Charles as my roommate. His presence at the celebration meant the world to me. Charles had played a pivotal role in crafting my speech working alongside me as it came together.

As part of my oration meant to inspire, I included a favorite fable about a hotdog seller. The original author remains anonymous, so I'll paraphrase, but the timeless wisdom remains intact as a solid reminder of how we influence others.

> *There was once a man who lived by the side of the road and sold very good hotdogs. He was hard of hearing, so he had no radio. He had trouble with his eyes, so he read no newspapers, and of course, he didn't watch television or see the news on the internet. But he sold very good hotdogs.*

*He put up signs on the highway telling everyone how good they were. He stood on the side of the road and cried out to all who passed, "Buy a hotdog. They are the best in town."*

*And many people bought his hotdogs, so he increased his meat and bun orders. He bought a bigger stove to take care of all the extra business. He finally got his son to come and help him out with his business.*

*But then something happened. His son, who was well-educated, said, "Father, haven't you been listening to the radio or reading the newspapers or watching television or seeing the news on the internet? There could be a recession coming. Inflation is higher than ever; nobody agrees on anything, and everybody thinks they're right. The foreign situation is terrible. Our domestic situation is even worse."*

*Whereupon his father thought, "Well, my son's been well-educated. He reads the papers, listens to the radio, watches television, and is always on his phone getting the latest information, so he ought to know."*

*So, his father reduced his meat and bun orders, took down all his advertising signs, and no longer bothered to stand by the side of the road to promote his hot dogs—and his sales fell almost overnight.*

*"You're right, son," the father said. "We certainly are about to have a recession."*

\* \* \*

Charles and I progressed smoothly, but soon, new tensions infiltrated our budding relationship. Even with a boyfriend, it didn't occur to me to stop going out to the bar or the "club," as it was more affectionately known. The intoxicating attention and camaraderie I enjoyed there remained substantial and affirming. Being in a committed relationship reduced some of the usual drama, perhaps a lack of neediness made me freer to have fun and flirt here and there without concern about anyone's usual intentions.

One night, I found myself there on my own, as alcohol clouded my judgment like tonic water under ultraviolet black lights (try it sometime!), I succumbed to temptation and ended up in the bedroom of a winsome fellow named Kyle. However, he surprised me when he drew a line, perhaps due to my relationship status.

"Let's not start something we can't finish," Kyle cautioned.

"Okay... probably a good idea," I replied. *Well, there's a first.*

With that, I retreated home to Charles, burdened with tremendous guilt. I vowed to not reveal my indiscretion. Sure, too much booze had played a part, but it can't shoulder all the blame. The incident signaled unseen dissonance within me that couldn't be ignored. I was in a committed, loving relationship with an attractive, stable young man at peace with himself, who adored me. Despite everything appearing idyllic—especially to my gay friends—it still wasn't enough for me. *Seriously, what the freak is wrong with me? Cheating on him? Who am I really?*

When I had first ventured into the gay bar scene, there were several random encounters, many of which were fueled by alcohol. However, those incidents weren't as frequent as they could've been during such an enticing period of discovery. Put another way, I hadn't been the "town pump," nor did I ever want to be.

It's crucial to understand that despite my struggles and insecurities, I was nurtured in a stable home by loving and committed parents. Loyalty, monogamy, and faithfulness were values I'd prized from an early age, and it only seemed natural to honor them in any relationship. Perhaps that sheds more light on why I was so distressed after betraying Charles. As far as I knew, he remained blissfully unaware of my transgression... until now, I suppose. The realization of my illogical inner conflict intensified doubts about my identity and the man I was evolving into. *Why is it all so difficult?*

\*\*\*

In the throes of my first official relationship, moments arose when I needed to remind myself of my inexperience. At twenty-two years old, I hadn't experienced any kind of long-term relationship, so having a boyfriend required some adjusting. The unchartered territory of a committed, live-in relationship unveiled a plethora of unforeseen challenges that we'd either grow through, or apart.

As my relationship with Charles progressed, it became apparent I had control issues. Or, as I prefer, a *control orientation*. Was it simply a personality trait, or perhaps a conditioned response ingrained in me under my strict father? Regardless of its origins, the inclination challenged my bond with Charles.

One of the ways the orientation manifested itself was when Charles did something to upset me, you know, like washing the dishes wrong or forgetting something important. *Oh wait a minute, didn't this also happen with Dale?* Instead of talking it out, I reacted with an abrupt emotional shutdown, withdrawing into a shell of silence. My self-imposed isolation could persist for days: no talking, no connection, simply coexisting in the same space, devoid of emotions.

The "Mr. Freeze treatment," as I've come to call it, hurt Charles, which I suppose might've been something that didn't bother me that much. It was a desperate and controlled attempt to elicit an apology or change his behavior. And that's often what happened.

To Charles's credit, he refrained from retaliation through his own anger or control tactics, saving our conflict from further escalation. Over time, he adapted to the recurring cycle, awaiting my thaw out and a return to normalcy.

In retrospect, I recognize the cruelty and selfishness embedded in my actions, and I admit it was a behavior I needed to outgrow. It did finally happen, but not while I was with Charles. And I later learned that my dad was also prone to similar tactics in his younger years. *We are similar in many ways, Dad!*

\* \* \*

Most who knew our real story could feel the chemistry between Charles and me—perhaps even those who accepted our roommate scheme. Despite our mutual attraction and strong commitment to each other, our relationship weathered bumps and bruises like most relationships, I suppose. But the undercurrent of dissatisfaction never really went away.

Due to financial limitations and my growing openness, Charles and I soon downsized into a modest one-bedroom apartment with a rather bleak parking lot view, situated only a few blocks away from the city center. A garden-variety alcoholic named Arthur managed the building; his slurred speech didn't once hint at any reservations about two young men sharing a single bedroom in his domain. *Maybe this will be the fresh start we need.*

# A Whole New World

An undercurrent of discontent in my first-ever gay romance surfaced at random, like the Loch Ness monster. A frequent occurrence was whenever I received a little attention or flattery from some random guy, turning me into a bright yellow sponge eager to soak it all up. The consequence was self-imposed humiliation (guilt) as I denied my commitment to Charles in those vain pursuits.

Most efforts failed to suppress the insatiable desire for validation from other attractive men, which caused a spiral into despair, regenerating my desire to seek fulfillment from others. Furthermore, lust's intensity fluctuated with the present condition of my relationship with Charles. If we were fighting or I was freezing, it worsened, casting a foreboding shadow over the contentment and pleasure of a loving and intimate partner.

One night, sleep eluded me as I lay beside Charles, pondering The Revelation that my friends Curtis and Gary had shared with me only a few hours earlier. I was initially excited about what I'd heard with answers to questions that had haunted me for so long. But there in bed, my enthusiasm gave way to a tempest of turmoil brewing within me, raising questions about the trajectory of my life. Doubts gnawed at me like ravenous piranha.

> *Was I still happy with Charles?*
> *If so, why do I keep looking at others for more?*
> *Why does everyone I know think I've got it made?*
> *I know Charles loves me, but is this as good as it gets?*

It was undeniable within a span of a few months, I'd fallen deeply in love with Charles, and he felt the same. On one hand, I'd gained enough confidence and self-acceptance of my sexuality that I was willing to move into a one-bedroom apartment with my gay lover only one month earlier. On the other hand, I still wasn't willing to be all in and all out loud, marching in parades or storming city hall for my rights (which would've been consistent with my long held public service interests).

Over the previous month or two, it seemed like the shine had begun to wear thin on what we had. I wondered if Charles had been unfaithful, although it was only a feeling. Perhaps it was projection blamed on my wandering eye, or I could have been reading and reacting to his unspoken response to my growing discontent. And it only made everything worse. The evidence suggested the bliss we once shared had waned, yielding to a yearning for something different, something greater.

I was in that state of mind and heart during The Revelation when I talked with Curtis and Gary earlier that evening and stumbled upon a potential escape route. They proposed possible freedom not only from the conflicts of a fading gay relationship but also from years of painful struggle as I wrestled with my persistent and unwanted same-sex attractions. Merely the hint of such lasting liberty seemed impossible to ignore. *But what about Charles?*

Inflicting rejection and emotional pain upon my boyfriend was an arduous contemplation that tormented me. Ache settled into my heart and stomach as what seemed true became the only way forward. The relentless clock ticked downward toward the inevitable moment of truth: Disclosure.

\* \* \*

Paramount was how and when to engage Charles about an issue that would've been unimaginable only months prior. Apprehensive he'd be angry with me for sharing such a radical concept with him, I also realized it would reveal my discontentment in our relationship. *He's going to be livid!*

It took two more weeks, but finally, only nine months into our zealous relationship, I mustered the courage to inform Charles about my stirring conversation with Curtis and Gary and that I wanted to explore the possibility of not being gay. My hands, clammy with nervousness, remained at my side. I fully expected his vehement rejection of such outlandish notions—and me—as I recounted all I'd learned from my friends, and I braced for impact.

Instead, Charles's reaction was an antithesis of what I'd dreaded. He asked many questions about the support group and the root causes and paid rapt attention to all I shared with mind-boggling intrigue and openness. *Wow! So relieved!*

"I'm also interested in finding out more about this, Todd," he offered, as I tried to steady my reeling self, shocked he would even go there. *Hold on... he's eager to end us? That can't be right.* After more discussion, we decided to go together to our first group meeting. *Can this be real?* Nothing was said about the obvious implications for our relationship. *We'll figure it out later, I guess.*

We met Curtis and Gary on a Tuesday night at the entrance of an old downtown office building; an overly relaxed security guard ensured we all sign in. Curtis suggested we use fake first names only. *Hmm... Siegfried? Rock? So clandestine!*

The meeting itself felt surreal and awkward. A small group of various men—and one woman—perched on stackable chairs forming an irregular circle in the middle of an over-illuminated room. The space featured musty gray carpet, white-trimmed gray walls, and large windows facing the busy street below.

Brief introductions gave way to a short inspirational talk from one guy who seemed to know what he was doing. Everyone took turns talking about their problems, careful not to talk over each other, as per the rules. We "prayed" at the end. I was told I could simply sit and listen while everyone did that, so I did. One thing I appreciated was everyone's sincerity about wanting something different from life. No one wanted their sexuality to dominate their lives, and it sounded good to me.

Charles was more comfortable with the religious feel of the group. He owned a Bible and spoke of his beliefs early in our relationship. I wasn't interested. In fact, the sight of his Bible in our bedroom made me uneasy. During one romantic interlude, I tossed a shirt to remove it from my line of sight. *Ok, I'm not in the mood anymore.*

As others shared during the meeting, I heard parts of my story in theirs. And what a hodgepodge it was. A bus driver. A business owner. A recent college grad. A retired teacher. An old bachelor. Two were parents. Many walks of life were present in our little group of twelve, all religious. Nonetheless, I felt free to be myself and those dear ones seemed to quickly understand me and some of the reasons I'd never fully settled into a gay identity. Soon, Charles and I looked forward to attending each week.

The meeting format followed the fifty-plus year old A.A. model with a "step talk" every week, led by somebody different. Our focus was obviously not alcoholism, so the group was called "Homosexuals Anonymous" and had fourteen steps instead of twelve. Like A.A., there was no fixed leadership to help prevent control issues and leadership identity conflicts and promote a grassroots culture.

After a few meetings, others in the group became emphatic about Charles and me getting our own places to help "reduce temptation." He and I agreed, and decided to formally break up so we could continue down the new path. I was determined to walk it out, believing with all my heart if I put in the effort and gained more understanding, I could be truly happy living the life I wanted.

* * *

My Aunt Dagney had resided downtown on her own since her husband's passing. She had an extra bedroom and offered it to me, an opportunity I grabbed. I was employed at a prominent petrochemical company in an office tower a mere two blocks away. My Aunt's huge heart, infectious laughter, and adept kitchen skills all contributed to my adoration for her—delighting me in our living arrangement. Her building boasted a compact workout room, where I adhered to my post-workday routine with a sense of duty.

Almost every evening after my workout, Aunty had a delicious dinner waiting. I felt cherished and pampered, and I loved our times of connection and laughter. Living with Aunty enabled my physical rejuvenation and desired weight loss, largely because of daily workouts and regular balanced meals. *Things are moving in a good direction!*

Aunty had first met Charles at my SAIT graduation and became fully supportive—another reason to love her even more. I was uncertain if she understood my newfound path away from Charles and being gay, but it seemed inconsequential. Charles visited on occasion, and he and Aunty got on like a house on fire. She was also fine with Charles being in my room to watch TV and even staying overnight occasionally.

Charles and I were often more than friendly during those late-night visits, especially after the unexpected results of my new fitness program. As I've shared, flattery had long proven to be my kryptonite. It became exceedingly challenging to maintain a clear boundary between our platonic and erotic interactions, but we kept trying, with some success and lots of failure.

After a few months, Auntie's health was declining, and it was determined best for me to move out while she explored housing and care alternatives. I was so appreciative of spending quality time with her, making it a win-win times two. But the time had come to move on and my heart ached yet celebrated so many happy memories to treasure forever.

I found myself in a charming vintage apartment in a two-story walkup building on the edge of a trendy neighborhood called Mount Royal. Hardwood floors, unique built-in cabinets, large windows, and southern exposure all meant I prized my new home despite missing my aunty.

Charles also liked my new place and visited often, staying overnight from time to time—a choice *not* helpful in reducing temptation. Despite our newfound direction in life, our mutual feelings and attraction persisted. As a result, many occasions of group sharing time included candid confessions of how we "fell" (as in, off the "wagon" of sobriety) during the past week. *Will you tell them, or will I?* Nodding heads and understanding faces affirmed their care for us every time, offering unwavering support and encouragement to persevere—a refreshing and empowering experience.

The managers of my Mount Royal apartment were a young couple who lived directly above my unit. The wife possessed a heavy gait to rival a Clydesdale. It was evident she never wore slippers and often engaged in demanding projects at opposite ends of their apartment. The relentless pounding reverberated through my living space, nearly driving me insane. With great reluctance, I eventually bid farewell to my trendy little apartment. *Perhaps I'll ask everyone to pray for her on Tuesday night.*

During a visit with Charles, a couple of months after moving apart, he seemed determined to validate my convictions and desires to not be gay.

"So, you're sure you want to do this? You honestly believe people can change?" he inquired, leveling his handsome gaze upon me, awaiting my response. I was surprised he was even asking.

"Yes, Charles, of course. I believe it, and I want it," was my conviction-filled reaction. "Why? Don't you?"

"I'm still trying to get there, Todd. I'm really not so sure," he admitted, hesitant and honest. For the first time, I contemplated moving forward without him, and I held him even tighter.

About a month later, subtle hints led to a candid exchange to reveal Charles had ceased resisting his same-sex attractions and instead embraced them without hesitation. He disclosed he had met a doctor, and they'd already been romantic. His confession stirred an unexpected cocktail of betrayal and jealousy within me, spiked with solemn sorrow.

Advice from my support group was unambiguous: cease all contact with Charles for the sake of my well-being. Our time together dwindled, and I learned he'd feigned interest in the support group because it was what I wanted and where I'd be. But we all knew that being in the group without a true desire for change almost assured little to no growth or healing of the wounds that changed us. *Did he really give it a chance?*

Yes, I had my ups and downs from the beginning, but I didn't waver in my desire for a different life. I was so exhausted by the secretive double life and the constant battle to navigate my path alone. Our weekly support meetings included Bible readings, which I found inspirational. I couldn't deny the authenticity of the others and their belief in God's plans for their lives if they stayed faithful.

Sadly, there wasn't a seat on the bus for someone with a different destination. Charles had told me if his choices meant he would spend eternity gnashing his teeth in a lake of fire, then he was okay with it. In more ways than one, I had to let go of Charles—and my hopes for him—so he could live the life he wanted. It was heart-wrenching, but it was the right thing for both of us. Our emotional bond had been strong and I still cared about him, so it helped to know he'd met the doctor who also thought he was pretty special. Coming to terms with the final separation took months and would have been impossible without the loving support from others in my group. It also required reminding myself often about my ultimate objective to one day be free of the issues that had caused so much pain and suffering.

# Aren't All Homosexuals Anonymous?

I never chose to be gay. I didn't want to live a gay life. Unwelcome feelings of curiosity and attraction to other boys crashed the party of my young life without any invitation from me. Feeling different from my brothers and all the other boys was difficult, but *pretending* I didn't feel that way was unbearable. What's worse, in the early eighties, there were few well-known (and respected) gay role models.

But it was widely understood that *coming out* typically meant someone had finally confronted himself, wholeheartedly embraced a gay identity, and made some sort of declaration about their decision. Even in my sheltered upbringing, I overheard tales of polarized family reactions: either acceptance or rejection. The heartbreaking stories of individuals victimized by severe rejection from parents and families were seldom offset by heartwarming accounts of one being fully embraced by loved ones.

All through the journey, there was only one real "choice" ever presented: keep it hidden (remain in the closet) or come out. So, as you know, I did come out to my family, and their response was supportive; my dad did not reject me as I feared. But on the historic evening at the bar with Curtis and Gary, I'd encountered an incredible revelation: the existence of an alternative.

At its core was the understanding a man could choose how to respond to his attraction to other men based on his understanding of the origins of those feelings. And even more amazing was I would no longer have to face or hide my struggles alone and in secret. It was an extraordinary gift to me, although, at the time, I wasn't sure *who* was doing the giving.

An author named Max Lucado encouraged me early in my journey through his wonderful book, *No Wonder They Call Him the Savior*. Lucado's heartfelt portrayal of this man called Jesus had me weeping through every beautiful chapter.

Max Lucado offers a persuasive assessment of the single most destructive force in my life, from his book, *Fearless:*

> *"Fear never wrote a symphony or poem, negotiated a peace treaty or cured a disease. Fear never pulled a family out of poverty or a country out of bigotry. Fear never saved a marriage or a business. Courage did that. Faith did that. People who refused to consult or cower to their timidities did that. But fear itself? Fear herds us into prison and slams the doors."*[3]

\* \* \*

An important premise in our Homosexuals Anonymous group was it would be three to five years of hard work before we would witness significant transformation. It's true I translated the premise into an enticing promise of sorts. The alluring assurance I could reshape my sexual orientation was potent enough to propel me forward week after week, through countless challenges and setbacks, steadfast in my pursuit.

It never dawned on me there was little evidence of transformation from anyone in the group, well, at least the outward, visible kind. Frankly, it became disheartening to get together and endure repetitive stories from the same people week after week, recounting their relapses after ill-fated choices, me included. Yet, it didn't deter my resolve to stick it out and give it everything I had because the glimmer of hope for change was enough for me. *Maybe one day I will be like all the other boys.*

The group often pointed to an intense connection between God and his omnipotent ability to transform us when we remained faithful. The idea compelled me, even though I lacked a clear understanding of who God was. Though he sure seemed patient, reportedly listening to our weekly group prayers that often lasted longer than my waning patience.

Gary had frequently invited me to join him as a guest at his church, and I finally took him up on his offer one Sunday. It was the first church I'd been to, aside from a few weddings and a memory at five years old when I clung to my grandmother's hand, bored out of my mind. Gary was active in his church choir, which piqued my interest, as I'd long enjoyed singing. It was a Presbyterian church who leased space within a school, necessitating setting up and tearing down every Sunday. It wasn't much more exciting than my childhood church experience with Nan, and I struggled to stay awake during some sermons. But the people were friendly and there was the choir. *Count me in!*

Ever the entrepreneur, I felt our generic support group needed some corporate branding. True, we were an anonymous group operating under a covert code name, but what harm could there be in distributing business cards to others who might be interested? I thought we could do better than "Delta" as our organization's name.

When I chanced upon a scripture verse from Romans during one meeting, it resonated within me and encapsulated the spirit of my driving motivation.

> *"Therefore, I urge you, brothers and sisters, in view of God's mercy, to offer your bodies as a living sacrifice, holy and pleas-*

> *ing to God—this is your true and proper worship. Do not conform to the patterns of this world, but be transformed by the renewing of your mind. Then you will be able to test and approve what God's will is—his good, pleasing and perfect will."* —Romans 12:1-2 (NIV)

The word *transformed* leapt off the page, captivating my attention. Inspired by its power, I proposed the name "Transformations" for our support group. Alongside that, I designed a simple logo featuring seven vertical rectangles side by side in a row, starting with a black box on the left and leading to a transparent box on the right. When I unveiled my mock-up to the group, it was met with sincere appreciation for my creativity.

However, it was later determined introducing a new brand didn't quite align with the ministry's anonymous, low-profile approach. So much for that, but I trusted the judgment of the more experienced participants and got over it because I didn't want to be distracted from my purpose.

My behavior underwent a gradual yet significant transformation, driven by growing weariness of confessing my downfalls every week during accountability time. The addictive nature of my actions was becoming clearer as I realized that those actions often didn't feel like choices… it's just what I did, or what I *wanted*, i.e. the anticipation and exhilaration of someone new. It wasn't until I became aware of the motives behind my actions that I realized the need for different choices to get different outcomes.

Moreover, I became convinced real progress was impossible unless I took decisive action to stop acting out on my same-sex attractions. The best approach was to not put myself into the risky situation in the first place. Waiting for my order at the drive-thru window is not the right time to resist the temptation to eat fatty foods. *This is a lot harder than giving up fast food.*

With the decrease of compulsive masturbation and pornography, my understanding of the underlying issues deepened through insightful step talks and thought-provoking conversations with senior members of our group. The journey came with a steep learning curve, challenging my perspectives and propelling me toward personal growth and self-discovery within a Christian context.

\* \* \*

The strength and success of the program was working through the fourteen steps over and over until their inherent wisdom becomes one's new reality, similar to A.A.'s highly regarded approach.

The first H.A. step refers to our powerlessness over the struggle and acknowledges the reality of unmanageable emotional lives. The second step recognizes the need to believe in God's love, forgiveness, and acceptance—especially considering our past misdeeds. Step three highlights our troubled lives and suffering, which were always under God's watchful eye, with all working for eventual good, whereas the fourth emphasizes believing God has power far greater than our struggle and a plan to heal and restore us.

Step five acknowledges the deception that led us to believe lies that trapped us in an identity that wasn't His plan. The goal was explained in the sixth step: an identity in Him through Jesus Christ, as our faith perceives Him. Step seven encourages trusting God and bolstering our faith, believing with confidence He will reveal His plan for our identity in him, in his perfect timing.

From there, the H.A. steps transition toward practical application, as the eighth step builds on the new awareness of forgiveness without condemnation, motivating a "fearless moral inventory" to expel fear and resolve anger toward others. Step nine focuses on "housecleaning" by confessing our wrongs while relying on God to identify and eliminate negative character-based obstacles. The tenth step promotes wisdom-driven amends directed to those who'd harmed us.

Step eleven revisits the impact of fear in our lives by emphasizing God's triumphant nature over all that hurt us, supporting the twelfth step's admonition to seek healing, health, and balance in our relationships. Step thirteen stresses the need for confident and steadfast prayer and Bible reading to cultivate our relationship with God and embrace his guidance. The final and fourteenth step recognizes the inevitable fruit of a spiritual awakening as the shared truth of our transformative experience—in God's unconditional love—and to continue practicing the steps throughout our lives.

I won't elaborate on the original H.A. founder here, but like all of us, he battled his own demons and succumbed to temptation, compelling the ministry to find new leadership. During my involvement, the new H.A. shepherd was a sincere fellow named John, who loved God and exuded the kindness of a TV grandfather, like the old guy on *The Waltons*. We met John when he came up to lead a conference, and I liked him right away.

John offered us encouragement with ease, and his inclusiveness was inspiring. I appreciated he discerned something greater in me than I knew, and I held nothing but respect for his leadership. It was surprising to be asked to organize one morning's worship time, but with Gary's help, it all came together.

John faithfully kept the H.A. ministry going and growing as a labor of love for many years. Thousands and thousands of people were encouraged during their faith-filled journeys over the years because of him, including me.

One final word before we move on to the rest of my story. Many on this path, including me, were fixated on the goal of a sexual identity transformation. However, a Bible verse helped to reframe my ambition in a Christian context. Even as the battle raged on, I hadn't yet made sense of what it meant to be "first justified, then sanctified, finally glorified." But I had a hunch I was more like a Gentile from this verse who desperately hoped for something more.

> *"For this is the will of God, your sanctification: that you should abstain from sexual immorality; that each of you should know how to possess his own vessel in sanctification and honor, not in passion of lust, like the Gentiles who do not know God;"—I Thessalonians 4:3-5 (NKJV)*

# Intimacy Cravings

About five months into my support group meetings, I was having a tumultuous day at work riddled with misunderstandings and self-doubt. Thoughts of the Tuesday night drink special at a local gay bar assailed me. Free-flowing booze meant most of the men—including me—would be uninhibited and affectionate. The yearning for masculine intimacy welled up within me, and later, all it took was a friend's casual invitation to meet him there. I was soon on my way to feed the wolf of affirmation addiction a mere snack, and perhaps test my resolve… in that order.

However, as with most gay bars, anyone who dared to arrive before 9:00 p.m. would find the place empty and eerie until the regulars made their fashionable entrances. At the appointed hour, the bar exuded an unusually desperate vibe, with only a handful of patrons scattered about. The pulsating dance music echoed between the stark walls of the long, narrow, dimly lit room. No sign of my friend, the sole reason I'd ventured out that night. *But was it?*

I made my way straight to the bar, promptly ordered two vodka tonics for the price of one and guzzled them down with reckless abandon. Being punctual at work the next morning was a concern, along with the longing to not entirely fall back into old habits. That night, I vowed I'd maintain the prime directive and not go home with anyone.

A guy at the other end of the bar may have noticed my rapid consumption and was kind enough to order the next round for me. He then slid into the narrow space beside me, which really wasn't space at all. Doubts about my vow crept in, and I wondered if I'd be confessing at my next meeting, even with my best intentions.

Generous Geoff was a new twenty-something face, and he looked pretty good to my twenty-something ego—though I'd never be caught dead in black spandex shorts (unless on a bicycle, that's different.) The way Geoff considered me as we leaned against each other at the bar made me forget about everything else as his attention and designer cologne enveloped me. That handsome fellow wanted me, and the realization ignited desire.

Shortly after the third double round (tequila shots that time), the bar had filled up, and I was well beyond controlling myself. If they allowed it on their dance floor, I was doing it with everyone. *Damn those drink specials.*

In that wild scene, my desperation clung to me like a leech, yearning for a lifeline—any lifeline—to validate my worth as a man, my desirability as a man by a desirable man. Amidst the throngs of other sweaty males, each seeking the same elusive prize, I found myself basking in a cyclone of carnal attention.

Enticing offers and my compromised condition aside, I somehow held the original line. But I don't know, perhaps the *right* one hadn't come along. Or perhaps someone was watching over me. *Who can say for sure?*

I think I stumbled homeward several blocks and crash-landed in my bed, alone, with only a few hours remaining before rise and shine. One or more retching calls were made on the big white porcelain telephone; I'll confess that more than Geoff supplied me with free drinks. I couldn't even guess how much sleep I got that night.

I'm not entirely sure how it happened, but I was on time for work, dressed (in work clothes, thankfully) and nursing a pounding headache on top of a serious shortage of slumber. Sordid memories of the previous night assaulted me, a relentless barrage of flashbacks threatened to overwhelm. Seeking respite, I retreated to the washroom, hoping to sidetrack the turmoil within. *Make it go away.*

\* \* \*

As briny tears smeared my face, my head slumped into my hands, the rest of me perched on a toilet in the staff bathroom on the eighth floor of a Calgary office building. My heart wrenched with a quelling surge of guilt and shame.

For the first time in my twenty-three-year, self-absorbed existence, a profound sense of condemnation and sorrow pierced the depths of my soul. With a sickening thud, I recognized I couldn't go on living that way.

In the solitude of the empty washroom, unfamiliar feelings of bottomless regret coupled with an overwhelming sense of wrongdoing over everything I'd done the night before. And what I allowed them to do to me. My heart was crushed with remorse.

Amidst desolate despair, something greater and deeper began to draw me in with an unearthly embrace. An unlikely sanctuary—devoid of formalities and structure—where my pounding heart began to somersault as my chest heaved with uncontrollable sobs. My nose and eyes were all running as I tried in vain to wipe away the emblems of my emotional upheaval.

In that sacred moment, I knew with unwavering certainty He was real. He had called my name and wrapped His loving arms around me right there on the company toilet. Next came a holy awareness that the exact same Love chose to sacrifice His only Son, took my place and died for me to fully cover every nasty thing I ever did… or would ever do. Immense gratitude overcame me as shudders raced up and down my tingling body. Finally, in my heart, I knew that I could *live*, forever free of the shackles of fear, guilt, and shame, as His beloved son.

My heart rushed to answer His call, even as my mind raced to keep up with the magnitude of what was unfolding within the hallowed confines of the third space from the end. It was as if my being was suspended between condemnation and forgiveness. My self-serving choices and actions all deserved harsh judgment. But my tender-hearted Father revealed that all of me was worthy of His mercy because of Jesus. And nothing I could do would ever detach myself from His perfect love and mind-blowing grace. That, I understood in the deepest parts of my soul for the very first time, my heart bursting with warmth. *Wow, thank you, Lord. I love you too! Wow. Wow. Wow.*

The work break was long past over, so I returned to my desk but with a heaven-sent sense of insightful hope that everything was going to be okay. *Yes, I'll be okay.*

To be clear, I heard no promises all was going to be easy. I only knew a deep transformation had occurred, a change that remained to be understood fully by both my mind and heart. Then came the convoy of "ya buts" as my mind tried to convince my heart that God had somehow overlooked a few details back there.

> *Ya, but what about all I'd done? Who I'd done.*
>
> *Ya, but not just last night but all the other nights.*
>
> *Ya, but what about the women I've hurt and all the other selfish choices?*
>
> *If He only knew all I've done.*

The condemning thoughts spun within me like a maniacal carnival ride, threatening to consume me. But then, a sharp ringing from my desk phone jolted me back to present reality. It was as if everything was normal, and nothing extraordinary had occurred.

*Ya, but all this, He knew. Every single thing. And He loves me still!*

\* \* \*

An unexpected wedding invitation showed up about three months after my intense encounter with God's consuming love. My middle school computer friend Joe was set to exchange nuptials with a fiancée I'd not yet met. Joe and I had kept in touch over the years and even collaborated on a short-lived business venture related to his golf passion. It would be my pleasure to be with him to celebrate such a special day.

Being back in Saskatoon brought a mixture of melancholy and appreciation for many good memories, including those from my favorite discount store, Army & Navy, located downtown in an old Eaton's location. I'd planned to stay with John and arrived the day before the wedding. With some extra time on my hands, I visited my old haunt in search of some bargains and a trip down memory lane. A little bored and mischievous, I decided to not pay for a leather wallet I was admiring. *I bet I can get away with it, just like before.*

At the cash register, my hands trembled slightly with nerves and excitement. I paid for a few small items while the wallet remained hidden in my pocket. As I exited the main doors, a strong hand latched firmly onto my left shoulder and pulled my body backward.

"Excuse me, sir, but we're store security, and you need to come with us," a guard stated, his voice echoing as if from somewhere else.

"What, wait..." I peeped in disbelief, as two guards escorted me back into the store and up to a third-floor office. Seconds after they began questioning me, full reality set in. My hands dripped with sweat as I considered the consequence of my action: Humiliation.

*What will John think?*

*Am I going to jail?*

*What about Joe's wedding?*

*How would I explain what the hell happened?*

Try as I might, I can't explain what came over me while store staff were questioning me. I knew something drastic was needed, or I'd soon be on my way to the brig. It began with imaginary voices, causing me to twitch my head around as if to hear them better. Then, I widened my eyes as if those who belonged to the voices had become visible. *Maybe they'll think I'm a little crackers and let me go.* The actual voice of somebody in charge snapped me back to reality.

"We've called the police, and they're on their way," he said, telling me I'd have to wait. My peculiar body movements needed to continue for about thirty minutes or so until the officer arrived.

The policeman seemed kind and a little flippant, telling me he didn't want to have to shoot me if I tried to run. *I think he's being cheeky.* He escorted me through the store and outside to his cruiser, where he helped me into the back seat and took his place behind the wheel. My craning neck and shifty eyes could've caught his attention as he completed some paperwork while the car idled.

It appeared my ridiculous strategy wasn't working, so it was time to put my newfound faith to the test. *"God, I've really messed up here. It was stupid, and I'm sorry, for this time and all the others—all to prove I'm smarter than they are. Forgive me. God, spare me from the embarrassment of this. If You do, I promise it's the last time, and it'll be me and You together from here on. Amen."*

In that moment, the cop looked up and perhaps noticed my fallen, resigned face in his rear-view mirror. Or perhaps it was something else.

"Well, Todd, I think you've learned a lesson here today," the officer said as I looked at him in disbelief. "If you promise that's the end of it for you, I'm gonna let you go." His words rang through my racing mind and then punctured my contrite heart. I was going to lose it if I lingered much longer in the back seat of that squad car.

"Uh, yes!" with enthusiasm and a broad smile. The officer got out, opened my door, helped me out, and said to have a good day. *Wow, will I! Thank you, Lord, for rescuing me. You and I have a deal!*

It was difficult to see where I was walking through tears of gratitude. All that was within me knew that by His grace, my shoplifting addiction—and its root based in pride—was broken, allowing me to honor my pledge to this day. Meanwhile, Joe hadn't a clue how close I came to missing his wedding... well, I guess he could know now.

\* \* \*

While I was first intrigued by the psychological discussions of the root causes of same-sex attractions, regular readings from the Bible began to illuminate profound truths that transcended much more than my attraction toward men. I discovered a life framework that resonated deep within me, aligning perfectly with the family values instilled by my parents.

Perhaps my accidental early childhood education experience had a more profound impact than my parents expected. It all began with a miraculous opportunity for free babysitting, complete with shuttle service! A local church picked up kids for their Sunday school. Still in their twenties, Mum and Dad often indulged in lively late-night socializing on Saturdays. Consequently, they welcomed the offer to pick up their kids, take them away to church, and bring them back home a couple of hours later.

While Mum and Dad relaxed at home, we learned about the Bible and sang melodious songs still resonating within my memory, including the chorus, "Since the Lord saves me, I'm as happy as can be, my cup is full and running over." No doubt we encountered the captivating narrative of man and woman's creation in the Garden of Eden, along with God's plan to fill the earth. Little did my parents know God was preparing the soil for future encounters.

Another poignant memory was the presence of a meaningful poem in my childhood home. Nobody can seem to recall how it arrived in our life, but the special words touched everyone in my family and hold great meaning to this day. I was moved at a young age when I first read it and reading the last line brought tingling to my spine, even without an awareness of God in my life.

The enduring verse resurfaced as an inscription on a commemorative plaque we made for Nan and Granch's 40th wedding anniversary. "Footprints in the Sand" gained significance in our family, despite the absence of anyone practicing faith.

It's the story of a man who had a dream and observed two sets of footprints in the sand through the scenes of his life; one belonged to him, and the other to the Lord. Then the man noticed that the most troublesome scenes had only one set of footprints. It bothered him because the Lord had promised to walk with him through all of life, including the most difficult times. The Lord assured him He had kept His word and explained it this way:

*"When you saw only one set of footprints,*

*It was then that I carried you."*[4]

One final story from my childhood points again to how God was preparing the way for the revelation of His love and truth, using Nan and Granch as the catalyst. On one Sunday visit, my grandparents wanted to watch a favorite church program and invited us to join them. A popular and controversial evangelist named Oral Roberts was among those to first use television to share Biblical encouragement and hope. And hey, if a son is to become one of the most famous preachers of the 20th century, why not name him Oral? *Was another son named Print?*

Oral's son Richard recorded a song released by the ministry and a free forty-five record was offered as an outreach promotion. "Something Good is Going to Happen to You" became a hit theme song for their ministry. Its stirring lyrics refer to outcasts who were forever changed by their encounter with Jesus of Nazareth, promising transformation is available as we encounter Jesus.

After the record arrived in our mailbox, it was played a lot on our stereo. Upbeat with a catchy melody, I took to it right away and soon memorized the words that reflected something of my Sunday School experiences. A message of hope rang out from the song's lyrics, which still captivates hearts in our family to this day.

\* \* \*

Perhaps all those seeds sown during my formative years contributed to my yielding mindset almost two decades later. The Genesis account learned in Sunday school, now rang out as foundational and true: Man and woman, upon leaving parents behind, unite as one flesh to seal their bond, to bring forth children, and to fill the earth. There appeared to be little room for variations within God's intended plan for human sexuality and gender identity, as identified in the Bible. I wholeheartedly embraced the sacred truth of God's design for human sexual interaction within the confines of marriage between one man and one woman, as ordained and blessed by Him.

Also becoming clear was my support group friends were a little like the God of the Bible, intent on a supportive and loving relationship with me. However, my Creator's love transcends human comprehension, characterized by His holy and unconditional love. Nothing I could ever do or fail to do could diminish His perfect love for me. Again, like my supportive friends, an enthusiastic God cheered me on as I embarked on a journey of self-discovery, shedding the vestiges of my old self to embrace my true unseen identity in Him.

Through His gracious gift of free will, whenever my chosen behavior didn't align with His established values (also known as "sin"), I was tempted to hide from God *and* my support group. Yet, their steadfast care and acceptance demonstrated my inherent worthiness of love. Regardless of my choices, whether virtuous or flawed, they kept steering me back to Him. The weekly support rhythm softened my heart like a loving tenderizer, making me more receptive to God's presence and His divine plan for my life.

Within no time, I came to believe my ongoing sin would separate me from God if it were not for the sacrificial intervention of His son, Jesus Christ. On the cross, Jesus chose to endure the ultimate sacrifice, dying in my place to reconcile me forever with Father God. Jesus triumphantly conquered death by rising again and now sits at His Father's side, interceding for us. I believe with confidence that I, too, shall overcome death and rise again one day to be with Him forever. *Oh, what a magnificent day it will be!*

Various scriptures provided much more encouragement in my early faith journey, and in surrendering my gay identity, with one of the most significant being the Apostle Paul's words to the early church in Corinth.

> *"Don't you realize that those who do wrong will not inherit the Kingdom of God? Don't fool yourselves. Those who indulge in sexual sin, or who worship idols, or commit adultery, or are male prostitutes, or practice homosexuality, or are thieves, or greedy people, or drunkards, or are abusive, or cheat people—none of these will inherit the Kingdom of God. Some of you were once like that. But you were cleansed; you were*

> *made holy; you were made right with God by calling on the name of the Lord Jesus Christ and by the Spirit of our God.*
>
> *"You say, 'I am allowed to do anything'—but not everything is good for you. And even though 'I am allowed to do anything,' I must not become a slave to anything. You say, 'Food was made for the stomach, and the stomach for food.' (This is true, though someday God will do away with both of them.) But you can't say that our bodies were made for sexual immorality. They were made for the Lord, and the Lord cares about our bodies. And God will raise us from the dead by his power, just as he raised our Lord from the dead.*
>
> *"Don't you realize that your bodies are actually parts of Christ? Should a man take his body, which is part of Christ, and join it to a prostitute? Never! And don't you realize that if a man joins himself to a prostitute, he becomes one body with her? For the Scriptures say, 'The two are united into one.' But the person who is joined to the Lord is one spirit with him.*
>
> *"Run from sexual sin! No other sin so clearly affects the body as this one does. For sexual immorality is a sin against your own body. Don't you realize that your body is the temple of the Holy Spirit, who lives in you and was given to you by God? You do not belong to yourself, for God bought you with a high price. So you must honor God with your body."*
> —1 Corinthians 6:9-20 (NLT)

Everything was reframed for me through this passage because no matter how gloomy or desperate my circumstances were, hope was always available. No matter the nature of my sin—whatever I placed higher than Him—there was a standing offer to be transformed and more like Him, simply by calling on His name and being changed by the Spirit. This truth made me want to sing out loud. *Wow, Lord, You are so good!*

Those verses also helped me see that my selfish ways and preferences enslaved me and that my body belonged to God as His temple. Grief struck my heart as I considered how often I'd dishonored His temple. *Forgive me, Lord.* The weighty passage contained formidable challenges; my ambition to conquer them kept me going! *It's worth reading over and over.*

Within a few short months, I gained a profound understanding of God's true nature and the unfathomable depths of His love for me. As I reflected upon twenty-three years of life, I couldn't help but acknowledge the numerous signs from Him to capture my attention.

But none of it meant my same-sex struggles weren't real or that they instantly subsided because they did not. I still longed for tangible masculine love and affirmation beyond the platonic connections with my group. The battle was arduous and turning away from the acceptance and validation I received from other men proved far more challenging than the promotional brochure had conveyed. (Okay, there was no brochure—I'm being cheeky.)

A perpetual tug-of-war between desires led me astray on occasion, drawing me back to encounters with strangers, which made it difficult to honor God as Paul implored. As usual, many of those situations involved copious amounts of alcohol, which only compounded my poor decision-making. *Maybe I have an alcohol problem.*

# Buddies and Butch

Weekly accountability in the support group reduced my erotic same-sex behaviors, including acting on fantasies. As the months passed, I found myself growing more confident in openly sharing my struggles. The sense of safe vulnerability helped normalize the nature of my plight, reassuring me I wasn't so special or unique. Melancholy came whenever a member dropped out, but new faces soon yielded familiar stories with sincere appreciation for being heard, seen, understood, and supported.

As a keen observer and compulsive leader, I couldn't ignore members returning week after week with sorrowful tales of how they fell since their last meeting. Something was missing: Mid-week accountability. So, I proposed what I called the "buddy system," a concept that came with a few hurdles given our vulnerable population.

The foundation of a multi-step program support group is anonymity, hence the "A" in the title. It's a critical principle that protects everyone's privacy, allowing them to seek transformation without the debilitating fear of their stigmatized life-controlling addiction being discovered. The "code" says when you spot someone in public from your group, you're supposed to disregard (ignore) them to maintain mutual anonymity. Privacy is one of the key factors across decades of success in Alcoholics Anonymous, and it applied to our group as well.

So, you can imagine the scene when a know-it-all bumpkin like me suggested a new approach that challenged the old system. My suggestion to mitigate the inherent risks of the buddy system was for people to choose a buddy with whom there was no attraction or chemistry. But you may wonder why I would go through all this trouble, so let me explain.

The main difference between A.A. and H.A. was the addiction focus. Those of us in H.A. didn't focus on substances but rather on uncontrollable behaviors and fantasies involving others of the same sex. As a side note, a correlating battle with alcohol abuse or addiction could also be present as I've somewhat experienced in my journey. It was recommended to gain some sobriety from alcohol before changing one's focus to dealing with unwanted same-sex behavior, which I believe would have helped me progress faster in my journey. *But you're sovereign over all things, Lord.*

It's a perennial paradox that healing the affirmation-seeking drive behind unmanageable erotic same-sex behavior is often achieved through healthy same-sex interactions. The overwhelming fear and associated risks of pursuing those vital relationships paralyze many, depriving us of essential experiences that heal.

After all, it seemed all the other boys didn't accept me because I felt so different from them. I'm grateful to God that I was able to pursue and benefit from a few non-erotic relationships. Had I been more honest and transparent in those relationships, I may have enjoyed increased acceptance and more rapid healing.

That unavoidable catch-22 may explain why many of us got stuck—or abandoned completely—the pursuit of a non-sexual identity in Christ helped by non-erotic same-sex connections. I was convinced the secret to true masculine transformation was held in healthy connections with other men. My proposal for our group bore the potential to increase affirming interactions between members, support the healing journey, and increase ongoing accountability during the week.

Enough members supported the proposal, so we went for it. I gave little forethought to who my buddy would be but ended up choosing Butch, pushing past my uneasiness about his flamboyant sarcasm. He was about fifteen years older and had blond hair, a nice smile, and was friendly. Even with his pleasant, youthful appearance, Butch didn't appear to be the sort of person I'd be inclined to approach. But something drew me to him—perhaps it was God.

As per our guidelines, my physical attraction to him wasn't like that, but he was a mature follower of Christ, balanced and healthy, and a fun guy who loved to laugh. In time, we developed a profound friendship I never saw coming, and it transformed me and the course of my life.

Butch owned a well-established retail store, and we would occasionally discuss his business challenges. My entrepreneurial spirit loved to engage those concerns and help where I could in marketing-related tasks. Butch was also a talented musician who played the piano like nobody I'd ever known. His generosity and encouragement opened a door for creative self-expression through my singing voice as we spent time together at his piano.

The most remarkable thing about Butch was his tenacious and genuine love for the Lord. He grew up in a Pentecostal family and was heavily involved in church as a pianist. His wonderful parents instilled a desire for a dynamic and enduring relationship with Jesus, even with his identity struggles from an early age. He'd joined our support group a few months before Charles and I showed up and was keen for change, demonstrating the commitment to get there. Our Saturday morning brunches became a treasured tradition that persisted for years as a tremendous source of regular encouragement and connection. You'll soon hear much more about Butch and our many adventures together.

That summer, I got the bright idea to help guys in our group learn about football. Many of us missed out on masculine bonding experiences with our father figures and had little knowledge of sports, including me, as I've shared. Teaching was appealing to me, and I loved to learn, so I took on the project with eagerness. Hilariously, I'd never played football and had only seen a handful of games, thanks to the safety patrol and the PEP Club. But I was a good researcher, so I rolled up my sleeves to get the job done. *No, we don't need uniforms.*

We began with a field lesson in a local park rented from the city. Handmade neck signs displayed various position names, such as quarterback, running back, etc. Of course, a fight broke out over who would be the tight end or wide receiver.

There we were, about a dozen of us, rambling about in a school sports field off Highway 1 in Calgary. We attempted a few plays with an actual football while I ran around shouting out all I had recently learned, laughing out loud with those who weren't taking it quite so seriously (i.e. Butch). They were fantastic sports and everyone played along, but it's unlikely the lesson stuck or that anyone would advance to the Hall of Fame. The goal was to try something new, face fears, and remove some of the mystery and confusion surrounding the manly sport. On that front, our team scored big time.

At some point during my H.A. season, I received a powerful illustration that deeply affected me and crystallized my desires. I was told to envision myself as an observer sitting at a table in a busy restaurant. A few tables over, two elderly men sit across from each other at a small table, engaged in their private conversation. One of the seniors sits up slowly and leans across the table as the other also leans forward. They meet in a passionate kiss. As an observer, how does the scenario feel?

"I'd feel a little repelled and probably look away," was my immediate response. Then came illumination from my friend.

"In gay life, it's the *very* best you can hope for, Todd. That's it."

From where I sat, the observation held no *hope* at all. Sadness settled in my bones. I didn't want my life to look like that. So, I resolved to give it everything I had to "work the program."

When Charles and I were going through our on-again-off-again trials a couple of months after joining the group, it intrigued me to seek out his reaction to the illustration. His immediate response settled any doubt about our looming divergence.

"Heartwarming," he said, emphasizing our dissimilarity and how we were heading in opposite directions. He asked what I'd thought, and my response brought him clarity on my position. It seemed the hourglass of our relationship had officially tipped; the sand was falling. *Lord Jesus, keep him safe.*

Weekly meetings and step teachings continued as a big part of my life for about two years. The faithful work and practical wisdom of the steps advanced my mission in an extraordinary manner as new truths became my reality. Ongoing accountability helped break the addictive cycle of weekend bar outings and related behavior. But it was becoming clear there was more involved in winning the war to resolve my masculine insecurity and core identity issues.

\* \* \*

If I've ever met anyone who epitomizes the gift of hospitality, it's Butch. There's no doubt his mother's cooking and frequent hosting as a way of life influenced him—we all owe her immense gratitude. Meal preparation and having people over to enjoy it seemed as easy as breathing for him. However, it was *how* Butch made people feel in the presence of his hospitality that put him in a league of his own.

I once enjoyed a group study of a book by author Henri Nouwen that delved into hospitality as a spiritual discipline. His book brought immense clarity on how the hospitality gift (or discipline) is expressed uniquely, affecting me to this day. Its essence lies in making space for others—strangers—where transformation can take place. The philosophy is well embodied in a typical Christian retreat center setting, an important part of my story in later years.

Butch's supernatural ability to welcome strangers around his dinner table was delightful to behold—and some of us were indeed strange and delightful. Each person touched by his generous hospitality experienced a change stemming from the unconditional love found there. The same can be said about God's unconditional love; once encountered, it elevates us humans into truth and potential in Him. Butch has loved more souls in that way than I could ever count.

Our support group was invited many times to Butch's lovely home. Those occasions were filled with abundant food, drink—and laughter courtesy of his irreverent sense of humor. Butch often derived great satisfaction from shock humor, colorful gestures, or risqué words, and we loved it. The special gatherings fostered stronger connections within the group. *It feels so good to belong!*

Official policy discouraged socializing outside of weekly meetings due to temptation from risky emotional connections, but our happy little group continued to gather. Comfort and safety in the presence of like-minded, supportive friends was like a big warm blanket on a cold winter day. The freedom to discard social masks, and simply *be,* was an instrumental element in my growth journey. When asked about the wisdom of those gatherings, Butch's response was predictable.

"Screw the anonymity code!" he exclaimed with his patent flourish and cheeky grin.

However, as valuable as it was, a dark side emerged from our frequent gatherings. Many of us became overly comfortable in those sheltered and familiar settings. Our similarities and common goal meant we encountered little to no social tension in those situations. For example, it was improbable someone would say something hurtful or reject another for disclosing sensitivities about his struggle. It was completely safe to be with others who were similar.

Some members grew uncomfortable with the idea of venturing forth into scarier social circles, such as a men's Bible study, prayer group, or social event. Avoidance of settings beyond our comfort zones often meant we were prohibited from receiving essential affirmations from men different than us. Men who were secure in their masculine identity represented significant healing opportunities for those of us who weren't. To sidestep those types of transformative social opportunities would hinder the healing journey, and it was discouraged strongly.

We learned of a term applied to men and women who once identified as gay but then sought freedom through transformation and identity change as followers of Jesus. "Ex-gays" was the label they gave us. Frankly, I was about as enchanted by the new label as I was by the old one, but it was succinct.

It turned out our little socializing support group had created its own "ex-gay ghetto," where we were, indeed, free to be ourselves. However, we were much less likely to be released into new God-ordained identities. The false sense of community created tension for some in the group, and they moved on.

Those who remained continued in the socializing, but sadly, occasional transgressions occurred, resulting in three steps forward and two steps back for some, me included. So, it remained crucial for us to seek intimate, non-erotic friendships with men who were secure in their maleness. Failing to seek those men impaired our growth process while denying them the unique blessings of walking alongside us, something that could often be overlooked. As with everything, finding the balance based on truth and God's direction was key.

\* \* \*

Not all my social connections were linked to support groups in those days, which was helpful when one is trying to assimilate into the general male population. One such unexpected friend came along through a work connection because he needed some graphic design services. Mason was a handsome, dark-haired fellow with a radio voice and an appreciation for humor—we were destined for each other.

We clicked right away, and I found myself sorting through feelings of attraction and wondering about his interest in me. The time soon came for me to share my story with my new friend, and I was a nervous wreck. As usual, it was a do-or-die situation that was sometimes prompted by the wrong motive. *Lord, give me Your strength to do what's right.*

I'd found there were generally two motives in such situations. First, the nasty fear of rejection triggered an urgency to share my story as soon as possible before emotional ties were formed. That way, potential hurt decreased because the new friendship candidate was unable or unwilling to befriend someone who might put the moves on him or for other reasons of his own.

The second common motive was the desire to find out if there was any chance of similar feelings in the other friend. It's an unfortunate consequence of same-sex attractions—the inevitably wacky dynamics of friend-making. The second motive was more likely when there was a measure of physical attraction, and the measuring spoon was a large one. *Maybe he's open?*

With Mason, my motivation was a little of both. So, when the time seemed right, I shared an overview of my journey and explained the nature of my healing journey. Mason was understanding and accepting, and his heterosexual orientation and commitment to his wife were obvious.

Fortunately, Mason and I were able to get past the awkward stage in short order, and I was truly encouraged that a friendship with such a great guy was even possible. The affirmation and healing that came from being his friend was an unexpected blessing. I came to have great affection for Mason and remained grateful nothing romantic or worse was part of the mix. *Thank you, Jesus!*

Mason was also open to matters of faith, which added more depth to our interesting conversations. He had some Catholic school experience and was aware of what mattered to God, another reason to like him. Supportive of me and my choices, I could count on him to listen with a loving heart whenever we got together.

Our strongest common bond was a shared entrepreneurial spirit to seek out opportunities and solutions. Mason had a good full-time job when he began the side hustle that initially brought us together. He hoped the project would allow him to leave his j-o-b (entrepreneurs spell that word out in disdain) as it evolved into a thriving business, with my assistance of course. We never got there due to financing issues, but it was well worth the shot.

Over the years, we were involved in a few hit-and-miss ventures as our paths crossed from time to time. One of the more enlivening opportunities was our work together at a radio station that had lost its news team. Usually up for a challenge, I dusted off my SAIT education and jumped in to help keep the news machine going. Pulling that off was beyond satisfying and I thrilled in the excitement of live broadcasts. Mason eventually built a new team, and the time came for me to move on. I was grateful for a unique and rewarding radio newsroom experience, enhanced by the opportunity to bless my dear old friend.

Something I've long admired about Mason is his tenacity. Many personal and business challenges have tried to take him down, but he gets back up and keeps going. I give thanks to God for Mason, and after thirty years, our friendship still reminds me of God's goodness.

# Growing Faith

It's impossible to predict or anticipate the sequence of key events in one's faith walk. A little like a carnival ride that endures, my journey to deeper faith in God has seen twists and turns with highs and lows. There've been periods of darkness and light that triggered both white-knuckles and outstretched arms. But I'm buckled in tight and so grateful that the Lord will always be the divine Operator of an attraction called Surrendered Life.

Right out of the gate, music appreciation was persistent as it reverberated throughout my life. In the summer prior to the two-year mark in my healing journey, Butch had introduced me to a fellow musician named Rex, who still lived at home with his parents a few hours away. A believer near my age with same-sex attractions, Rex occasionally accompanied us to dinner or a movie when he was in town, and I relished our time together.

A retreat to a nearby mountain lodge was orchestrated for much-needed relaxation. We played games and made each other laugh, but the dynamics within our three-way friendship had become thorny and posed difficulties. Perhaps my attraction to Rex complicated matters even though we all sought to resist same-sex behavior.

Our weekend retreat offered a neutral, remote setting to sort it all out, like when the G-7 meets. The three of us resolved to address the concerns and fortify our friendship by crafting written guidelines outlining how we'd better engage one another and resolve conflicts. In hindsight, it all seems ludicrous, but it was sensible then. However, attempts to recall and implement the conditions of our accord presented challenges that made it even more awkward, until the guidelines finally faded away.

During one visit, Rex gifted me with several Christian music cassette tapes that I thoroughly enjoyed on my home stereo. Within weeks, I'd memorized most of the lyrics and found inspiration in the uplifting messages of hope and truth they conveyed. My connection with God intensified whenever the music filled my modest studio apartment in downtown Calgary, and remarkably, none of my neighbors ever complained!

One poignant melody arose from a tape I almost wore out by Michael W. Smith. Tears flowed whenever I belted out "Place in This World", and my heart resonated as I implored the Lord to reveal His plans for my new life. In those moments, I knew He was with me, comforting and loving. It was as if Jesus and I were holding hands, verse by blessed verse. Over time, He and I held hands a lot.

Rex soon moved to Calgary, secured an impressive job perfect for him, and joined Butch and me for the launch of a new ministry you'll hear about later. Sadly, Rex withdrew after a few weeks, telling us it wasn't for him. In no time, he crossed paths with a fellow who proved to be quite alluring. Following a brief courtship, he went all-in, and they got a house together. As I pen this, they're still together over thirty years later. I remain uncertain about Rex's spiritual journey, but I give thanks to God for him and his musical passion, which played a major role in nurturing my fledgling faith.

* * *

As an analytical thinker, I gravitated to the forces of logic that reigned throughout my life. After all, my Myers-Briggs® personality type[5] confirmed at eighteen years old I was a dominant thinker who preferred logic over values when making decisions. However, the ingrained approach was challenged upon the arrival of an unscientific and unpredictable framework of faith. *Does not compute!*

Within the context of my growing irrational faith, my quest for logical order and conclusions became a fool's errand. Decisions were still based on logic, but faith demanded its veto power as I submitted to God and His will. There were times when God's Spirit prompted me toward what seemed like nonsense. My faith was tested whenever I was called to override my intuition with obedience to His promptings, and I failed at it more often than I care to admit. I needed God's Spirit to provide clarity and guidance every day—loudly—and fill me with more faith so that I could even look the other way—His way.

Within the first year of my healing journey, I had stumbled upon something called a "One Year Bible." Butch had already gifted me with my own NIV version, but the organized approach of this book intrigued me. Daily prepared readings included a group of various verses, designed to help one complete the entire Bible within one year.

But something odd happened... I couldn't restrain myself! During a visit to my parent's home one Christmas, I was glued to the book, devouring much more than the prescribed daily reading. All the Bible stories and lessons surged to life within my hands. My heart stirred over and over again, growing my newfound faith exponentially. My One Year Bible turned out to be more like a three-month thrill ride of inspiration! As an avid reader herself, Mum observed my love and obsession for my new book about God and perhaps the Lord planted seeds there. *Will she be open one day?*

\* \* \*

Meanwhile, my topsy-turvy life roared onward. Questionable moral choices unfolded over many a weekend, but I cherished attending church on Sunday mornings. The warm embrace of belonging beckoned my hungry heart, a stark contrast to the bar scene that used to feel more welcoming. At church, no one wanted anything from me, and my well-coiffed hair and coordinated attire held minimal importance.

Unexpected circumstances meant I was moving again, that time to my own place near downtown. Butch suggested I check out a nearby church situated perfectly for a Sunday morning leisure walk, and he joined me the first few times.

The Full Gospel Church was larger and more established than my previous congregation, with lots more friendly, welcoming people. *Bonus: I'm not falling asleep here!* I reveled in warm hugs from Pastor Fenn, received on the front steps and through his preaching. Week after week, tears streamed down my cheeks during Sunday sermons that seemed to be custom-tailored for my receptive heart, as if God Himself was serenading me with His truth and love.

Infused with a variety of exceptional music, the congregation included a couple dozen vocalists who took turns with special songs during Sunday services. Sometimes, the selections were folksier, and other times, contemporary, and I loved it all. I was often moved closer to God's heart as the inspiring music washed over me.

Eager to enlist in the choir, I was in time to take part in the grand Christmas musical production called *We Beheld His Glory*. My inability to decode sheet music wasn't a problem because gracious guidance from fellow tenors enabled me to master my part. We rehearsed twice a week, and two final performances guaranteed ample room for friends and families.

As we approached the midpoint of our first live performance, what seemed to be an ethereal multiplication of voices joined in during an ensemble section. It was as if another choir had materialized in our midst, a remarkable delight for the ears and spirit! We all exchanged bewildered glances while continuing to harmonize, and afterward, some speculated a heavenly chorus of unseen angels had joined us. *Wow, that can actually happen?* The supernatural event amplified my faith and sent my spirit soaring for months. *What an amazing God we serve!*

Pastor Brian and his wife were in charge of the choir, and our camaraderie blossomed over time. After one practice, Brian asked if I would speak with them. *Oh no, what did they find out?* They surprised me by asking if I was willing to speak to the church. *Seriously?*

So, I haven't told you yet about my public speaking "career," which began at an early age. Almost every assembly or production at my schools had involved me as the host or narrator. I had a good speaking voice and always took it seriously, so frequent engagements over many years helped me gain much experience by the time I'd reached my early twenties. But it had been three years since the pinnacle opportunity of my address to SAIT students at graduation, so I was feeling a little rusty.

When presented with the invitation from Pastor Brian, it seemed instinctive to say yes. *But wait… speaking in front of a church? Where educated men of God stand?*

"Wow, I appreciate that! Can I get back to you?" I answered, trying to exchange my initial anxieties for honor and humility.

"Sure, Todd, that's not a problem," Brian replied. "We know you'll do great!"

After some encouragement from Butch, I timidly accepted their invitation. Those were uncharted waters, but I crafted my "speech" with the same diligence as usual. But, for the first time, I used my Bible as my primary resource. The message painted the picture of God as the master artist, meandering through His creation galleries, with each of us showcased as His Master-pieces. Even when we were as still as statues or framed canvases, He loved to be with His created ones so He could closely admire His craftsmanship.

My foray into church presentations was well received. Butch pointed out later there were one or two minor "theology" hiccups attributable to my newfound faith. *No worries, I did the best I could.* One congregation member approached me in tears after the service, her heart stirred as I read from the Bible. She declared I'd been given special authority and anointing, and she was grateful for my message. Her words heartened me greatly, fortifying my confidence and faith in a bold new arena. *Thank You, Lord Jesus, for Your faithfulness!*

\* \* \*

Prayer was an intriguing and mysterious practice early in my Christian walk. It wasn't difficult for me to understand the concept that God listens when people talk with Him. I'd witnessed lots of healthy group prayer and soon became comfortable enough to participate. But my confidence in personal prayer was something that needed building, occurring only with encouragement and practice.

A close friend named Carl had received news that his recent promotion resulted in a transfer to a remote town in northern British Columbia. Carl also had same-sex attractions, but he was on a different path than me. Nonetheless, we'd grown close through much time together, and I enjoyed his bright, sarcastic wit and humor. Word of his upcoming move was saddening because I knew there was little chance of me visiting him in his new home.

Carl and I never talked much about God or his faith, though I knew he'd been raised Catholic. He didn't attend church, and I never observed any practices or habits suggesting he was even open to God. But that didn't stop me from praying for him.

After he moved away, I began praying He would lead Carl to a church where he felt welcomed as part of their community. It was an unusual thing to be praying for, given that Carl hadn't darkened the doorway of a church the whole time I knew him.

Within a few weeks, I learned Carl was attending a local church and was happy to be there. Over the moon with joy and overcome by tears at the news, I was convinced God loved Carl way more than I did and that He had heard and answered my prayer. *Thank you, God!*

Another standout memory was when I'd heard on the news the famous singer Gloria Estefan had been involved in a terrible bus crash. I was familiar with her music for sure, but I wouldn't have considered myself an uberfan by any means.

However, the emerging details about Gloria's life-threatening injuries moved my heart with surprising concern and compassion. She'd fractured her spine, and the word was she might not make it. Doubt started me off, but faith kept me going as I lifted Gloria up to God in prayer, that He would save her life and bring healing.

Word soon came her complicated surgery had been successful, and it appeared she would not only live but be physically restored and able to resume her career. That's how it turned out, and I believe God used the unforeseen circumstances to show me again that He answers prayers. I don't doubt there were possibly millions of others praying for the exact same thing, and perhaps every one of them was encouraged to believe like I was.

Butch had long held a soft spot for my brother Greg, and when he'd learned Greg had not yet accepted Christ, he began to pray. One night we sat side by side in the living room praying together for Greg, and I was able to witness Butch pour out his heart before God. He was pleading with the Lord to bring Greg to acceptance of Him in his life, assuring his eternal destination with Jesus. I was privileged to partner in prayer with my friend for the benefit of my brother.

When news reached us that Greg was attending church with his family, the Lord filled my heart with awe as He reminded me of the faithful prayers He had heard and answered. *We praise you, Lord!*

\* \* \*

Butch had long attended Calgary's First Assembly church, and he got word Pastor Tom was planting a non-traditional church across town. Tom had cultivated a wildly successful ministry event called "Tehillah Monday," lending palpable energy and leadership to the new gathering. It didn't take much convincing from Butch for me to go and check it out. *Who's more non-traditional than us?*

Westside King's Church (aka Westside) emerged in a former curling rink on the growing west side of Calgary with a picturesque view of the Rocky Mountains. The rink had been converted into a rental hall, and Westside secured offices and space for its Sunday services. The new church thrived within a short span, and hundreds convened every week to be part of the new movement.

One magnetic lure of Westside was Pastor Tom's unwavering commitment to transparency, made more poignant as a recovering alcoholic who often spoke about his struggles. It was an endearing attribute, and I enjoyed his solid biblical teachings infused with life lessons and illustrations that amplified their impact and endurance.

Music worship at Westside was top-notch in quality and there were many times I experienced what I came to know as the moving of the Spirit, an unusual sense of God at work in our midst. One Sunday, the band was repeating the chorus of a familiar song, and I felt warm all throughout my body as I sang along. With my eyes closed, a strange sensation came over me with a vision of being slowly elevated from where I stood. But it wasn't up into the air, more like being lifted up about six inches or so.

As I realized what the Lord was doing in me, grateful tears rolled past my cheeks as my heart swelled with more love for Him. Father God was healing me of my insecurity about my less than average height, not because I'd asked for it, but because He loved me. From that point forward, I grew in sincere appreciation of my unique physique as an intentional gift for His purposes. *Thank you for how You made me, Lord.*

I loved the Westside church family, gravitating toward youth ministry under the passionate vision of Pastor Wayne. Every week, our youth leadership team gathered to eat before all the youth showed for the evening's activities, creating special camaraderie and fellowship through sharing and prayer. Wayne was passionate and compulsive in his outreach to the community, and I also volunteered at his pet project, The Cave.

City youth flocked every weekend to The Cave, located inside a converted commercial space. They enjoyed loud dance music, ping-pong matches, and snacks under the management of loving Christian leaders. Serving at their Friday nightclub (without alcohol) offered me some redemption from my bar-hopping past, as it yielded an unexpected healing opportunity for me. *Hey, no spandex!* Later, I helped develop an operations manual to serve Wayne's franchising aspirations for additional outreach centers; however, I'd moved on before its fruition.

It wasn't long before I shared details about my unique faith journey with church leadership, who then invited me to share my testimony from the stage during a Sunday service. Jitters were on a rampage, but I pressed into Him as He faithfully upheld me and guided me into an astounding experience of openness that resonated with many.

Overwhelmed, I wept as people lined up to pour out tearful gratitude for my courage. On that day, I was liberated from fears of rejection and ridicule as I admitted my same-sex struggles in a public setting. Instead of shame and condemnation, I basked in my church family's affection and acceptance, especially as many confessed their own issues to me. *Maybe it's true I am loved and not so different from all the other boys.* I was so grateful to God for such an important springboard to further healing, reigniting my commitment to pursue His plan and intentions for me.

Westside hosted another vibrant ministry called Abba, a homegrown spiritual healing program that had quickly grown to serve hundreds across many churches. No, the name didn't reference the 70s uberband, but rather an endearing Hebrew word for Father God used to suggest His daddy-like love and generosity. Abba held weekly gatherings that broke into smaller groups of men and women. Butch was familiar with the founder of this ministry, and he highly recommended it to me.

By then, I was nearly an expert in small group endeavors and willing to volunteer as a leader of a men's group, despite my persistent apprehension about their response to my struggles. Instead of rejection, I encountered full acceptance from those men who valued my vulnerability as a catalyst for deeper, sincere interactions for everyone in our small group. My Abba leadership season brought me increased healing and growth and represented a pivotal step toward seamless integration into my faith community.

The combination of my support group experiences over the years convinced me most of us can mature and overcome immense pain and grief through Christ and His work through others in small groups. I saw firsthand that small groups were an exceedingly rare opportunity for genuine recognition and acceptance of our own truth. To come out from hiding and be known for who we are and all we have lived through is to find healing.

The incredible ride began when I said yes to Jesus, allowing Him to love me as we sat together in my muck and shame there in the third stall from the end. The sincere love and acceptance received from others in my H.A. group made me more receptive to His love. Then, the same acceptance from my church family and my Abba group also negotiated further healing in my life.

It took a lot to convince me I was fully lovable, inside and out. But God didn't give up on me as He guided me through all I needed to agree with Him, and I still need reminders to this day. Being seen and known by others enabled me to mediate His healing to others as I mirrored my own receipt of it, a living trophy of His grace. With all my heart, I believe you can also become a living trophy of Grace no matter what life has brought your way.

Also, during my six-year season at Westside, God had kindled a passion within me to explore my inherent teaching abilities. At the time, I grappled with my career path because of a large array of skills, talents, and interests. My dilemma prompted rigorous research on spiritual gifts and confirmed I had a God-given teaching gift. One manifestation of a teaching gift is an innate drive to investigate topics of interest, even more so if there's even a hint it could lead to teaching others on the same topic. My fellow educators will resonate with that truth. *Sometimes I can't help but teach!*

Pursuing knowledge for the sake of others is precisely what occurred during my research into spiritual gifts. A complementary spiritual gift of administration facilitated the creation of an easy, navigable outline for a course designed to help others discover and unwrap their spiritual gifts.

Westside accepted the proposal to offer my new program to the congregation (originally called the PEP Workshop) and eight people showed up for my first class, including Butch of course. Soon, the workshop expanded to incorporate clarification on gift categories, snowballing into additional related modules as the Lord led. I remain so grateful to Westside leadership for entrusting me with the development and instruction of those courses. Their openness and God's provision created cherished memories of hundreds who were —and still are being—transformed by His faithfulness through life-altering awareness of divine plans for our lives.

Sadly, I had wandered without aim from one shiny job to another for a large part of my life. Meandering had contributed to my pervasive dissatisfaction with life and my unhealthy pursuits. My internal strife subsided as clarity surrounding God's intentions for me crystallized, equipping me with tools and activating the passion to serve Him in that manner. It's difficult to imagine how much more challenging my sexuality struggles may have been had He not provided transformative clarity on my Calling at the same time. *Your timing is perfect, Lord!*

One of the many byproducts of years of volunteer service was gaining perspective on the tasks and projects that floated or sank my boat. Sure, I wasn't compensated in pay, but I received much satisfaction along with clarity of my aptitudes, i.e., giftedness. Volunteering is a win-win strategy that can yield remarkable insight into who God made us and where He plans for us to serve, and I believe the church is the ideal place to do this. But if our church isn't wired that way, then we must seek out other non-profit organizations for service opportunities to help us find our place in this world.

* * *

The dynamic leadership team at Westside King's Church was eager to embrace new ministry ventures for Kingdom expansion. When an individual proposed an idea, swift approval often resulted, especially if funding wasn't required. As a SAIT student, I recalled the presence of chaplains using office space offered by the student's association to support the spiritual needs of the student body.

I had assumed that training or education would be mandatory for a chaplain designation. However, a chat with Pastor Tom clarified that training was not required, and I was surprised to find myself suggesting Westside sponsor me as a SAIT chaplain. The prospect of providing care and support within a Christian context to SAIT students enticed me, especially given my obliviousness to the value of such support while I was a student. Westside leadership endorsed my self-funded proposal and plans followed with the Student's Association. I agreed to meet often with Pastor Tom for accountability.

In no time flat, I had become a campus chaplain! I was responsible for setting my office hours, so I began with only two daytime slots, helping me to ease into unfamiliar terrain.

I got through my inaugural week with nary a visitor in sight. Even with my connections to the student association office and posted hours, nobody seemed interested in chatting. One time, I managed to reel in a passerby, who consented to my prayer offering. I considered tramping around campus (perhaps in the garb of a monk or white-collared preacher) to connect directly with students. However, I was wary of missing a student who actually sought help after showing up at my office in my absence. It was all disheartening, but I chose to trust the Lord. If He wanted to bring people, He would. But He didn't. And I couldn't understand why the door had opened in the first place. That is, until later.

Early the following year, the SAIT staff liaison for the association contacted me, perhaps unaware I'd abandoned my chaplaincy. He invited me to deliver the invocation as part of the platform party at the graduation ceremony. I couldn't believe my ears! The school hosted two grad ceremonies to accommodate substantial numbers of graduates and their families. Both events transpired at the Jubilee

Auditorium, presenting a rare opportunity to reach roughly five thousand people with the reality of God's love.

I accepted the invitation with enthusiasm, envisioning my return to the same stage where I'd stood as a valedictorian speaker eight years prior. *Oh, what would I say now to the hotdog man?* Ironically, it had also been the stage on which Dionne Warwick performed her hits while I was on a date with Charles. *Lord, remind me often to say a little prayer for him.*

The invocation was well received and helped set the tone for the entire ceremony. My favorite part? Shaking the hand of each graduate as they crossed the stage to receive a diploma. It was such a special privilege to bless each one!

Follow-up invitations to reprise my role surprised me the next year and, astonishingly, once more several years later, a truly humbling gesture. Those extraordinary occasions to serve God and the students in such a manner carved themselves into my memory, and I can only hope seeds of truth were planted for the Lord's purposes.[6]

\* \* \*

An Orlando trade show beckoned Butch on business, turning into a discussion about a Florida vacation. As with many of our projects, it began to take on a life of its own. I'd vacation time saved up from my job and soon figured out how to experience an epic five-week vacation touring the Sunshine State with my best friend.

A rental car helped us traverse many other parts of a fascinating state that's home to four different tropical climate zones. There's a lot to see in Florida so we were grateful for the opportunity to have more than a month to make our mark.

While in the Miami Beach area, we were mesmerized by the people-watching on Ocean Drive, especially as the sun set on a vibrant nightlife. Our eyes were caught by a handsome young man who'd removed his shirt to show off his tanned, athletic physique. We smiled and walked past him, praising the Lord for such breathtaking workmanship. About thirty seconds later, I felt a rare prompting and wrestled with understanding the motivation behind it. I turned to Butch and shared what was on my mind.

"I think we're supposed to talk with that guy," I suggested, my voice tentative and perplexed. My mind was trying to convince me otherwise because approaching that good-looking playboy seemed like a terrible idea.

"Well, you don't have to say that twice," replied Butch, with a snorty laugh I'd heard countless times.

More talking with Butch allowed me to share my concern and then affirm my sense the Lord was up to something. Nothing of the sort had occurred to me before, let alone with my best friend and in such a distracting setting. We turned and began the short walk back to the spot where handsome guy still stood.

His name was Chris, and he was friendly, perhaps a little too friendly. We chatted for a bit before he suggested we get off the strip, and we obliged. I was still feeling cautious because the situation had the potential to go further south than we already were. We found a quiet spot and enjoyed getting acquainted, starting with us sharing our story with him.

Like many others, Chris had assumed we were a couple and was surprised to hear of our efforts to surrender our gay identities to Christ—he'd never heard of anyone doing that before. He shared that he, too, struggled with his same-sex attractions, and as an east-coast cop, he didn't feel safe talking about it with others.

Chris came from a Catholic family and admitted he hadn't nurtured his faith since childhood. Butch and I were able to encourage him with the truth of God's love for him, no matter who he dated.

We enjoyed about an hour together before he had to go home and get ready for his shift. As we parted with warm hugs all around, his twinkling eyes and bright smile suggested God had encouraged that golden-brown stranger through our time together.

The Lord also used the unforeseen meeting with Chris to grow my faith in a new direction. It helped me realize I could hear His promptings and I could rely on His strength and courage to respond… if I could set aside my lustful self. It was an uplifting experience that ended well. *Help me to hear You more, Lord!*

\* \* \*

More than six years passed after I'd said yes to Jesus when a friend helped open the door for an exciting job as a producer at a new Christian television station. It was an awesome opportunity for several reasons, including a long-awaited return to my trade to put my first-rate education to the test. Joining the startup team of the trailblazing project was nothing short of exhilarating. I could barely contain myself as I shared the news with my roommate, who didn't seem quite as enthused as me.

"Todd, are you sure this is God's plan?" he clarified, showing only some tentativeness due to my obvious excitement.

"It's impossible not to see He's lined me up for such a time as this," I replied, appreciative of Butch's concern yet surprised he had any doubts at all. With a little more discussion, I won him over, and it felt great to have his support. *Let's do this, Jesus!*

A move to another city signified a fresh start for me and a big change in my relationship with Butch. The news was more difficult for him, but with time, we both embraced the potential benefits of time apart to help detach from unhealthy emotional bonds. A bittersweet parting, for sure.

In the world of television, a producer title can come with much ambiguity, and the role is often customized based on needs and relevant skills. My responsibilities included producing and hosting an entertainment news segment for the morning show, video editing as needed, and administrative support for the general manager. I was delighted my SAIT training would be put to good use in a Christian environment—a beautiful combination of my long-held aspirations with my maturing faith.

Friction soon developed with the director of the morning show. As the general manager's young, handsome, confident son, he enjoyed privileges other staff didn't have. It's unusual for me to dislike anyone—especially with a profile like his—but the two of us often clashed in arguments, gnawing at my confidence. Dormant triggers from past bullying were awakened, stirring up unwelcome emotions and insecurities. *Why, Lord?*

Many occasions for creative work brightened my days, but the lack of singularity in my job focus made it challenging to prove myself to others, especially the boss's son. Our conflict cast a shadow over everything, causing me to wonder if I'd made a terrible mistake in uprooting myself accepting the position.

One transformative afternoon, as I edited a segment that would air the next day, a viewer's words of heartfelt gratitude drifted down the corridor from an on-air monitor in the other room. She'd been watching a show we aired from another station and called in to express her appreciation for how helpful it was to her faith journey.

As I eavesdropped on the woman pouring out her heart in thankfulness, tears formed and fell down my face. My heart ached and rejoiced, causing me to praise the Lord's faithfulness right there in the editor's chair without fully understanding why.

It took some processing with loved ones before I realized the soul-stirring encounter was the Lord calling me to serve Him through my work, somewhat like the call received by the disciples who dropped their fishing nets to follow Jesus. At twenty-nine years old, I knew, like never before, that the focus of my work would always be to fulfill God's purposes.

About two months into the job, I had a surprising conversation with the station's founder. He asked about my interest in ascending into management. During our dialogue, I voiced my dissatisfaction with station operations. I also lamented the absence of team prayer, a true paradox in my mind, given our mission to cultivate Christian faith in our viewers.

Irony peaked a few days later when I was summoned by the general manager, only to be informed of my dismissal mere days before the conclusion of the ninety-day probationary period. My boss's mysterious awareness of my job dissatisfaction helped to highlight the necessity of discretion in the workplace. It was a lesson painfully learned in an environment where I'd hoped for a reprieve from secular workplace politics.

My termination pay yielded a much-needed three-week retreat at King's Fold Retreat Centre near Calgary. The serene, hospitable backdrop offered space and time for introspection and creativity in full view of the breathtaking Rocky Mountains and the Snake River winding through the valley below. An unexpected diamond-like gift had emerged from what appeared to be a lump of coal, though a regrettable detour occurred, worth sharing a little later.

* * *

Almost a year after the lights faded to black on my Christian television career, God began to stir in my heart a calling to full-time ministry as a pastor. After getting confirmation from loved ones, I prepared to attend a local bible college. An attempt to raise financial support yielded enough encouragement to register for the spring semester and begin an exciting new chapter. *Me, a pastor?*

Most of my classes were stimulating and relevant, and I appreciated the connections made with various professors. But it was what God revealed during one of the foundational classes that triggered a course correction. More specifically, a chalkboard eraser flying past my head caught my attention rather than the intended target. I was the only "mature" student in the class, and it was difficult to assimilate. I also didn't feel safe enough to disclose my sexual struggles, so I kept them hidden. It seemed my enthusiasm and commitment were waning faster than the speed of that eraser. *What am I doing here?*

I completed the first semester but failed one class because I didn't complete a reading—not a good sign. Matters were made worse when it became clear additional financial support wasn't possible through donations or a student loan. After chatting with a school counselor, I determined my formal biblical education would come to an end.

The following year, I was invited back to teach my spiritual gifts course[7] in the pastor's class, an encouraging footnote on a puzzling detour in my journey. The positive response to the class also served as confirmation my coaching and workshops were gaining favor and needed more attention.

Through the ups and downs, my relationship with God flourished through those encounters, with many aspects resembling a faith-building fast track. Despite the presence of my same-sex struggles, they no longer wielded the same authority and impact as before. Still, further healing was imperative to find greater liberty to pursue God's will in my life.

The following words from the Apostle Paul to believers in the Roman church inspired me toward something greater and possible in my life.

*"So, you also should consider yourselves to be dead to the power of sin and alive to God through Christ Jesus. Do not let sin control the way you live; do not give in to sinful desires. Do not let any part of your body become an instrument of evil to serve sin. Instead, give yourselves completely to God, for you were dead, but now you have new life. So use your whole body as an instrument to do what is right for the glory of God. Sin is no longer your master, for you no longer live under the requirements of the law. Instead, you live under the freedom of God's grace."—Romans 6:11-14 (NLT)*

# Overjoyed Over There

Only six months after I had entered my new relationship with Jesus, I learned that Nan and Granch were planning a trip to England. Somehow, the idea surfaced I could join them. The idea of a big trip together to connect with our British family was enticing.

Nan and Granch generously agreed to cover everything except my flight and anything I did alone. We would rendezvous in Toronto for our overseas journey to Gatwick Airport, where my granduncle and family would collect us before driving to Hereford. As I've shared, Nan was born and raised in England within a large family. An abundance of relatives awaited my maiden voyage across the pond, and I was eager to meet them all.

Speaking of maidens, my part-time job then was operating an old-fashioned telephone switchboard for an answering service. My former co-worker, Reg, had secured a management position there and landed me the job, which I enjoyed despite the varied hours. Aside from Reg, I stood as the lone male on the payroll and found much amusement in the company of all the switchboard damsels.

As my impending British invasion loomed, a hilarious suggestion arose at work: I should seek a maiden of my own during my tour of the United Kingdom. Hence, the Great Canadian Duchess Search was launched! Given his foreknowledge of me and my ongoing struggles, Reg found it all quite amusing.

From various locales scattered across the British Isles, I loyally mailed postcards to the ladies, chronicling my eccentric pursuit of a wealthy duchess to wed. My updates rang with sarcastic wit and tongue-in-cheek humor. Upon my homecoming, my switchboard damsels presented me with the entire collection of postcards, preserving the memories and hearty laughter we all shared. Reg may have laughed most of all, who knows what he may have relayed to my co-workers. Despite our different paths in life, Reg and I have kept in touch over the years, and we've managed to enjoy some chuckles and snorts about days of old.

My overseas adventure was spent mostly in the company of my loving grandparents. I relished meeting everyone and reuniting with the dear grandaunts who'd visited Canada during my childhood. Many meals and even more laughs were appreciated by all.

In a bold twist, I ventured out from our home base in Hereford, for a day trip via British Rail to savor a meal in Scotland. It proved interesting but uneventful, as I kept to myself, choosing to let fear have its way in favor of safety.

You see, as a struggling young adult exploring a foreign land on his own, countless temptations loomed. *What will I do if a guy is too friendly with me?* As mentioned, I was only six months in my new walk with Jesus, so the sea legs of my faith were wobbly. As a result, I deemed safety paramount during the long five-hour ride each way, donning headphones, window gazing, journaling, and reading as I made my way to Glasgow and back.

While in Glasgow, I located a pub for a late lunch, then reboarded the train to return to Hereford, where I lodged with Auntie Sylvie, concluding a full travel day without any slipups. Scotland now crossed off my bucket list, and the only person I met was my waitress. Safety was precisely what I'd accomplished.

*** 

Our English holiday lasted almost two weeks, permitting several family outings and some more exploration on my own. I soon resolved to call on Paris and accomplish an uncharacteristic achievement at the same time—zero meticulous planning for an overnight trip, in favor of improvisation and comfort-zone stretching.

I cannot stress enough the magnitude of that decision at that time in my life. Always methodical and organized, the inflexible habit persisted in almost every role I undertook. Maintaining control appeased my anxieties; if I dictated the details of every event, then nothing could harm me, right? *Bollocks!*

A solo foray into a more foreign country without a room reservation would've been unthinkable in my world. But my motivation was to expand my zone of comfort, an attempt to embrace the axiom, "Nothing changes if nothing changes," and propel my growth and healing process.

With adventure on my mind and a wannabe, carefree heart, I boarded a train bound for the white cliffs of Dover on the southeastern coast. From Dover, I climbed on a commercial hovercraft for a gripping ride across the choppy English Channel to Calais, France. From Calais, I commuted via rail toward the heart of Paris. Frightfully aware of troublesome temptations, I remained vigilant and absorbed in my journal. The three-hour trek proved harmless, culminating at the Gare du Nord station at 5:00 p.m. on a Saturday.

Familiar train station noises encircled me as though they were in my native tongue. Less than half-armed with high-school French, I prepared to gaffe my way into dubious Parisian accommodations.

Lo-and-behold, a large sign in English appeared from above with a vibrant red heart, declaring, "Paris Loves Youth." It directed my attention to a popular booth on the platform, and I beelined into the long queue. I awaited my turn, rubbing shoulders with scores of dashing young men from distant lands, enveloped in a nearly visible cloud of French cologne. *Eyes forward, eyes forward.* At last, it was my turn to talk with the attendant, ready to help locate my lodging for the night.

Most patrons were young and steered toward thrifty hostels. Visions of a crowded dorm in a French guesthouse induced a curious mélange of terror and excitement. I elected to play it safe, splurging on a private room, counting the additional cost as well worth the added security. The rarity and lure of a private bathroom sealed the deal. After all, I was in Paris to explore the sights from my bucket list, not test my resolve. If I was going to dip my toe in anything French, it would be the River Seine.

My determination to push past my comfortable boundaries screeched to a standstill when I opted for my first meal at Lé Burger King, where Lé Whopper's Parisian price tag was higher than a car payment. I was grateful nobody had the bright idea to translate the name of an iconic American sandwich. *A meal worth every greasy franc!*

The Eiffel Tower was an awe-inspiring marvel, especially at night when its countless lights transformed beams of steel into mesmerizing magic. I maintained a low profile, keeping my interactions with strangers to a safe minimum. A pair of young men down by the river looked quite chummy, embracing each other with affection, displaying minimal concern for onlookers. The foreign sight sparked intrigue and revelation—some Paris citizens obviously lived in stark contrast with my fellow Calgarians, perhaps even most Canadians.

Upon returning to the hostel, I discovered a raucous party underway in the lobby bar. *Nope, not for me. But maybe? Nope, I am not like all the other boys here.* Eyes down, I darted through the gauntlet and up to my private room. It felt like the right thing to do. *Thank you, God?*

The next morning, extra time before catching my train allowed me to enjoy one of myriad sidewalk cafes. With chairs arranged facing the street, optimal people-watching ensued. Yet again, I yearned for more focused practice on my conversational French before squandering the remainder of my precious time in France. I mustered courage for my impatient waiter, attempting to order from the menu with limited success, then eating what could've been something they scooped from the intestine of who knows what. *Well, I tried.*

Gare du Nord appeared the same as it did the night before, but the spirited trip back across the channel was even more thrilling due to powerful winds and towering waves. Our craft mostly hovered over the treacherous whitecaps instead of rough sailing on the stormy surface, birthing a powerful metaphor for later recall. A few hours later, I found myself back in Hereford with another extraordinary adventure under my unfashionable belt.

\* \* \*

Before I had left for England, Butch suggested I contact his friend, Ian, and explore the possibility of accommodations at his London home during my visit. Ian was a lovely sales representative who visited Butch's business, and I got to know him through occasional meals with Butch when he stayed with him.

Pleased to oblige my request, Ian arranged to meet at a pub before we would head to his flat. Ian was an older gentleman who held no allure for me, rendering it a low-risk situation.

However, the unexpected unfolded as we discussed plans for the rest of the evening. Ian was a little curious himself and proposed we visit nearby gay bars. Keen to avoid those venues for many reasons, his suggestion took me aback given Ian's awareness of the battle to embrace a new identity. Grateful that Ian didn't press the matter, I suggested a more prudent alternative—enjoying the remainder of our delightful evening at a quintessentially British pub, which we did.

During the stroll home, we passed a bar Ian knew to be gay, and he again asked if I wanted to check it out. *What exactly did Butch tell him?* The bar's energetic bass and animated lights beckoned almost as much as the welcoming lads out front, and we paused for a few moments as Ian stared at me for a decision. *Lord Jesus, help.* Once again, I declined, and retreated home unscathed.

In the morning, Ian departed early for work, leaving me with instructions on securing his flat upon my exit for the day. I navigated through the lockable latches on all doors between his unit and the front of the complex. But Ian had overlooked one crucial detail—the front door, which locked from both sides, using a key I didn't have.

So, as the door to Ian's flat closed behind me, it bolted securely, and I proceeded down the stairs to the front entrance. There I discovered that door was also inaccessible. Confined to the cramped stairwell, I was without a phone or any means of contacting someone. With no glass window to shatter for escape, I resigned myself to the snug space, perhaps for Ian's entire workday.

It was a peculiar sensation, actually. The situation's absurdity struck me funny, and I was grateful panic didn't overwhelm me. Instead, I perched on the stairs, serenading myself with songs as the hours crept by. Hunger had been satisfied at breakfast with some toast, averting the need to cannibalize my left arm.

A little after lunchtime, I detected activity near the front door. I slid open the mail slot, imploring the angel who appeared before me. Mercifully, the woman knew Ian and how to reach him, securing his help. In less than an hour, a flustered and sheepish Ian showed up, releasing me from captivity with repeated apologies.

I was grateful to get out, but in all honesty, the circumstances didn't trouble me. Instead, I pondered what the predicament could've provoked in me and instead leaned into grace able to respond better. Choosing grace was made much easier as I pondered how He extended the same to me despite countless mistakes and similar rescue situations. *Thank you, Jesus.*

\*\*\*

One other unforgettable incident happened during a stroll the next day (with a door key in my pocket) while Ian was at work. I had donned my Olympics CTV jacket knowing it would pique interest of many, owed to world-famous insignias. I admit I still enjoyed the attention garnered by my jacket, reflecting upon its magical powers that brought Matt into my life in such a memorable manner.

As I strode down the London sidewalk under the midday sun, I noticed a handsome young man approaching me. Our eyes fleetingly met as we passed, but we both continued on our way. Intrigue gripped me, and I couldn't resist looking back over my shoulder, only to discover him doing the same. *Is it the jacket?* Then we each carried on walking, drifting further to about a half-block apart.

Every single painstaking effort made on this vacation to prioritize protection and defy temptation coalesced in a singular moment. My heart pounded like a drum while thoughts churned at the speed of sound.

*What did I really want?*

*Was it me who wanted this, or someone else?*

*Why would God even allow this to happen?*

Before I could deliberate further, another look over my shoulder revealed the young man had halted, pivoted to face me, and I did likewise. Our world paused as if caught in a timeless painting. Something leaped within me without my permission. He exaggerated a shrug, conveying an inaudible, "Well, mate?"

With no further wavering, a decision crystallized. I turned away, upholding my determination, walking taller without looking back. And sometimes, it's that simple: turn away.

My gracious host allowed me to later recount the tale as I reveled in the triumph that better illuminated my priorities. I felt confident the Lord was my helper, bolstering my tenacity in an unforeseen encounter. Left to my own devices, the episode could've transpired differently, culminating in a profound sense of defeat and failure.

A different choice would have cast a pall over the rest of my vacation and subsequent reunion with my brothers in the faith. But instead of woeful tales of relapse, I'd be celebrating a God-given victory over my self-driven desires. I treasured the rewards of having made challenging, even sacrificial choices, attributing all credit to God and His faithfulness. *You are so good!*

The balance of the holiday progressed smoothly and included memorable road trips on narrow country roads and extensive sightseeing through Wales. Safe and sound, my grandparents and I returned to Canada, chock-full of cherished memories to keep us reminiscing for years.

In retrospect, I remain convinced the series of obedient decisions in favor of God's leading made early in my Christian walk established a firm foundation from which my faith blossomed, and blessings flowed. The rewards of knowing God's will and remaining obedient far outweigh anything the world offers me!

# Naked for Jesus

As I mentioned, my healing journey taught me to appreciate the cruciality of stepping outside my comfort zone. We learned that facing our fears often puts us on a fast track to expanding the boundaries of our comfort and in some cases, wiping out such comfort zones altogether.

Remember that disrobing in front of a group of men had been a long-held source of binding anxiety, due to unresolved trauma from childhood. In dread, I'd realized a central component in my healing journey: I needed to come to terms with my body image and fully embrace all of myself, as God designed and created me. *Oh boy.*

About four years after meeting in H.A., Butch and I had become roommates after Gary (my bar friend) moved out. By then, Butch was the best friend I'd never had. I came to understand he found me more alluring than I saw him, and perhaps the lack of mutuality was a blessing, as our relationship might have become something quite different.

Over time, Butch became more familiar with my issues than anyone ever before, yet he loved and accepted me like Jesus. My buddy had an unimaginable impact on my life in many ways. One significant contribution to my healing was his influence on my body insecurities. As trust increased with Butch, non-erotic physical freedom also increased by us being naked together in showers or hot tubs. Over time, those casual occasions ushered in profound self-acceptance of my unique male body and all its shortcomings.

The most transformative event was an excursion to Wreck Beach in Vancouver, British Columbia. A secluded beach near the

University of British Columbia campus, it sits below the main road that skirts the Pacific Ocean. Butch suggested we check it out when we were visiting near there one summer. I was petrified. Why? Because Wreck Beach was a nude beach. I'd rather tear out each of my fingernails with pliers and savor them as a gory salad topper than bare my all on a beach teeming with nudists—or anywhere public, for that matter. But Butch can be very persuasive, or encouraging, depending on one's mood.

As we parked near the beach, thoughts of escape simmered in my mind, my heart pounded furiously, and my stomach a whirlpool of anxiety. "Oh, I forgot my swimsuit" wouldn't work this time. There was Butch, grinning ear to ear, offering much-needed reassurance. He'd frequented Wreck Beach and appeared to be well beyond any body image issues. However, my insecurities had crippled me most of my life, rooted in fear of ridicule and rejection as a man and friend. Yet, we forged ahead. *Lord Jesus, help me.*

Still dressed, we descended the long, high embankment through the towering coastline cedars providing welcome shade in the summer heat. My chief concern was, of course, "Well, when exactly will I be forced to get naked?" Or put another way, "How long can I put it off?" *Do nude beach bylaws prohibit all clothing? Maybe just my undies?*

I'd like to tell you we stormed the beach like Normandy. But instead, Butch steered us from the bottom of the stairs to several enormous cedar logs, an ideal semi-concealed place to collect myself and disrobe. I'd have preferred to remain clothed as we sprinted to our intended beach location, eyes forward, peeling off everything like it was on fire… stop, drop (forget the roll), and flop—face down —into a book. But my dear and loving friend Butch dissuaded me. I attributed my tiny morsel of courage to his presence.

In my exasperated, trance-like state, I didn't notice Butch had already stripped before we had even hit the sand. But he was so gracious with me. I drew a deep breath, uttered another silent prayer, and gazed at my buddy's... eyes.

"You could at least look the other way," I suggested, laughing nervously. Butch laughed with gusto. Seagulls mocked me with their squawking as my flaring nostrils let an abundance of salty air into my heaving lungs.

"Oh, Buddy, you can do this," Butch declared. "Buddy" was his nickname for me as a nod to the H.A. buddy system that brought us together as friends. *Thank you, Lord, for my buddy.*

There in the shadow of the giant logs, the big reveal couldn't be delayed any longer. I shed all my clothing and prepared to traverse the hot sand with speed and determination, keen not to roam about any more than required. We arrived at a nice spot near another large cedar log and spread out a blanket to lie down. However, I surprised myself with enough ease to remain seated so I could survey and absorb my strange surroundings... and catch my breath.

The most extraordinary aspect of the nudist beach became apparent in an instant: none of the guys there gave an actual shit. Nobody did. Not about me. Not about my body, or my penis. None of it. The startling revelation was beyond freeing for the newest Wreck Beach virgin. But I couldn't help but wonder if the good Lord had made more of me above average, perhaps some attention would be mine? *But what am I thinking, would that actually be a good thing?*

The wonders on a nude beach were quite amusing. An eclectic assortment of people scattered about, each with unique body types. Most were older, overly tanned individuals, which helped. Of course, a handful of younger athletic types caught my attention, but contrary to my fears, there was no physical response whatsoever. Preoccupied with their own affairs, most were disinclined toward socializing, also helpful. Various extraverted peddlers zigzagged across the shore dodging crashing waves, selling questionable items that remained a mystery to me. The vendors knew many of the regulars and seemed to monitor everything.

In under thirty minutes, I'd adjusted completely and focused on more important things such as applying sunscreen to my bits and pieces without appearing lewd. I could hardly believe the extreme angst leading up to the outing and how quickly it all dissipated like my Diet Coke tipped over in the sand. But still, it was a remarkable achievement, and my heart overflowed with gratitude and amazement. *Bring on the healing, Lord Jesus!*

A word of caution: a similar experience may not be suitable for everyone, and it should only be considered as the Lord leads and with proper support. Genuine dangers existed on that beach, including alcohol and other substances, most in plain view. Return trips to such an indulgent setting would have likely raised my curiosity and my defense condition, so I think once was enough. After all, I guess it depends on one's unique issues and healing journey. For me, the entire therapeutic experience was an incomparable watershed moment in my self-acceptance journey, for which I remain thankful to God and appreciative of Butch.

But even if my racy romp on a nude beach with a trusted friend and Jesus holding my hand had never happened, I was still grateful for other healing opportunities.

When I was younger, I often refused to remove my shirt on a public beach because of my insecurities, but it changed after I pushed forward with small, uncrowded beaches and supportive friends. The life lesson to push the envelope was vital to stretch and grow into space I didn't yet occupy. Otherwise, I'd have remained quite safe in my neat and tidy comfort zone. It's why they call it that —it's comfortable there!

Expanding beyond those margins was, and remains, critical especially for someone predominantly constricted most often by fear. It's that straightforward, but it also takes time and patience.

* * *

Joining a gym was beyond helpful in fostering healthy acceptance from other men in a public setting. SAIT offered discounted gym memberships to alumni through the student's association. Although the location wasn't ideal for my commute, the price was reasonable, and I was fond of their modern workout area as well as the campus atmosphere. Another impressive feature of their gym was a spacious steam room inside the men's locker room (the women's locker room likely had one also).

Many might think such a steamy spot wouldn't be the best choice for someone struggling with same-sex attractions, especially early in the healing journey. However, being further along and committed to abstaining from sexual behavior, it seemed safe enough for me, especially given the potential reward of more healing.

I've long delighted in warmth and humidity, whether manufactured or natural, and a steam room wins over a dry sauna every time. That one was huge, with two tiers of wide benches, perhaps to better accommodate school teams. Once inside, ample vapor obstructed the view for others, which enabled me to be bolder in my nudity as I stretched out on the bench. The heavy steam barrier also helped curb temptation to gaze too long at any one thing.

One afternoon, the helpful haze failed to fully conceal a remarkably athletic young man who opted to stand in front of his bench rather than sit or lie down as most did. With only me near, he shifted and stretched several times at about six feet away. His actions were peculiar and somewhat annoying fodder for improper thoughts or worse.

Instead of yielding, I asked God for help to tune the guy out so I could mind my own business. I thought about singing a worship song out loud but held it in. To my delight, I successfully achieved a personal triumph without giving in until he left. Each instance of such victory was akin to fortifying new muscles, helping me transform and grow in my resolve to honor God and my commitment to Him.

Another "feature" of the locker room was the pole showers. If you're unacquainted with its unfortunate yet space-saving design, it comprises a single large pole equipped with multiple showerheads and faucets. There's no refuge to be found when only one other man arrives for a shower, let alone several.

Had I encountered that horror earlier in my journey, it would've triggered nightmares and quite likely a hard no. However, knowing Jesus was with me, I mustered the courage to use the sadistic contraption every time I visited the gym. With time, it became less daunting; through each use, I built transformative muscles and banished fear.

One day following a workout, I stood alone at one of the three pole showers, more at peace than ever in my public nakedness. As I glanced toward the lockers, something caught my eye.

A trashcan at the end of a changing bench sat between two rows of empty lockers. Emblazoned on the side of the white plastic pail, somebody had used a felt marker to scrawl the words "Men's Locker Room." I'm unsure what drew me to hold my glance and skim the words on the pail a few times before something extraordinary occurred. A deep ethereal voice enunciated the words a few times in my head, "Men's Locker Room," before the arrival of unexpected thoughts led to a revelation.

*Men, as in, you know, "Men."*

*A place where men belonged.*

*Wait, that's me.*

Like cold, fresh water on gasping, dry soil, the transformative message was received, seeping to the depths of my being. Tears streamed down my wet face, and I wholeheartedly received the affirmation, which I'm convinced was from the loving heart of my doting Abba Father.

A scene that had menaced me for so many anguished years was transformed into a landscape of healing and redemption, just because He lives. *Yes, I am a man, and I belong here. Thank you, Jesus!*

\* \* \*

Nakedness comes in various forms, even while remaining dressed. One significant night, I'd given in to the pull of temptation and ventured out to 318 with friends. It was a slow night, an unfamiliar older gentleman at the bar struck up an engaging conversation while I was getting a drink. His name was Gabriel, and he seemed a trustworthy man of unmistakable kindness and curiosity.

I entrusted Gabriel with many of my life accounts, including recent adventures and discovering faith, my desire to reject my gay identity, and my progress thus far. Our dialogue flowed as I recounted what I'd learned about potential root causes of same-sex attractions, captivating Gabriel's interest.

After a great deal of intimate one-way sharing and baring my soul, I felt raw and vulnerable, unmasking myself in front of a veritable stranger. For an hour, I'd done almost all the talking and learned almost nothing of him or his story. Our conversation seemed to pause on its own.

Gabriel gripped my shoulders, so I faced him directly. *Whoa, what's this?* His words, ominous and loaded with solemnity, etched themselves into my soul.

"If you have a choice," he cautioned, his voice brimming with sincerity, "do not come this way." One of those sobering statements prompting a proper and equally weighty response from me, right?

"Wow, okay," I muttered, a testament to my proven ability to form coherent thoughts at the drop of a dime.

Recognizing I was grappling to absorb the weight of his solemn admonition, Gabriel simply nodded his head as he gazed deep into my eyes. It was as if he saw his words being planted within the depths of my exposed being. *Not sure what to do here.*

Our unexpected exchange bore a sobering effect on me, prompting me to consider an exit from the bar. So, I expressed my gratitude for Gabriel's company and our poignant conversation before extending an appreciative hug, a natural gesture for me. Gabriel welcomed the friendly embrace with warmth, and with that, our encounter ended.

My friends weren't ready to leave, so I headed home alone. Along the way, I believe the Lord helped me accept Gabriel's word as His own. As a result, a renewed determination to resist the allure of the bar scene was mine, as was increased openness and desire to hear His voice. *Help me to remember, Lord. I always have a choice.*

# Expanding Horizons

Healing continued through my H.A. support group, mainly through weekly accountability and implementing the wisdom of the steps into my daily life. Many in the group also benefitted from our extracurricular activities and social interactions, as I've shared. But it became clear that connecting with others beyond our little cluster was important, even beyond local churches and the vital benefits of integrating there.

More than a year had passed in H.A. when I learned of an organization based in the States hosting annual ex-gay conferences. Hundreds from around the world flocked to them to worship, attend workshops and lectures by ex-gay leaders, and partake in unparalleled fellowship. Most delegates struggled like us and were joined at the conference by loved ones and various ministry leaders.

Exodus North America originated in the seventies, expanding into a vast and active network of diverse ministries across the USA and around the world. The annual Exodus conference continued for thirty-seven years as a dynamic platform for fellowship and training and became a source of revenue for the ministry as it grew in the early years.

The Exodus conference occurred in the summer and moved to a different city each year, increasing exposure and accessibility to people throughout North America. A group of us from H.A. journeyed to Exodus 16 in Toronto, drawn by the rarity of a Canadian location. The idea of having friends with me—Butch especially—provided great comfort, but my insides churned at the thought of such a public event with so many other strugglers. An entirely new experience in an unfamiliar place where anything could happen. *Who will I meet? How will I handle temptations?*

Soon after our arrival on the university campus in downtown Toronto, my nervousness translated into eagerness. The sight of hundreds of individuals like me gathered to learn and fellowship was exhilarating. And I must confess, the spectacle of countless attractive, God-loving men held more allure than I expected. Not that I was entertaining any untoward ideas, mind you. But there was something invigorating about the prospect of meeting men who understood and shared my struggles without the usual trappings of dance floors, copious levels of alcohol, or spandex.

It quickly became clear the electric Exodus environment harbored myriad dangers. Organizers meticulously outlined boundaries in a code of conduct bolstered by frequent reminders to keep everybody safe. Delegates were warned to be careful about spending excessive time with a new friend during the week.

However, a shiny new friendship was precisely what I'd hoped for, savoring the fading tabooed thrill of meeting someone new. A chance stirring of mutual chemistry, staying up late, and sharing laughs and life stories. The benefit of blessed boundaries is that they ensure everyone's safety, making a new connection feel like a guilt-free, zero-calorie romance... but with all the original flavor! *Anybody else thinking this too?*

As it turned out, two-for-one vodka tonics were nowhere to be found, reducing the risk of falling prey to another takedown and three steps back. There was great wisdom in combining a curfew and fixed bedtime, trusted support from battle-tested brothers, and a secure environment shielded from the outside world. Well, mostly. A few activists who opposed the ministry of Exodus did burst into one of the evening sessions, but they were escorted away by campus security and on we went. *Lord, bless those ones with Your truth and love.*

One of the most awe-inspiring features of Exodus 16 was partaking in frequent worship services in Convocation Hall, where the perfect acoustics made each occasion transcendental. The beautiful lyrics and melody of one song we revisited throughout the week moved me like never before. "As the Deer," written by Martin Nystrom, is based on Psalm 42 and represents an expression of our desperation to have God as our primary desire, as deer long for water.

> *"As the deer pants for streams of water, so my soul pants for you, my God. My soul thirsts for God, for the living God. When can I go and meet with God? My tears have been my food day and night, while people say to me all day long, 'Where is your God?' These things I remember as I pour out my soul: how I used to go to the house of God under the protection of the Mighty One with shouts of joy and praise among the festive throng. Why, my soul, are you downcast? Why so disturbed within me? Put your hope in God, for I will yet praise him, my Savior and my God."*
> —Psalm 42:1-4 (NIV)

\* \* \*

Over the years, I've treasured eight annual Exodus conferences, encountering hundreds of the kindest and most sincere people one could ever know. All of us sought something better for ourselves, motivated to resolve the relentless inner conflict and dissatisfaction with our gay identities by seeking God's guidance and peace. But there were other dark forces at work.

Despite all the safeguards at conferences, we still heard disheartening tales of the wayward souls who succumbed to temptation and were asked to leave the conference. I give thanks to God that wasn't my experience, but I understand how it could happen. The moment me and my new friend realized we shared erotic attraction is probably a moment too late.

The cat-and-mouse game has begun, testing how close to the edge I can get with gushing flattery and compliments. Then come the enthralling battlefield legends to reveal one's interests on the sly, much like a wriggling worm on the sharp end of a rusty hook in front of a ravenous trout. Throw in occasional touches to the shoulder, arm, or knee, with an engaging smile and unbroken eye contact, and I may be doomed. *Lord help me to break the old behavior patterns.*

Each year, standouts among the crowd emerged. Guys who drew the most attention from the others, Exodus virgins especially—wide-eyed, slack-jawed, easily distracted, bumping into everything, not unlike energetic puppies. A great place for an early look at the new standouts was the special workshop for first timers. Its primary purpose was to familiarize newcomers with the environment and help them to form initial connections with others, so they didn't feel like outsiders.

However, the problem was the workshop also familiarized newcomers with the environment and helped form initial connections. Sure, it helped break the ice, but it increased risks for more vulnerable delegates. It's a fair representation of the event's delicate balance—a unique healing environment fraught with the risk of setbacks—and an unavoidable tightrope in the unique ministry setting.

Some years, standouts included guys known from previous years who'd become extra attractive that year. Steve, a blond muscular man with a contagious grin, was one such fellow for me. It seemed certain that since the previous conference his spare time had been spent at the gym. As a leader in his ministry, Steve evoked a sense of safety, reinforcing the healthy barrier between leaders and other delegates. I admired Steve from afar, marveling at the liberation with which he carried himself.

During general sessions, Steve would casually drape his well-toned arms over the backs of the adjacent chairs, exuding self-assurance and comfort. I couldn't help but wonder how it would feel to sit by him with his lovely arm behind my shoulders... *left or right arm, doesn't matter.* Though I didn't witness any hip-checking for a coveted spot next to Steve's arms, the possibility didn't seem far-fetched.

That scenario also exemplified the growth-versus-risk tension tightrope: potential healing from safe, public, physical affirmation, wrestling against the risk of romantic stirrings or thoughts through the same healing gesture. I determined making a decision in such situations required a close and brutally honest examination of my motive. So no, I was not among those who jostled for a cozy cuddle spot next to the enchanting leader named Steve. Besides, I'm not sure I'd know a proper hip check, even if it hit me.

The reality of finding other delegates attractive prompted organizers to offer a caution to newcomers: admiring someone from a distance for too long increases the likelihood of placing them upon a pedestal. I found it true the more time I prized someone like Steve from afar, the better the chances he'd become a difficult distraction. From a distance, Steve appeared to have it all, even though he likely did not.

The key was to be proactive and introduce myself to dispel any illusions of supposed perfection. The cardinal rule? Never confess or even hint at my own attraction to said person. Or worse, attempt to discern if the magnetism was mutual. It was solid advice that worked well for me on many occasions. Sadly, others co-opted the strategy with nefarious intentions or were in a state of heightened vulnerability when poor decisions followed, leading to impropriety, a canceled registration, and an early flight home. Those *outings* of a different kind were difficult for everyone involved, especially if they were part of a ministry group that was left reeling with the aftereffects.

"Well, if Jonny wasn't able to resist temptation, what hope do I have?" asked a delegate, convinced his leader was far beyond those trappings. It was always tragic, and Lord only knows how many similar situations occurred that remained hidden and trapping them in undisclosed shame.

In retrospect, I believe I came to terms with the unavoidable risks associated with vulnerable delegates. As mentioned, the healing and life-changing rewards vastly outweighed the dangers. A sincere commitment to following and submitting to Christ, coupled with a strong support system, was essential. Those two things represented the sturdy boat and lifejacket essential to navigating the risks that towered like massive boulders on a whitewater rafting run. In my later years, I became heavily reliant upon those dynamics as I stepped into volunteer and leadership roles at Exodus conferences.

\* \* \*

At my first conference, I was dazed by all the workshop offerings for various streams of interest, but I appreciated the breadth of programming because it soon gave me something to look forward to at future conferences as I matured and healed in my journey.

Topics exhibited a wide range within various categories, tackling subjects such as surviving codependency or abuse, cultivating spiritual disciplines, personal finances, devising practical steps to start an ex-gay ministry, music ministry, responding to the pro-gay agenda in the love of Christ, and dozens more year by year. Being able to choose workshops relevant to my present situation year by year was a tremendous blessing, and I was encouraged to know specialized support for more sensitive issues would be available when needed.

Seasoned ministry leaders and noteworthy Christian figures discipled delegates with adeptness through transformative educational training experiences. Many ministry leaders walked their talk, experiencing various degrees of freedom from the life-controlling outcomes of their same-sex attractions. I appreciated the exposure to people further along in their journey because we had few such role models in our circles. Getting to know those Exodus leaders was so encouraging and, in some cases, more important than the topic of their classes.

First-timers were encouraged to embrace the fact it was impossible to attend every workshop of interest. Exodus offered recordings of all workshops for purchase, allowing delegates to enjoy the sessions they missed and share them with others. It helped reduce the pressure for achievers like me while encouraging a reasonable pace during the conference. It was okay not to get to every class and take a break on occasion to digest all the Lord was revealing; many of us needed help to give ourselves permission to do that.

One year, several of our group were enroute to a popular workshop on how to stop compulsive masturbation. My friend Gary from Calgary informed us not to wait up for him, as he had to "take care of something first." We howled!

The teaching from that workshop was immeasurably helpful to me, offering evidence of the harmful nature of reinforced fantasy with uncontrolled behavior, along with practical advice to observe the warning signs and underlying forces. Fantasy occurs in our minds, no doubt, and pornography is a toxic fuel that feeds fantasy and starves our souls. The emotional and relational destruction using porn causes is devastating and must be considered and addressed as soon as possible in the healing process.

I've observed ignoring or delaying victory over porn usage significantly slows the healing process and, in some cases, derails it. Its importance must not be underestimated. The Apostle Paul tells us we are more than conquerors through Him who loved us (Romans 8:37), so much so He was willing to take our place of death on the Cross. *Thank you, Jesus!*

Most often, I used masturbation with fantasy or porn to satisfy urges and sexual frustration in addition to other rewards. There's also a biological element that sneaks up on us when we use porn through the release of a chemical called dopamine, like a heroin or crystal meth rush to the brain. The effect ensnares us in a compulsive cycle of addiction and for many, the resulting shame can become a debilitating spiral downwards. My journey has included various seasons of both mountaintop victories and valley hardships. The first time I achieved a 30-day period of abstinence was a tremendous boost to my confidence and faith. I am convinced life is fuller and more joyful and I am a better follower and servant of Christ, a better mentor, and a better friend while I remain free from the bondage of the dark influences that steal my joy.

I've learned to recognize the triggers that prompt the desire to change my mood and consider using porn and fantasy. For example, consider the acronym H.A.L.T., which represents four states that increase our vulnerability: Hungry, Angry, Lonely, and Tired. I appreciated the workshop leader's challenge to seek out healthier alternatives to change my biochemistry when needed, such as nature walks in the sun, listening to music I enjoy, and yes, even a cold shower. *Help me, Lord!*

But past increasing awareness and a desire for growth, I believe the most proven method to overcome the use of pornography and fantasy for sexual gratification is accountability. I've tried filters and monitoring services, and there was some success, but that effectiveness disappoints in comparison to the strength of an emotional connection with a safe man who lifts me up and cheers me on.

Not only can that relationship offer freedom and healing from porn addiction, but it sets the stage for additional relational healing that's unique to non-erotic, same-sex friendships focused on Jesus. I also found it helpful to consider the battle for sexual purity is more pervasive than I knew, reminding me, in this way, I was indeed like all the other boys.

Another Exodus class helped me gain a biblical perspective that framed the foundation of traditional Christian sexuality. While I was averse to trite expressions such as, "It was Adam and Eve, not Adam and Steve," understanding God's unchanging intention for creation and human sexuality brought an immense amount of peace and assurance into my life. I respect that God revealed His sacred plan for sexuality clearly in His Word, even though much debate and reinterpretation continues to this day. *Lord, forgive us.*

Other conference dynamics required careful consideration to avoid possible setbacks. We could share dorms to help reduce costs, and we could choose our roommates in advance, typically a friend from home. Doing so helped waylay the temptation to hold on-campus auditions and shack up with someone who might be too much of a distraction.

However, some delegates I knew were brave (or faith-filled) and asked Exodus to pair them with a roommate. I must confess, it was stirring to consider meeting someone to share my room and join me in all-night chemistry-fueled conversations. *Maybe one day?*

A strict daily format was a conference standard, beginning with recommended devotional time, followed by breakfast, and the morning general session framed by music and corporate worship. Next were one or two workshops, then lunch, two or three more workshops, and supper. A full day wrapped up with the evening general session, again with worship, and finally, fellowship before turning in.

The schedule resulted in jam-packed, exhausting emotional days punctuated by occasional special events and leisure time to explore local attractions. In later years, the schedule condensed from a full week to three or four days, conforming to related trends in our fast-paced world.

Mealtimes presented excellent opportunities to mingle even though we often gravitated toward familiar faces. I tried hard not to feel rejected when my friends dined with others, soon understanding its importance and then doing likewise. Evening fellowship before bedtime became a precious tradition, providing a forum to discuss the day's events and "God-sightings."

Safe connections established during meals became a crucial social aspect of the conference. Unlike the extremely extroverted Butch, I required subsequent conferences to form connections easier, that were safer and more meaningful and often resulted in special ministry and mutual personal growth.

The unique opportunities to socialize and learn alongside a diverse group of people from all corners of the world proved to be an exceptionally powerful instrument in my healing journey. The most significant benefit stemmed from the realization I wasn't as unique as I believed, and my struggles were not as shameful as I told myself.

Honesty and vulnerability regarding my pain and accumulated fear—first with myself and then with trusted others—proved to be the single most effective action in empowering me to accept myself fully as God does, warts and all. Of course, that practice is best within a local Bible-believing church and a small group alongside a specialized ministry. However, even for those well connected within their church or a local ministry, the Exodus experience had an undeniable, ability to blow the doors off our limited and self-focused mindsets.

\* \* \*

Numerous individuals stand tall as my Exodus heroes, attending many conferences to offer insightful encouragement. Some of those heroes led ministries or provided related services, while others were leaders of Exodus-affiliated ministries with their clients in tow. Our group wasn't linked with a referral ministry, so we relied on our own ability to remain connected with each other and the people we knew from previous conferences.

Exodus-affiliated ministry leaders who served as volunteers or speakers traveled to the conference with other staff and clients. Their primary mission was to shepherd the men and women in their charge, facing myriad challenges. Those great heroes impacted hundreds or even thousands of delegates over many years and are worthy of much celebration and praise for their faithful service to our King. *Maybe that'll be me one day!* Please allow me to introduce a few of my heroes in the faith to you.

The first time I heard Joe Dallas speak, I was astounded to learn of his past as a pro-gay activist, given what appeared to be an unshakable security in his masculine identity. He aligned more with my stereotype of a manly football coach than a gay pride, flag-waving advocate. Yet, Joe's inherent gentleness drew people in, only to be walloped by his uncompromising stance on Biblical truth. It's no wonder his workshops and keynote speeches were among the most sought-after at Exodus conferences.

Joe's insightful wisdom and Biblical straight-shooting inspired and motivated me to work harder in my journey. As I listened to Joe, the weight of my struggles diminished. I contemplated the greater calling God had for me, a calling far beyond my battle with compulsive masturbation. Joe continues to inspire me as a beacon of God's truth, thriving as an author, speaker, podcast host, and ordained pastoral counselor.

Frank Worthen, often hailed as the founding father of Exodus, was a cherished speaker at the conferences. His tender and low-key demeanor and profound love for God and His people—particularly those in turmoil—made him a paternal figure to many of us. His steadfast wife, Anita, actively contributed her own dynamic leadership within Exodus, blessing countless individuals. Though Frank has since passed into the presence of Jesus, Anita maintains sweet connections with many from the Exodus community. I can't even imagine where I'd be if it wasn't for the sacrificial and faithful service of the Worthens and the countless others who've stood on their shoulders to bring Heaven closer.

As one of the most engaging and likable Exodus instructors, Sy Rogers captured hearts and minds after being disarmed by his flamboyant persona. It was obvious to me the Lord was especially fond of Sy, made even more apparent when I saw how committed he was to his relationship with Christ. Sy's testimony was significant; he lived briefly as a woman with plans to transition, scuttled when the hospital closed the program down the same day his surgery was scheduled. Sy was convinced God had intervened to prevent him from moving forward with those life-altering plans.

Sy's distinctive delivery and no-nonsense approach blended humor with unequivocal truth and left all of us in stitches as we praised the Lord. His frequent use of phrases like "Listen, sunshine" during his talks endeared everyone even more.

We hung on every word of wisdom drawn from his inspiring testimony that revealed a well-seasoned union with the Lord. In 1988, Rogers told a reporter for the Chicago Sun-Times that the ex-gay movement was not anti-gay,

> *"If you want to stay gay, that's your business... But the bottom line is, you have a choice to overcome it. You can change. The goal is God—not going straight. Straight people don't go to Heaven, redeemed people do."*[8]

Sy's passionate discussions on global issues, reflecting his extensive international ministry experience, broadened our perspectives. Sy's impactful talks were often met with a standing ovation from appreciative men and women.

One year, while serving on the conference team, I was treated to a ride with Sy across campus. I was struck by his integrity; he was exactly the same person in my golf cart as he was on stage, with the added touch of his genuine care for me as his driver. I was inspired by his humility and compassion, marveling at his determination to remain transparent enough so we could see God's fingerprints on his life more readily. *Maybe one day, Lord!* Now in the loving arms of Jesus, Sy's legacy continues to resonate and inspire.

My first encounter with Dennis Jernigan's worship leadership occurred at Exodus 17 on the campus of San Diego's Point Loma Nazarene University. Less than three years into my healing journey, a transformative shift occurred within me during those sessions of worship. I felt I could trust Dennis without hesitation to embody God's heart through his music. Themes from his original worship songs spoke directly to the core of my struggles. Gratefulness-filled tears flowed freely down my face as God's Spirit ministered to my heart through his music.

In the quiet space between songs from the Brown Chapel stage, Dennis shared stories of his own same-sex struggles, drawing me closer still. While basking in soothing melodies filled with God's unconditional love, understanding and encouragement covered me as certain life-changing truth formed in my mind:

*My Father God loves me, and He understands my struggles, without condemnation.*

*He's cheering me on! When I fall, Jesus picks me up every single time.*

*He calls me to trade my painful reality for so much more than I can see or feel.*

*All this because He made me, and He loves me completely. Perfectly.*

I know in my heart those truths can transform you too!

For the remainder of that conference, I almost knocked people over to get to the general sessions and immerse myself again in God's love while singing together with hundreds of His beloved sons and daughters. To say I became a Dennis Jernigan fan is an understatement and his soulful music inspires me to be who He says I am, to this day.

\* \* \*

Success stories and testimonies abounded during the general sessions for all delegates, bringing guaranteed cheers and thunderous ovations. I believe the reason the Bible upholds the importance of sharing our stories is because His transformative work within us amplifies His magnificence, drawing others closer in. Yet, the pursuit of traditional heterosexual marriage often took center stage as the ultimate emblem of God's favor and one's personal triumph. It was regrettable that a goal of wedded bliss had morphed into an idol for many, as illustrated by overly enthusiastic reactions to announcements of engagements and weddings.

As a result, the most coveted badge of success in the quest for heterosexuality became entering marriage—or for some, staying in one. Parenthood added even more luster. The achievement of marriage served as "proof" that true change had transpired, the brass ring most of us wanted. Celebrations of chaste celibacy and singleness were rare, although a venerable few in the celibate underground were known to be content in a celibate lifestyle.

Please don't misinterpret my words. According to Scripture, God's sacred design for humankind has at its heart the family unit, beginning with one man and one woman, joined in holy matrimony. He also commands us to multiply and fill the earth.

However, the Bible also reveals—or doesn't disprove—that several heavy hitters remained single in their powerful ministries. The most significant single showcased in Scripture was obviously Jesus, followed by Paul, other apostles, and various prophets.

In retrospect, I question the negative repercussions of the Exodus focus on marriage. I wonder how a more vibrant celebration of those faithful and joyful in their calling to singleness could have altered perceptions and eased the suffering of many. Moreover, is anyone permanently or irrevocably called to singleness, like the marriage vow before God? Perhaps we'd all fare a little better with less emphasis on pursuing matrimony and more on honoring singleness, however long the season.

As a baby Christian in my early twenties, assimilating into church culture without succumbing to the pressures to conform proved challenging. Echoing the culture of Exodus, adult singleness within church communities felt like purgatory, with "liberation" granted only through finding *the one*. Sermons that celebrate, discuss, or discern the call to celibacy and chasteness are exceedingly rare. I contend the broader Christian community could extend greater support and understanding to those struggling to be content and at peace in their season of singleness, regardless of its duration.

Nonetheless, almost a decade after Jesus wooed me away from my gay lover, I would be blindsided by the challenge of singleness. But instead of a well-crafted sermon, God used a country music song to usher me deeper into His will. But that story requires a bit more two-stepping on a crowded dance floor to get there.

# Deeper Healing

Not unlike ocean tides, healing journeys ebb and flow for all of us. The real challenge is to embrace those conflicting undercurrents as part of the journey, instead of being distracted by them and become discouraged. For deeper healing in my own life, I recognized the need to dive into more understanding.

It had become evident that whenever my own real unobserved traits (not seen in myself) were exhibited in an attractive man, the allure often became irresistible and seductive. Helpful advice was to immediately give sincere thanks to God for creating such a specimen and ask Him for a revelation and gratitude for the attributes He gave me. Over time, the allure diminished as corresponding addictive behaviors reduced, i.e. fantasy, masturbation, acting out, etc.

The cannibalistic attraction I mentioned earlier can be based on literal or perceived truth. For example, I am a big-boned person, described as husky. While weight and body concerns plagued me much of my life, I've maintained a large frame despite my short stature of only five feet eight inches. However, I often underestimated my stature due to the self-perception rooted in my longstanding insecurities, causing me to believe I was not a big guy. In fact, I laughed right out loud when someone called me that the first time. *Not a big guy.*

I think of Leonard, a thoughtful member from our H.A. group, who once expressed his broader understanding of the same-sex dilemma in a memorable way.

"It's like two guys hooking up to get something from each other neither one has," he said during his sharing time in one of the meetings. The profound nature of his words had its way with us in the room before the meeting resumed.

Leonard had expressed the truth that men living with deficits in masculine affirmation are generally ill-equipped to supply critical male affirmation for each other. However, I find it difficult to deny there was zero positive effect. As I've shared, I give some credit to my intimate connections with Charles (and Matt before him) with providing unique physical affirmation that contributed to my healing.

But still, there was no way to discard the deeper longing that remained unsatisfied within me. Understanding that dynamic also explained why I fell into the trap of pursuing others in my subconscious search for affirmation, resulting in hurtful choices and an addictive cycle that became life-controlling.

Based on my own experience, I remain convinced that my unsatisfied longing was to connect with my Creator as His son, perfectly made by Him. It was also clear to me that the road to healing a same-sex affirmation deficit must include intimate, non-erotic same-sex friendships with male role models and peers secured in healthier masculinity.

\* \* \*

It's widely believed nearly all boys face varying intensities and frequencies of same-sex impulses, whether acted upon or not. My own exploration of this topic with others reinforced the principle, at least those willing to be honest and vulnerable. Accordingly, it would prove beyond beneficial for us strugglers to hear from more courageous men willing to admit their own experiences with openness and honesty. Available statistics on those who act on said impulses are contested broadly and challenging to confirm.

Nevertheless, in the late 1940s, the controversial sex researcher Alfred Kinsey pioneered a continuum scale to denote sexual orientation, ranging from zero to six, where zero is heterosexual exclusively, six is homosexual exclusively, and three is equally heterosexual and homosexual.[9] *Wait, my sexual attractions slide on a scale?*

Upon first acquaintance with the Kinsey scale while I was part of the H.A. group, I experienced renewed hope. The notion that sexual behavior—akin to all other behaviors—hinged on an individual's choices and remained subject to change seemed grounded in reality to me. I couldn't ignore the certainty that myriad factors (seen and unseen) had influenced all my choices throughout life. Therefore, accurate and consistent predictions by anyone about my choices (voluntary and involuntary) would be challenging and improbable. So why would my sexual behavior be any different?

Kinsey's debatable data gave me pause for brief period to consider settling into a bisexual identity based on my conflicted experiences, some of which you'll soon hear about. However, my ongoing studies of God's Word along with continued teaching from respected authorities brought me to the ultimate conclusion that God's plan for human sexuality did not leave room for that variation.

\* \* \*

Following two years of diligent work on the steps and increasing sexual and alcohol sobriety, a four-year H.A. veteran named Thomas discovered a California-based ministry for ex-gays, offering an intensive, holistic healing experience. Thomas was a little older than me, with dark hair, glasses, and an average build. He leaned toward being more serious, but when we tickled his funny bone—a challenge both Butch and I often attempted—his bright face and belly laughter were a just reward.

Thomas felt called to complete his training to spearhead Living Waters in our region, extending invitations to our group's members to partake. I didn't hesitate, but only a handful of my brothers from H.A. joined, including Butch, and I continued to occasionally attend the H.A. meetings to maintain connections there. *I'm ready for the next step, Lord!*

Those meetings, hosted within the welcoming confines of a local church, marked a refreshing departure from the code words and secret location that had become normal to us. "Living Waters" was a logical next step beyond drop-in accountability meetings. The program's requisite six-month commitment to weekly attendance and rigorous engagement in scripture study underscored its effectiveness.

The program was based on Andrew Comiskey's book *Pursuing Sexual Wholeness*, and it defied anonymity. It was a welcome relief because I felt ready to strengthen connections and step out from the shadows, especially with other believers. I wasn't shouting anything from the rooftops, but I found myself more grounded in my faith and willing to address my struggles more openly.

The Living Waters gatherings began with singing worship songs together, then transitioned to the week's lesson from the book. Teaching was followed by prayer time before splitting into gender-specific smaller discussion groups, and fellowship time wrapped it up.

A combination of nervousness and excitement carried me into the first meeting, where about twenty-five men and women spanning diverse demographics were present. Those folks differed from the typical H.A. attendees, appearing less edgy, more stable, and rooted in their faith. *Thank you, Lord, for these committed brothers and sisters.*

I devoured Andrew's book much quicker than the recommended one chapter per week. Each page rang out with undeniable—often uncomfortable—truth and insight, captivating my attention. Immersing myself in every aspect of the weekly meetings brought immense satisfaction, especially in the unfamiliar dynamic style of prayer that seemed odd at first but soon became meaningful. Thomas enlisted my help in managing hospitality, and I served with enthusiasm. Guided by passion and unsatisfied with the status quo, I sourced unique teas and delectable treats, aiming to delight everyone each week.

My H.A. journey had been a critical step in my walk, equipping me to overcome my destructive addictive behaviors—weekend bar hopping, excessive alcohol use, and fleeting sexual encounters. There, I first encountered God's unwavering love through other Christians. My support group was an excellent springboard into healing and a new identity in Him, helping to displace my self-serving, pleasure-driven lifestyle.

In Living Waters, almost everyone had surpassed the addictive cycle of bar-centric behavior, and some never had sexual encounters at all. But don't assume our paths were fast steered straight, especially mine. However, the frequency and intensity of poor choices receded week by week, filling me with immense gratitude for reclaiming a sense of life balance.

The majority of my fellow Living Waters students yearned for deeper spiritual healing, addressing the wounds that precipitated our destructive behavior. United by faith and determination, we persisted through difficult days and the sore reality of our pain-filled pasts to allow Jesus to bring the healing that only He can.

All facets of Living Waters esteemed those who committed wholeheartedly to doing the hard work, digging deep, and journeying through all the hindrances holding us back from the fullness of life intended by our Creator. It so happened our common denominator was same-sex attractions.

\* \* \*

The inspired methods behind Living Waters were used by God to reframe my struggle through a revelation of its nature—and *my* nature, without Jesus. After all, it's exceedingly difficult to overcome life-controlling wounds and habits without first knowing how they got there. Those discoveries allowed me to face my pain and suffering with others under the authority of the highest power of them all.

Comiskey maintains that instead of efforts to stop or change same-sex attractions, the goal ought to be an integrated identity in Christ. Our obedience to Him brings dynamic spiritual maturity and the byproduct of rightly placed sexuality under His authority, a concept that resonated deeply within me. Therefore, my "sexual reorientation" would become a journey of emotional, intellectual, and spiritual development as my Creator reforms and rejuvenates me. *I need You with me, Lord, on this narrow and difficult path.*

Living Waters hinges on the unwavering authority and inerrancy of God's design for humankind, meticulous in its details as found in the Bible. That foundation was one of the largest factors that influenced my embracing the program. The Genesis creation account unveils the first man and woman, both created as a reflection of Him —fully masculine and fully feminine. Male and female polarity complement each other on spiritual, physical, and emotional planes, fulfilling His objectives and generating new life in accordance with His will (Genesis 1:26-28). Marriage encompasses God presiding over the husband, who presides over his wife, as expounded by the Apostle Paul in 1 Corinthians 11:3. Jesus underscored the sanctity of the marriage covenant between male and female, encapsulated as "one flesh" (Mark 10:6-9).

# NOT LIKE ALL THE OTHER BOYS

The following words from Andrew Comiskey gave me hope and a sense of security as I realized I longed to trust God's authority over what the world was saying.

> *"God's image is reflected in the merging of true maleness and true femaleness. I believe as well that the Christian life can be aptly described as the complementary rhythm of the true feminine and true masculine. Believing both leads me to wrestle with the conclusion that gender realities are somehow rooted in God and His creation. [Bible-based] gender isn't merely a cultural prescription; it's essential to all people in every culture who seek to reveal God in their personal identity and relationships."[10]*

But my pursuit of relational wholeness was obstructed by masculine self-doubt causing relational insecurity that triggered an endless cycle of concurrent internal and external responses. Internally, I withdrew emotionally from my dad and male friends, missing out on connections that would've given me hope and security. Externally, the perception of my uniqueness occasionally became amplified in social circles, which may have threatened others who became bullies.

For some, pre-conditioned prejudices or one's own masculine insecurity—or curiosities—increases the threat, and points to the origins of the term "homophobia" (now broadened to include most anyone who doesn't support gay rights). All these forces combined to intensify my insecurities, especially when I felt ostracized and shamed, repeating a devastating cycle of withdrawal. According to Comiskey, the outcome is a defensive detachment from perhaps all aspects of masculinity, with a profound impact. It hit me like a ton of bricks.

> "Detachment from the same-sex parent, from same-sex peers, and ultimately from one's own gender wholeness is the primary root of homosexuality."[11]

The popular "born this way" notion gave me pause during my journey and even prompted an unexpected detour you'll hear about later. Based on her life's work, Dr. Elizabeth Moberly weighed in years ago with remarkable clarity, pointing us back to the need to seek healing from the wounds that changed us.

> "It is true that no one is born a homosexual, but no one is born a heterosexual either, and it is vital that we should do justice to the significance of pre-adult development in God's plan."[12]

\* \* \*

It's important to note detachment wounds from childhood can be addressed as an adult, in fact, it's strongly encouraged if the same-sex parent is willing and able to participate. As a perennial camper and mountain enthusiast, Dad enjoyed frequent trips to the mountains as he'd done ever since childhood. *Perhaps it's a Norwegian thing.* An annual hike was an opportunity for the Ringness men to camp and meander up and down remote trails in the majestic Rocky Mountains.

For years, I declined the invitation to participate for a few reasons, the least of which was my disinclination toward cold, damp, arduous physical activity. I suppose another reason was I simply didn't feel man enough to be part of such a trek because I doubted my worthiness on male turf. After a few years of my healing process, I finally recognized the benefits of that type of connection, but I wanted to ease into it with a trip for only Dad and me.

Our first camping experience in Yoho National Park included a hike through the woods, but there were more laughs than anything else due to my resolve not to take myself so seriously. Dad was ever gracious, coaching me through woodchopping and fire-starting as he'd often done. Fortunately, skinning rabbits wasn't on the program.

As the full opposite of an accomplished frontiersman, my self-acceptance was boosted through this shared adventure and made me feel closer to Dad. It gave me enough courage to participate in the all-men family hike the following year. That was a miserable camping experience with heavy rain and temperatures so cold we were surprised we didn't see snow. God's sense of humor showed up as we arrived near the top of the mountain hike, where a little teahouse (yes, a teahouse) appeared before us like a heavenly mirage.

It didn't take me five minutes to ensconce myself for a piping hot peppermint tea and biscuit, sweet-talking Dad into staying with me to appreciate some civilized refreshment while the others hiked on ahead. Regardless of how it felt at the time, those life-giving experiences built upon the foundation of healing in my family relationships and with myself as a unique man who was loved as he was. My heart didn't stop singing for weeks!

Upon completing the six-month Living Waters program, we commemorated our achievements with a graduation, where I was delighted to receive my certificate from my friend Thomas. While not quite as grand as my SAIT graduation with thousands of spectators, my Living Waters graduation ceremony may have been more significant because I was equipped for life-changing transformation.

I appreciated the sense of conclusion offered by the program, distinct from the perpetual cycle of H.A.'s fourteen steps, a distant memory. I'd acquired the comprehension and resources necessary to walk in freedom from life-controlling addictions and other trappings of the gay identity, and excited to pursue the recovery of my true self who existed before the woundings. However, none of it would be possible without a robust walk with Jesus and exchanging my will for His will, every single day.

As I learned to examine the origins of the feelings and thoughts that routinely influenced my choices, I became better equipped to implement transformative measures to regain control in my life. Through the involvement and baseline authority of my King Jesus, the outcome was new empowerment that enabled me to reclaim a sense of self-worth and understanding. The simple goal was to become healthy enough to enjoy God's gift of free will and consistently make choices to honor Him and yield abundant new life. *Yes, but simple isn't always easy.*

# The Struggle for Obedience

One might think the pathway to healing and recovery is simple and straight. But as I will continue to illustrate in my story, that just isn't how it happens, for anyone. Yes, there are milestones of discovery and epiphanies mixed with watershed moments of healing. But the battle of the flesh in our former ways and thinking bring about many unfortunate opportunities that contribute to the struggle, experienced by anyone pursuing transformation and Christlikeness. Those were frequent revelations of how very much I so desperately need a Savior.

We all knew the potential risks of socializing in our support groups. But as I've shared, I'd been successful in avoiding those perils and managed to have healthy connections with many brothers in the Lord, especially through the group gatherings Butch hosted.

I'd received an unexpected phone call from Miguel, a kind young man from our H.A. group, inviting me to his home for dinner and a movie. Knowing there would be no alcohol at his table, I accepted the gesture because Miguel's friendliness, warm smile, eager laughter, and twinkling eyes had often beckoned.

As we watched the movie together on the couch, Miguel's unexpected tender touch to my hand sent an electrifying sensation throughout my body, coupled with a mix of genuine surprise and excitement. Our connection deepened that night, marked by mutual affection and tenderness, yet neither of us made a move for even more—that night or afterward—given an awareness of our mutual goals. *Father God, why does this keep happening?*

The encounter with Miguel would become the last of those experiences, at least for a while. Upon reflection, I recognized a meaningful aspect of connection was simply being "unmasked" together. I realized unsatisfied curiosity, generalized masculine and body insecurity, and a need for male affirmation drove me, consistent with the wise teachings of Andrew Comiskey. Perhaps I could have saved myself and others a lot of additional heartache by trusting all that God had revealed during that season and adjusted my behavior accordingly. *Thank you for your mercy, Lord.*

\* \* \*

Butch and I share a great fondness for Mexico—its people, culture, tropical climate, and relative proximity often beckon. While in the San Diego area for Exodus 17, we hopped across the border to Tijuana to make my first foray into the magical country. Butch's history with Mexico dates back decades as his family had ventured south several times over the years. A couple of years after becoming roommates, Butch led me to Puerto Vallarta for the first time, a memorable experience in more ways than one.

Lush tropical mountains plunged into the azure ocean in a spectacular tropical locale, first made famous by the film, *The Night of the Iguana*, starring Richard Burton. Another film shot in the region was called *Predator*, starring Arnold Schwarzenegger, and featured a remote jungle location near Mismaloya, a village to the south.

During our visit to El Eden near the original *Predator* movie set, Butch rested nearby while I made my way across the top of a simple dam that formed a small swimming area at the top of the stream. Except for us, the area was abandoned. Something beautiful and transcendent occurred in those moments. The tropical humidity, the peacefulness of the jungle, the gentle wind through the trees, cool water moving over my feet all combined to fill my spirit to the brim with His peace. From then on, it was my "happy place" that beckoned in my mind whenever my waters were troubled. *Thank you, Lord!*

On the south side of Puerto Vallarta lies the Zona Romantica, or "Romantic Zone," boasting a high concentration of gay bars and restaurants, earning a reputation akin to San Francisco. At Butch's suggestion, we lodged there, enjoying the breathtaking vista of lush green tropical mountains plunging into the azure Pacific coastline.

To be clear, neither of us was keen to meet anyone special or get into any trouble. I appreciated the atmosphere of the so-called "gay-borhood" offering safety and comfort in the company of friendly, non-threatening folks like us. Additional risks were minimized because most everyone assumed Butch and I were a couple, which didn't bother me much. *Better safe than sorry.*

Our quaint hotel faced the main gay beach, teeming daily with hundreds of gay men of all shapes, sizes, and ages. The beach restaurant offered an aggressive three-for-one drink special right before sunset, and their margaritas were exceptional. If Butch hadn't accompanied me, I might have found myself in a difficult situation.

A charming young man named Kevin surfaced while Butch and I were cooling off and conversing in the ocean. He rose between us like a sea creature, startling us both.

"Oops," he sputtered, wiping salt water from his eyes, possibly to better view his intended quarry. In no time, Kevin and I hit it off, agreeing to meet later for dinner. Butch wasn't too excited about my decision, but I'd become a man on a mission. *Maybe it would be like we met at Exodus, but better without those pesky boundaries.*

Butch was enjoying the sights from the balcony when Kevin arrived to pick me up. While in the bedroom getting ready, we gave in to chemistry and became better acquainted on the bed. We needed to clear out and get to dinner, so we pulled ourselves together. A thin blue and white square foil package had fallen out of Kevin's pocket and lay on the bed before he quickly scooped it up.

"Oops," he offered in the same charming manner as before. "I guess I'm optimistic," he added.

I didn't know what to say, so I insisted we leave for the restaurant. *Uh-oh, danger ahead?* Kevin had reserved a private table on the beach, which perhaps wasn't the best choice since the scene felt like it was wrapped with the warm fuzzies of a tropical romance. But I steered our conversation to my Exodus experiences and shared freely about what I'd learned and experienced since I'd left Charles to encounter Jesus about six years prior.

Kevin appeared curious about what I was sharing. *God, are You planting seeds?* I believed furnishing him with all the background info and my commitment to abstinence, might help cool his jets so he'd be okay with only a nice dinner out with a delightful new friend. However, the booze was flowing as usual, and it tipped the scales enough for me to accept his appealing invitation to return with him to his hotel.

The private hot tub on the ocean-view balcony invited nudity and much affection. But the presence of abundant alcohol, mutual chemistry, and a resort setting did not result in Kevin and I having sex. *How is this even possible?*

Perhaps it was our earlier conversation and sharing my journey or something greater. An unusual childlike innocence prevailed as we joked and laughed and enjoyed each other for a few hours in a way I'd never experienced. Kevin had an early flight out, so it was time for me to go. I called a taxi to return to the hotel, where an unimpressed Butch wasn't in the mood for chit chat.

In later reflection, the near-miraculous maintenance of a sexual boundary fostered a noteworthy epiphany and another significant turning point in my journey. Quite by accident, I'd discovered another level of intimacy with a man that felt healthier without typical sexual expression. The result for me was new awareness of unique healing affirmations in male-male intimacy that couldn't be ignored.

Please don't get me wrong. I didn't begin seeking out repeats of similar situations, nor do I advocate comparable behavior because it would almost certainly lead to a major setback. I share that story to illustrate an aspect of my personal transformation. I couldn't have imagined the surprising outcome of such a risky situation, nor that it would cause me to see non-sexual male intimacy as potentially virtuous and achievable, becoming a source of tremendous hope.

Would I willingly put myself in a similar situation again? Not at all, because it would be unwise, and downright foolish with alcohol in the mix. And private social nudity isn't a good idea anytime. But public nudity, well, that's different! *Wait, is it? Lord, I need You!*

Another profound moment during our Vallarta vacation occurred late one afternoon as Butch and I relaxed on our balcony overlooking the beach. As the waves crashed beyond, I observed the throngs of gay men socializing, laughing, tanning, and flirting, all trying so very hard. *Did I belong here or not?*

Andrew Comiskey's eloquent words come to mind.

> *"...We were like little boys working hard to fit into men's bodies, struggling to prop up an image of masculine appeal in order to attract the lost father of our youth. But morning after morning revealed the impoverished capacity we shared to view one another beyond our childish need."*[13]

But given what I'd experienced with Kevin, I couldn't help but wonder was it all bad? I found myself asking the Lord why I was there and what He wanted from me. As the fading sun prepared to set for another night with all of creation waiting in awe, a divine message resonated within my heart.

"All they need to know is that I love them," God whispered. I sat in silent reverence, tears rolling down my unsuspecting, bronzed face.

"What's wrong, Buddy?" Butch asked, noticing something had come over me.

I recounted what I'd heard from Father, moving Butch also. I told him that I didn't understand the meaning or purpose behind His message but trusted it would make sense in His perfect timing.

\* \* \*

Almost four years after I'd begun my healing journey and just a month after attending Exodus 18 in Boston with Butch, I landed a sales job at a start-up boutique advertising agency launched by a talented graphic designer. She was busy with lots of creative work and sought a salesperson to attract new clients. Her office resided in a shared space with a business magazine she designed, where I befriended an editor named Joanie.

One day, Joanie divulged she collaborated with two young entrepreneurs who owned a modeling agency and were debuting a fashion magazine to feature their models. *Now there's a smart idea.* Joanie had helped them initially but didn't want to continue as their editor. Joanie's curiosity was piqued when I told her about my role as a volunteer editor for the SAIT alumni magazine, and suggested I consider her position. I was immediately interested in the idea because I was struggling in my new sales job.

Joanie set up the interview with the co-owners to discuss my suitability as editor for their new fashion publication. It was a phenomenal chance to join their venture on the ground floor. Their first issue was in final production, and they needed someone to begin coordinating content for the second issue. *Wow, thank you Lord for this amazing job!*

The magazine's headquarters were in an old eclectic building near Calgary's downtown, boasting hardwood floors and exposed brick walls. The modeling agency was down the hall, where owners continued working as I took over the magazine.

As advertising sales grew, I expanded our team. Soon, the co-owners parted ways, but one wanted to keep and grow the publication beyond a city magazine. And with that, a new regional lifestyle magazine was born, and we moved into a larger office a few blocks away to accommodate growth.

With the owner's father as the sole investor, we secured $100,000 to launch the magazine under its new brand with a bi-monthly publishing schedule to gain traction before going monthly. However, within only six months, we recognized the need for five times the original investment because it was taking longer than anticipated to build the trust of major advertisers.

Though I loved startups and all aspects of magazine publishing, the venture proved incredibly demanding. A significant source of tension stemmed from the new sole owner—an experienced model turned inexperienced magazine publisher. He insisted on taking part in decision-making but lacked business acumen and relevant experience, trying to make up for it with enthusiasm and determination. A painful cycle ensued: good ideas, questioning, bad ideas, poor decisions, implementation, expensive rectification, and intensifying pressure to drive up ad sales as overhead escalated every month.

Throughout that tumultuous period, I treasured Butch's companionship as my friend and roommate. He often witnessed my arrival home from work, collapsing onto the plush living room carpet, overwhelmed by exhaustion and anxiety. Unbeknownst to me, my fabulous trademark hair had been thinning week by week. Premature baldness doesn't run in my family, so it was likely attributed to the work stress.

During my tenure in the fashion industry, I continued grappling with my same-sex attractions and insecurities to some degree. Despite encountering hundreds of industry people, including models and photographers, I was able to resist temptation. Well, aside from another hot tub incident during a promotional event at an upscale hotel in the rolling foothills of the Rocky Mountains.

Our generous host hotel covered all our costs and provided free-flowing drinks. *Uh-oh, Lord... but surely, I've healed enough to handle this?* As a goodwill gesture, I invited my friend and insurance agent, Owen, hoping to encourage an ad buy. An attractive, blond, exuberant partygoer, Owen had persuaded one of the female models with a saleswoman to join him in the bubble-filled hot tub right inside my hospitality suite.

"Naked or nothing, Todd! Naked or nothing!" Owen chanted as soggy clothes piled on the floor and the brimming tub overflowed. I did join the three of them, but I wasn't doing naked—thank you very much—no matter how much booze I had. It was a ton of laughs for sure, but it could've easily taken a sharp turn into trouble. *Do all the other boys do this sort of thing?*

The following morning, our hotel contact informed me of the water damage to the suite below us. She was pleased we'd enjoyed ourselves after taking her leave earlier in the evening, and I was grateful for our comp status and property insurance. *Lord, even when I'm foolish, You are so good to me.*

\* \* \*

In the early nineties, the "internet" was the Wild, Wild West, and America OnLine (AOL) was its only cyber saloon. AOL had expanded rapidly, and its mail and messaging system gained mammoth popularity in a short period. The friendly, computerized male voice exclaiming, "You've got mail!" upon logging in was enticing and addictive. A blockbuster motion picture of the same name released in 1998 reflected some of the intrigue and pitfalls of anonymous connections within a burgeoning online frontier.

AOL's most popular service was "chat rooms," themed virtual spaces for people to connect through online personas based on their interests. I'd previously stumbled upon personal rooms (think personal ads, but online) and discovered "M4M" signified men interested in other men. The endless allure of complete anonymity and privacy in an online setting with strangers from around the globe who shared same-sex attractions proved irresistible. I was beyond hooked.

When someone's persona triggered my interest in a chat room, I would simply IM (direct instant message) him, start a private conversation, and exchange photos. However, I soon discovered some users sent random, attractive photos of other men instead of themselves. Pro-tip: users with professional-looking headshots were probably not legit. Many photos were explicit to entice more explicit connections; my persistent body insecurities restrained me from going down that road. *Thank you, Lord, for insecurities that protect me.*

After exchanging photos, phone numbers could be exchanged when there was more interest, taking the connection "offline." Most chat rooms included a geographic identifier, i.e., M4M Calgary, to help users from around the world navigate to their interests.

It was easy to spend hours engrossed in AOL, "meeting" people and racking up phone line connection charges and online usage billed by the minute; more time online equaled more money for AOL shareholders which rocketed the company's growth. In some ways, the pay-as-you-go model benefitted me, as my limited discretionary funds curtailed my usage. But did I mention it was addictive?

Their platform was designed for ease of use, but I was hard-wired as a geek, so all of the tech requirements came naturally for me. For those not so computer savvy, like Butch, it seemed daunting, and a bit far-fetched to meet people online. *Probably a good thing.*

A popular travel strategy involved connecting with people who lived in other cities that would be visited in person, tempting because it promoted convenient access to anonymous in-person hookups. Not all chat rooms resulted in random, casual sexual encounters; genuine, quality connections with decent people were also possible. So, the strategy could be redeemed by healthier motives, such as a west coast road trip with Butch. The grand adventure was his idea, triggered by rumors that a massive earthquake would soon cause the continent's coastline to disappear into the ocean. Our expedition would be a farewell tour of sorts.

Prior to our departure, an intriguing yet lonely chap named James introduced himself on AOL inside one of the Seattle chatrooms. I found his pilot stories captivating and appreciated his entrepreneurial spirit. As it turned out, James owned a large company with hundreds of employees. He also owned his own plane and graciously offered Butch and me a tour while we were in the area, near the beginning of our west coast sendoff trip.

We met together at the regional airport (instead of a dark alley) and headed to the airport diner for a coffee. James was even more charming in person. He displayed kindness and gentleness—not at all the blood-thirsty, axe-wielding type. He reiterated his original invitation to take us on a tour and was genuine when he told us he was fine either way. The often-adventurous Butch didn't hesitate one moment longer, pushing me toward the hangar.

James's pride and joy was an amphibious aircraft that housed the pilot and a single passenger in the front. Butch selflessly insisted I take the front seat, reminding me it all was because of my efforts.

Nervousness—okay, my nervousness—subsided quickly as Captain James revved up with great confidence, taxied toward the runway, and propelled us swiftly into the air.

We escaped into a breathtaking flying tour of the Pacific Northwest under clear blue skies and sunshine, punctuated by a Space Needle flyby. *Does he own that also?* James surprised us with a Lake Washington landing—right in front of a 66,000-square-foot estate under construction. Although we weren't able to spot Bill Gates from the water, it was still a thrilling pit stop as James reignited the engine, roared us across the waves, and up into the sky to return to the airport.

Back on the tarmac, James suggested lunch, and we consented because it felt awkward to part ways right after enjoying his generous gift. Our lunch conversation focused on how Butch and I had met, so we learned very little about our gracious host. Like many others, James had assumed we were a couple and was surprised to hear we weren't. He posed many thoughtful questions that stimulated good discussion about our healing journeys. Only the Lord knows if He rooted anything within James that could one day yield a harvest.

Our delightful meal together at the diner was enjoyable, and James insisted on settling the bill. *Is this place his too?* We concluded our time together with heartfelt hugs and expressions of gratitude, promising to stay connected through AOL.

Driving away, Butch clarified newfound support for my AOL adventures and welcomed fellowship opportunities with all manner of wealthy men and their airplanes. Similar extraordinary experiences weren't replicated, but my AOL addiction was poised to yield one or two run-of-the-mill M4M encounters, along with a rather notable one.

\* \* \*

During my Living Waters days, Butch threw a Halloween party at his large penthouse. All right, perhaps it was me who urged his decision with my fervor for themed events and his place as a perfect locale. Our guests included support group comrades and a magazine co-worker with her friend. Butch's brother, his wife, and their friends also made an appearance.

Costumes were mandatory, with zero tolerance for sticks in the mud. Everyone was into it, showcasing an eclectic mix of getups—almost more colorful than the people wearing them—brightening up Butch's monochromatic decor with festive, vibrant hues.

A guest named Liam, new to our support group and only nineteen, donned drag and arrived reeking of alcohol. He didn't seem to have an "off" button, boozing it up to the point where something had to be done. My imbibing had been scaled back, so I agreed to escort him home. He got a little handsy in the car, and I confess I didn't protest the attention.

As we cruised along one of Calgary's main thoroughfares late on Halloween night, glaring headlights emerged in my rearview mirror and got larger as the vehicle roared up from behind. *What the hell?* My body tensed, my heartbeat accelerated. I braced for impact.

I turned to ensure Liam was buckled in, then glanced back at the mirror. The car had vanished. I scanned the road through every window, bewildered by its sudden disappearance. I wish I could claim I'd been praying so God would receive the credit for an intervention miracle. But something unexplained had transpired, leaving me to ponder how or even why. *Was that you, Lord?*

Upon arriving at Liam's house, I ensured his safe entry. Despite some resistance, he persisted with his drunken advances and alarmed me with his aggressiveness. A sense of spiritual unease settled over me, and I repelled him with extra force, declaring my departure.

I've since come to believe dark forces wield considerable influence on that annual event day, when people, typically inebriated and lacking self-control, give the devil more access than usual. To this day, I remain hesitant to partake in Halloween-related events, especially when they occur on the last day of October.

The aftermath of the unexpected encounter with Liam sparked concerns about my own HIV status, given my awareness of his. That was a time when HIV wasn't well understood, but a positive diagnosis often resulted in AIDS with the promise of new experimental treatments to delay its onset. Even the remote possibility terrified me, and my past activities made it undeniable I was at risk.

So, I scheduled an appointment with Dr. Neil to face it head-on.

"Why do you want the test, Todd?" he inquired, distracted by the computer on the desk.

"Well, I guess I have some things to tell you," I replied, angst-wrestling determination in my voice. In his white exam room, Dr. Neil was all ears as I told my story. I recounted immersing myself in the gay lifestyle and the bar scene as "an experiment" to see if it was right for me, you know, like the latest TV medications. Dr. Neil then heard me describe an extraordinary sequence of events: meeting Christians, accepting Jesus, and choosing to abandon a gay identity in obedience.

Obviously, I'd not seen much of Dr. Neil in a long while. I awaited his response with nerves tingling.

"I have to say, that's unique. I've had patients tell me they're gay, and I've had patients tell me they've become Christians," he explained. "But I've never had both from the same person in that order!" he exclaimed, chuckling. I joined the laughter and felt immediate relief, praying God would open Dr. Neil's heart to Him.

The HIV test results would take two weeks—an agonizing wait. *Why so long?* I envisioned my blood samples being transported via sled dogs to a secret lab buried beneath Siberia's frozen tundra. The waiting period verged on unbearable as I wrestled to find solace in God's care, trusting Him regardless of the outcome. *I know You're with me.*

After receiving Dr. Neil's call to come and discuss the results in person, I'd arrived early and sat in the parking lot, reviewing my circumstances in somberness. I knew if they can't do it over the phone, it's usually not good news. The car engine idled, providing some warmth on a gloomy winter day as I talked with the Lord. Even though I knew He was there, most of my body had lost feeling.

I recognized my reckless actions could've justified a positive diagnosis, upending my life. I beseeched Him for calmness and received it, a sweet reminder of His enduring love for me. Together, He and I faced Dr. Neil, who shared negative results. Nothing could have been more positive, for my life, my faith, and my hope in Him.

For reasons known only to God, I believe He shielded me, and I will cherish eternally the unmerited protection of my King. *I love you, and I live for you Lord!*

Despite repeating choices that didn't reflect my true desire, at my core I still wanted what God wanted for me. Nobody had mapped out my healing journey before I took the first step, and nobody ever explained the consequences of my selfish decisions before they were made. I was on an epic journey of faith and trust in my Heavenly Father towards an identity rooted in Him above all, with more disheartening detours than I could've imagined.

One of the walls in my childhood home had featured an eloquent poem that spoke to me in such a way that I committed it to memory. Perhaps something (or Someone) in me knew then how much encouragement would be mine as I recounted those stirring verses over the decades.

*Keep Going (Don't Quit)*

*When things go wrong, as they sometimes will,*
*And the road you're trudging seems all up hill,*
*When the funds are low and the debts are high*
*And you want to smile, but you have to sigh;*
*When care is pressing you down a bit,*
*Rest if you must, but don't you quit.*

*Life is queer with its twists and turns,*
*As every one of us sometimes learns.*
*And many a failure turns about*
*When he might have won had he stuck it out;*
*Don't give up though the pace seems slow,*
*You may succeed with another blow.*

*Often the goal is nearer than*
*It seems to a faint and faltering man,*
*Often the struggler has given up*
*When he might have captured the victor's cup,*
*And he learned too late when the night slipped down*
*How close he was to the golden crown.*

*Success is failure turned inside out,*
*The silver tint of the clouds of doubt,*
*And you never can tell how close you are.*
*It may be near when it seems so far,*
*So stick to the fight when you're hardest hit*
*It's when things seem worst that you mustn't quit.*[14]
—*Edgar Guest*


"*So let's not get tired of doing what is good. At just the right time we will reap a harvest of blessing if we don't give up.*"
—*Galatians 6:9 (NLT)*

# Crossing the Great Divide

My adult life included several positive relations with women, but physical chemistry remained largely elusive, often turning me into a non-threatening, neutered pal. It wasn't until I was in my healing process when I saw the importance of testing those waters from a place of curiosity and openness.

As one attempts to leave behind a same-sex identity, sooner or later, interactions increase with the opposite sex. There's no playbook to suggest how or when socializing happens, but its importance cannot be ignored. I believed my God-given masculinity would be reflected more fully in the presence of femininity, made difficult to experience if I only hung out with men and ultra-safe women. I also knew that some healing would increase opposite-sex attractions, reducing the anxiety that usually got in the way. What I didn't know was those opportunities would sneak up on me.

A cozy, main-floor apartment in the back of an old house on Calgary's 12th Avenue became my home after Thomas sold his place, about a year before Butch and I would become roommates. Despite its modest size and age, the ordinary suite met my needs, with a tiny galley kitchen, a living area, and my single Ikea bed.

Managed by a property management company, I noticed they needed assistance during the winter months. As I approached the property manager with an offer to shovel the sidewalks for a discount on my rent, I harkened back to a similar proposal at the tender age of sixteen. My offer was accepted and about half of a city block became my charge after every snowfall. I made sure of an extra shovel at the ready because more than once, Butch came to my rescue.

One sure thing about my buddy Butch, I could count on him after over-committing myself, a frequent occurrence. A true friend! It was Butch's prairie farming dad who had instilled in him a steadfast work ethic that he's maintained his entire life, so different from my citified upbringing.

My new upstairs neighbor liked to flip around her long, dark hair and flash her warm smile while we chatted from time to time. Her name was Veronica, and she claimed to be a writer, though I suspected it may have been aspirational. Every encounter with Veronica sparked attraction within me. She was feisty, slightly edgy, and intriguing, despite a nasty case of split ends. I often pondered the what-ifs, imagining knowing her better. But alas, my tenure in the apartment was brief, denying further possibilities. And yet, surprising seeds of possibility had been planted in the fertile soil of my changing landscape.

* * *

A small group of us from Calgary, eager to delve deeper into Mexican culture and language, embarked on a Spanish continuing education course. About four years had passed on my healing journey when I met Maria, our dynamic and spirited instructor, cute with dark hair, a nice smile, and an irresistible laugh. Every week, as our Spanish improved, an undeniable—and unexpected—spark lit between Maria and me. Her sparkling eyes and engaging Latina persona captivated me, and an unspoken attraction grew between us.

Butch and I hosted an epic theme party, bringing characters from *Star Trek: The Next Generation* into our spacious apartment. Using commercial trade show curtains, the penthouse transformed into the Enterprise as the stage for the evening's role-playing game. Each room featured color-coded drapery to represent distinct starship areas, such as the holodeck and Ten-Forward lounge. Our party progressed through those rooms throughout the evening, like a journey through space.

With only eight guests on the list, besides Gary (as Guinan) and my cousin Lola (as Lieutenant Yar), I was excited to invite Maria to join the adventure, casting her as the empathetic Helena Troy. Butch landed the part of Lieutenant Commander La Forge while I embodied Will Riker, the first officer, even renting a trombone as a fitting prop for my role.

A professional caterer served drinks and multiple courses, resulting in an ambitious, lavish celebration. Our cheeky caterer's assertive alcohol service soon shifted the party's atmosphere into another dimension. Everyone's dedication to their roles began to wane as we reveled in making each other laugh, trying on each other's costumes.

Maria was fixated on a line from her empathic character, using it ad nauseam all night. She was getting on Butch's nerves.

"If she says, 'I'm *sensing* something here,' one more time, I'm going to *sense* her off the balcony!" exclaimed Butch, in exasperation. More laughter all around as our faces and sides ached more.

As the evening wound down, I escorted Maria to her car, admiring her impressive self-restraint compared to all of us over-imbibers. Standing by her car, I hugged her, and she leaned up for a kiss. I was eager to meet her lips with my affection, something I'd thought about a few times.

But an unexpected sense of uneasiness washed over me, prompting me to pull back. *What's that about?* The only thing that made sense was my heightened awareness of being in public. After all, there we were, right there on the side of the busy street for all to see. I wasn't the only perplexed one.

"D'you don' like me?" Maria asked in confusion, with her adorable accent.

"Oh, I like you. I'm sorry, but it just feels strange in public like this," I replied. I assured her my feelings were mutual and I didn't understand my reaction, but it didn't help much. Maria shrugged as she got into her car and drove off into the night, obviously put-off.

I felt the same way as I returned to the apartment as other guests were departing. Gary remained behind, one thing led to another, and our mutual uninhibited condition led to getting too friendly in the bedroom while Butch was in the kitchen.

Livid is what best describes Butch's state when he found us, destroying the Ten-Forward lounge walls, sending Gary in a scurry out the door. An unfortunate outcome that again revealed how much easier bad choices were in conducive circumstances, with no regard for consequences. *Lord, forgive me!* Once again, my best friend's boundless grace had its way, the very next day.

Later, I realized the cause of my discomfort when kissing Maria on the street. My expressions of affection and intimacy had been almost entirely with men and in private or within safe, friendly settings. Romantic public displays were foreign to me, even counterintuitive. Mixed with a sprinkling of residual angst and shame from previous failed kissing attempts, it's a recipe for an upside-down cake that reminded me how I'm not like all the other boys.

If I'd understood any of this when I was with Maria, everything might have turned out different. But it became clear she wasn't interested in helping me to sort it out, so we stopped seeing each other. The bottom line, encouragement still won out because I knew my romantic feelings for Maria had been genuine, opening the door to hope and new possibilities. *Thank you, Jesus, but we've still got work to do!*

\* \* \*

# NOT LIKE ALL THE OTHER BOYS

The rapid growth of the Westside King's Church in Calgary had demanded a boost in its communications. I was eager to volunteer and spearhead a newspaper-styled Sunday bulletin and found myself teamed up with Jackie, an attractive communications professional with dark hair and sparkling eyes. We were set to design, pen, arrange, and distribute *The King's Court* for weekly publication, but the debut edition was the first mountain to conquer.

An exuberant and slightly bombastic woman, Jackie harbored an affinity for heartfelt laughter that often sprayed like automatic gunfire from her tall, slender frame. Our shared sense of humor fueled countless hours of merriment as we carefully pieced together the fledgling publication. The pressure of looming deadlines for the inaugural edition inevitably led us to hunker down in my bedroom office at Butch's penthouse, toiling away on the computer until morning's wee hours.

On occasion, the strain of our ambitious endeavor would cause Jackie's eyes to droop as she nestled into the comfort of my bed, leaving me at the computer to tackle the remaining tasks. While she slumbered, her vulnerable, innocent frailty enamored me because it was concealed beneath her competent and self-assured persona. Jackie was like a sensitive little sparrow, who'd been raised by mistake with eagles. I became aware of my burgeoning feelings for her, a revelation catching me off guard—such emotions still represented untested waters for me.

Jackie had heard all about my story when I shared my testimony at church. It made it even easier to be with her, dealing a fatal blow to my secret fears of rejection. She seemed unaffected by my past, remaining open and compassionate, which heightened my interest and increased my feelings for her.

Exploring my attractions seemed appropriate, so I invited her to a DIY pottery shop. We howled in amusement at our clumsy attempts to craft personalized coffee mugs for each other. But sadly, we didn't find ourselves tucked away in the dim back room, intimately entwined with each other at a pottery wheel, the melodic tunes of The Righteous Brothers underscoring the scene. Nonetheless, our creative date still evoked romance for me. *I like how this feels.*

To clarify, untamed sexual energy toward Jackie wasn't consuming me. Instead, we enjoyed harmonious fellowship, mutual platonic affection, and an ample supply of hilarity. And beneath it all, Jackie's sweet spirit called out for somebody to care for her, perhaps it could be me. Our shared company often brought joy, but I couldn't shake lingering uncertainty about her romantic perception of me, her hilarious, handsome new friend.

Five years into my healing journey, Jackie's unexpected entrance into my life landed me on an emotional roller coaster. More and more, possibilities crossed my mind, envisioning our connection as a potential springboard into the unexplored realm of heightened physical affection and attraction toward a woman. *Is there more here, Lord?*

Given my lack of experience in deciphering female signals, I mustered the fortitude to seek clarity in Jackie's feelings toward me, fortified by Butch's blessings. My plan was to commit my evolving emotions in writing via a fancy, water-colored, eloquent Blue Mountain Arts card and present it to her.

It would be the moment of truth: her immediate reaction to my emotional guts irreversibly on display, a clear and ultimate act to reveal all. Upon reflection, my efficient and ultra-safe wooing strategy might've been less than optimal, but the wheels were in motion. Everything turned and churned within me.

As Jackie pored over my heartfelt words one summer evening in the privacy of my dim bedroom, her eyes welled up with tears. *That's good, right?* She hesitated for what seemed like forever as my nooks and crannies dampened with anxious perspiration. Traffic sounds from the street below drifted through the open window, oblivious to the moment.

Jackie conveyed her thoughts with tenderness, highlighting her sincere appreciation for our friendship. One specific phrase stood out with crystal clarity.

"Oh, Todd, I think I'm just part of your process. But not your destination," Jackie concluded. My head got it, but my heart sank. *Well, shit.*

While difficult to absorb, her admission did little to diminish the bond between us. Unspoken tension on my end was free to dissipate within our interactions, replaced by even more comfortable familiarity. Although our relationship remained firmly within the platonic realm, her vital role in my transformation journey was unparalleled.

Years would pass before I comprehended the significance of Jackie's words that evening. I came to see her presence in my life served as an indispensable catalyst, illuminating my capacity to forge new and meaningful connections with women, tuning into their unique traits like I hadn't before. The welcome realization—and our enduring friendship—proved to be a tremendous gift that still fills my heart with joy and gratitude. Jackie was a critical element in my transformation process, something I could not have expected or even planned. For that, I remain eternally grateful to God.

* * *

All Exodus conferences had included my buddy Butch as my extroverted shield of protection, which made it easier for me to settle in and have more fun. But for the first time, Butch decided to stay home and not join me at Exodus 23 in Seattle—the first one to be so close to home. At first, I wrestled with his decision but eventually made peace with it because I knew he'd become a little more disillusioned and less hopeful for victory in his transformation.

During our season as roommates, Butch's journey included heartbreak with two different women, and I was glad to support him through that pain. The good news was he still loved Jesus with all his heart, it just wasn't known if a woman would get some of it too. That year, he wasn't inclined to return to the conference, or perhaps any year. *Lord Jesus, bless his aching heart.*

I had been getting used to not having Butch around since deciding it was time for me to be in my own place. He and I remained close, we maintained our Saturday brunch tradition and visited each other often. His absence at the conference would be felt in myriad ways, and not just by me.

My unexpected conference-single status would open the door for me to take advantage of the roommate-matching process, a long-standing curiosity. But I realized that I had become accustomed to relying on my friend, and venturing forth solo would be challenging enough without also stepping into the room-sharing-wilds. Butch's light had always shone brighter than mine, often drawing others to him before me, which suited me most of the time. *Less dicey.*

So, after much reflection, I chose to pay the extra money and get my own room at the conference because I believed it's what God wanted for me. And no, there wasn't a hot tub.

Exodus 23 began like all the others, and it was so encouraging to connect with old conference friends again, many of whom asked about Butch. Everything was going well when a young, vivacious woman caught my eye. Hailing from Melbourne, Australia, Emily had long sandy-colored hair, a pretty smile, and a killer down-under accent; she captivated me without trying. Emily exuded an appealing, understated femininity, and I found myself charmed. Even though she maintained a casual demeanor, I savored our conversations and occasional meals together throughout the conference despite her being in the company of women most of the time.

Emily and her friend Sara had planned a post-conference extension to their overseas trip, intending to travel near Calgary. Eager to stay in touch and connect again, I exchanged contact information and proposed to show Emily around my city—an experience I often relished with visitors. Underneath my cool exterior, I couldn't help but wonder if a deeper connection between us might be possible. I hoped she wouldn't misread me through my attempts to match her laid-back, Aussie attitude.

Another meaningful Exodus 23 connection was made as the event was wrapping up, that time with a man. Being on my own made me more open to getting involved and when the request came for helpers to tear down the meeting room on closing night, I responded with pleasure.

The conference director was friendly and approachable, and I ended up spending a chunk of the evening volunteering at his side. Our connection took hold quickly and he was intrigued with my perspective on conference logistics and potential improvements, and we agreed to keep in touch.

Upon Emily's arrival in Calgary, she joined me for sightseeing while Sara pursued other plans. A beautiful, early fall day bathed us in warmth and sunshine as we set off to explore the downtown park known as Prince's Island. Armed with my Canon SLR camera—a treasured gift from my Uncle Don when I'd begun my SAIT studies—I loaded the camera with Agfa film and anticipated capturing some great photos showcasing Emily's radiant beauty.

Playful banter and light horseplay ensued as we roamed the riverbank, tossing stones into the fast-moving water. I positioned the camera on a nearby rock, allowing us to pose for a timed photograph. In the seconds leading up to the photo snap, I gently tugged

Emily closer, but I sensed her unease. Ignoring her hesitation, I persisted with a few attempts, which later revealed the awkwardness in a few uncomfortable expressions captured in prints.

In retrospect, I saw my infatuation stemmed more from the image of being with a fun, attractive woman than from establishing a genuine connection based on mutual interest and shared values. Perhaps I was mistaken in thinking Emily's acceptance of my tour guide invitation showed more than a general interest in me. Social media wasn't available back then, but I may have hastily envisioned a photo of the two of us on Christmas cards heralding the news at least one woman existed who appeared to be interested in me.

Nevertheless, Emily and I shared a nice day together, meeting up with Sara at Butch's place for a lovely patio barbecue. Our laughter flowed freely, as it often did whenever Butch hosted. Grateful for our dinner and good times, the two travelers departed for their hotel.

Although we exchanged mailing addresses, neither of us followed up, and I came to view the experience as a loving lesson from the Father reminding me of the need to prioritize Him in my desires. I learned that at times, it may appear I can acquire my heart's deepest longings without putting in the necessary work as prescribed by God. *Important note to self.*

My Emily encounter served as a source of hope and another reminder the Lord could perform miracles no matter my mess. He had brought another attractive woman into my life who shared my love for Him, and who also empathized with my struggle—again eliminating the dreaded "when do I tell her" drama.

Though events didn't transpire as I'd envisioned with Emily, another faith-filled seed of optimism thrived within me. I stood in full assurance that the Lord was sovereign over all things as they work together for His good, in His perfect timing.

Even as my same-sex struggles percolated and sputtered, I had allowed myself to picture an ideal wife as I made my way along the path to healing and recovery. A fascination with American culture, politics, and business could be attributed to President Ronald Reagan, and Alex P. Keaton, of the TV show *Family Ties*. Someone similar in appearance to Alex's TV sister Mallory would be of interest, a pretty American woman (who could assist with citizenship, of course) dark hair, not delicate but sturdy, and with childbearing hips.

My experiences with women in my transformation process had clarified my vision, which included a love for Jesus and with a heart that sings for God. My dream girl aspiration was rightly restrained by humble awareness of God's sovereignty, lightly held and submitted to Him alone. But one thing I knew for certain was a surrendered life that seeks His will is still affected by freedom of choice and its perennial twists and turns. *Thank you for loving me through it all, Jesus.*

# Happiest of Christians

About six years into my healing journey and just a month after losing my television job, I learned of a group of Christians who had opted to abandon their pursuit of Jesus-inspired transformation. Instead, they'd decided to embrace gay identities and maintain their faith. A few had bypassed the transformation lane altogether, settling with the others into gay Christian identities. At first, the concept seemed silly to me—perhaps a desperate compromise requiring extensive justification through mental gymnastics to harmonize seemingly incompatible spheres.

However, as I delved deeper and contemplated my own condition—a Jesus-lover with strong lingering feelings of erotic attraction toward other men—I entertained the possibility for myself with caution. I'd often described my reckless faith as a wayward sheep careening down a mountainside, confident my Good Shepherd would correct my course as needed. It seemed to me embracing a gay identity would end all my struggles, and it was enticing.

I was grateful my beloved, free-spirited buddy Butch shared the same curiosity, ensuring I wasn't navigating alone. We plotted a trip to Vancouver, where I'd located a gay-affirming church and a community of believers who appeared to uphold their Christian faith while celebrating their gay identities.

The vision contrasted sharply with many stories of individuals compelled to abandon their faith to pursue long-term same-sex relationships. That sacrifice felt tragic to me, and I grieved for countless brothers and sisters in Christ who had turned away from Him because they felt alienated—or worse—from churches because of their sexuality.

Motivated by a blend of apprehension and intrigue, we resolved to visit an established gay church to observe firsthand how congregants navigated the delicate balance between traditional biblical faith and non-traditional sexuality. The gay church gathering took place in a former church building near Vancouver's bustling downtown.

Upon entering the structure with Butch, I first noticed the pervasive smiles and the collective effort to exude positivity. However, an underlying sense of inauthenticity lingered: it simply didn't feel real. While the congregation indeed rejoiced in song, it felt as though they were celebrating themselves more than their Creator or His Son.

As the service continued, the language and demeanor from the pulpit came across as if everyone was trying to convince themselves they were all okay and that everything was going to be okay. And the reason? Well, because they were gay. In that sanctuary, sexual identity seemed idolized, and God was a backrow passenger on their happy bus. Nonetheless, we remained until the end of the service. But Butch and I couldn't get out of there fast enough, and sorrow overwhelmed me for those people professing to love and serve Jesus, who doesn't suffer any other gods before Him.

Our introduction to gay church culture wasn't a great way for Butch and me to begin our healing journey detour to explore gay Christianity, casting a shadow of doubt over the possibility of enjoying a genuine gay faith-based community experience. That church was presented as a shining example of gay-affirming doctrine, so the off-putting experience left me dispirited to try again elsewhere.

Instead, I chose to focus on being open to same-sex intimacy with another man who loved Jesus first, seeking monogamy and long-term commitment. That time, the wayward sheep really went for it, believing He would order my steps and help me discern His will while living as a Christian homosexual—not the other way around—and figure out the shared community part later.

Our time in Vancouver allowed me to reach out and connect with my old friend Dale, who had moved there from Saskatoon a few years earlier. I was so encouraged to see he'd become a successful entrepreneur, public speaker and personal coach, not far from my own interests. I'd tracked him down through his website and we arranged to meet for a coffee. I also noticed the absence of a wife or girlfriend in his online presence. *You just never know!*

I'd determined I would share my whole story with Dale, because I had nothing to lose and possibly something to gain. We had a nice visit, but Dale had changed a lot, I guess he'd grown up since I knew him. The chemistry we once shared was no more. He still looked great and was now into healthy outdoor living, and not remotely interested in the matters of God. Despite his single status and me looking my best, he assured me once again he preferred the company of women. *Well, shit.* I guess he was in the "I always knew it" category, based on one comment.

"You always had more of a feminine energy," he said, matter-of-factly. *Well, sorry, but no, not a woman, and now, very much Jesus first and maybe a man who loves Him second.*

\* \* \*

During our quest to determine if it would be possible to honor God in front of and over same-sex identities, Butch and I had mapped out a road trip down the west coast, over to Las Vegas, and back up to Calgary. Our resolve to honor God first wasn't the only thing to be tested.

We paused in San Francisco for a few nights and found ourselves immersed in the notorious Castro district. It may sound odd, but we had no idea a flagship gay celebration was about to begin in front of our eyes. So, we found a spot on the side of the street near our hotel. But instead of celebration and joy, our first-ever gay pride parade was an unexpected exhibition that left both of us saddened.

The brash, in-your-face participants and pretentious floats and costumes (or absence thereof) caused us to feel further alienated rather than invoking feelings of inclusion, pleasure, and pride. *I don't feel like them at all.* Identifying with my own vulnerabilities, I was moved by those who were flagrant in their desperation to seek adulation and validation for their particular uniqueness. *But by the grace of God, there go I.*

Later, we wound up on a welcoming patio near our hotel, indulging in food and drinks as the uber-gay culture enveloped us. An enticing promotion offered discounted pitchers of alcohol and my resolve to have some fun pushed us over the edge, perhaps eager to numb the disheartened emotions that had been stirred.

As the evening wore on, our excessive boozing exacerbated our questionable decisions. With my prompting, we eventually made our way to various gay bars as part of our "research" project, inhibitions lower than the proverbial front step of every one of those bars. *Who knows, maybe I'll find Mr. Right.*

In one busy location, I found myself drawn to a charming, slender young man who showered me with attention. Unable or unwilling to resist, I accepted his invitation to join him at his nearby apartment. Butch followed us there and into the young man's bedroom. *Why is Butch here?*

Considering the young man's obvious interest in me, I insisted Butch return to the hotel, which he hesitantly did, but not without first getting a phone number. Watching him leave brought an unfamiliar feeling. Beyond then, my recollections blur.

Shrouded in shame, I reached out to Butch the next morning to rescue me from the awkward and regretful situation. Butch, with astonishing grace and love, gathered my belongings from the hotel and picked me up in the car before we headed out of town. He later told me he'd seriously considered dropping me off at the airport; he was so hurt and angered by my choices.

Our shared silence during the car ride spoke volumes as I grappled with the weight of my actions for miles. The experience stood as one of the most humbling experiences of my life, and the fact that Butch came through still as my friend seemed miraculous.

Overwhelmed with remorse, I felt utterly wretched and eternally grateful for Jesus's relentless mercy that shielded me from harm throughout the tumultuous night. The unyielding love and forgiveness from Butch impacted me as well. The dreadful night served as a potent reminder of how old habits readily resurface, particularly when fueled by my old chum, excessive alcohol. Also disturbing was how I treated my best friend in the middle of it all.

With resolute conviction and determination to not repeat such a scene, Butch accepted my heartfelt apology and forgave me. Our road trip resumed, accompanied by a sober and somber mindset. We reflected on the importance of our enduring Christ-centered friendship, the many lessons learned, and the strength we derived from our shared experiences. *Lord Jesus, never again!*

\*\*\*

Soon after I had been let go from the television station, I was at King's Fold for my three-week healing retreat. The discovery of dial-up internet access in my upgraded suite was unexpected. Heightened pain and vulnerability of recent events proved temptation too great, and I soon logged into AOL to check out the chatrooms.

A friendly fellow named Luke from Vancouver was intrigued to hear about my healing and recovery journey, especially since we'd met in an M4M room. Luke's profile suggested he was attractive and intriguing, and our connection was enjoyable as I opened up about the ups and downs of the past six years. I appreciated his curiosity and believed he might be open to hearing more about matters of faith, so we intended to keep in touch.

But just a few weeks afterwards, I had learned about the gay Christian group mentioned earlier which meant my horizons—and interest in Luke—were expanding. Fortunately, I'd already planned a visit to Vancouver and could meet Luke in-person. *Maybe he's the one.*

Upon meeting face-to-face for the first time over drinks, it was difficult not to notice Luke was indeed attractive and warm with a great smile and mild-mannered demeanor; our chemistry was instant. Luke wasn't out with his family, adding both intrigue and concern. He also said he'd been seeing a guy for a while but wasn't sure he was the right one. Innuendo progressed to candid descriptions of favorite activities. Mutual flattery and lowered inhibitions for the win.

In an ironic twist, I had kept in touch with Charles since he left Calgary and looked forward to seeing his new place. He'd gone out earlier, giving me the keys because I planned to return before him. So, there I was ready to know Luke better, but we couldn't go to his condo, so we headed to Charles's apartment instead.

It was a little more than embarrassing when Charles returned, calling out to me to buzz open the front door. Scrambling to be presentable, a quick introduction and Luke's hasty exit must have appeared suspicious. *Did I really just do that?*

Beyond the awkwardness of Luke, my visit with Charles allowed me to see he was happy in a new chapter of his gay life. Charles was tickled by the news of an apparent shift in my life—now open to a gay relationship—but I'm not sure he was buying it. Perhaps I wasn't either. Soon, Charles moved back east and there he found lasting love and has been with his adoring partner for almost twenty years. We still keep in touch and I truly desire nothing but long-term happiness for him.

\* \* \*

Many months after the encounter with Luke, I was about to exit an AOL M4M chat room when a captivating fellow named Larry reached out. His profile was enticing: blond, tall, and athletic. We struck up an online connection that didn't compare to past encounters. Unlike everyone else, Larry hesitated to reveal his photo because of privacy concerns. Undeterred, I promptly shared my picture, and he said he liked what he saw.

As our bond grew through many telephone conversations, I also found myself captivated by his alluring Texas drawl. Over time, I detailed my journey of coming to faith and my involvement in support groups to help me pursue a non-sexual identity.

Larry revealed his upbringing in an evangelical Christian household and an openness to the matters of God. However, he didn't relate to my acceptance struggles, even though he had only come out to his grandmother. When I shared the more recent development—my willingness to possibly harmonize my Christian and gay identities—I was astounded as he expressed firm support. *Wow, are you in this, Lord?*

Fueled by curiosity and our deepening emotional connection, I longed to see Larry's face. Eventually, he agreed to mail me a photo with the condition that I would hold off on the reveal until we were on the phone to share the moment together. He had mentioned he'd done some modeling, nearly overwhelming me with anticipation. *Maybe he's somebody famous!*

Larry's letter and photo arrived a week or so later, and we arranged the call so I could finally see what he looked like. Perhaps growing anticipation had skewed my expectations, conjuring an image of a perfect ten in my mind. The first glance struck me instantly with the stark contrast between fantasy and reality. Stunned and a little flustered, I called once again on my powerful ability to conjure the exact right words when needed most.

"Oh wow, look at how green the grass is there," I mused out loud.

"Huh?" puzzled Larry, his potential love interest's reaction not quite meeting his expectations.

In truth, the photo did feature his lovely Texas garden with verdant landscaping that contrasted the harsh northern realities of snow-covered brown lawns. But I realized how absurd my remark must have sounded, so I assured Larry post haste that I indeed found him attractive. The minor setback required adjusting my inflated expectations, and we carried on getting to know each other.

After a few months of online and phone connecting with growing intimacy, we finally agreed a face-to-face connection had been long overdue. We had progressed to candid conversations that included endearing terms for each other but not yet crossing the "L" word boundary.

Eager to further explore our budding relationship, we agreed to rendezvous in Las Vegas. The grandeur of Sin City, combined with Larry's family connections at a downtown hotel, heightened the excitement. He had made all the arrangements, including an airport limousine and an upgraded room where we freely enjoyed each other and a great view of Fremont Street. Larry's self-confidence was surprising and alluring, on full display there on familiar turf.

One of our relationship's most compelling qualities was Larry's genuine interest in me, which may sound funny. But I relished the attention he lavished upon me, and his charming, dry sense of humor generated lots of laughter between us. I had no trouble loving him back. *Lord, are you in this?*

Larry also grappled with balancing his faith and sexuality, so it was good to share my struggle with him, even though we rarely discussed spiritual matters. Despite the gay nature of our alliance, my goal of a faith-inspired, monogamous-type relationship offered an enticing sense of safety and appeal. It held a certain nobility, a vastly better alternative than returning to the unpleasantries of the roller-coaster bar scene.

Yet, as we roamed the streets of Vegas together, Larry's fondness for discretion matched my own, which meant our public interactions held the facade of a couple of buds hanging out in the entertainment capital of the world. Well, that's what I chose to believe.

As our weekend ended and we prepared to part ways at the airport, the bewildering challenge of losing my paper ticket left me stranded, unable to board the flight to Calgary. God and I had a little chat about the situation, but He didn't cause my lost ticket to appear, nor did He provide a plausible explanation for my predicament. *Nothing, Lord?*

With no available credit and Larry already en route back to Texas, I needed help. Butch hadn't been very supportive of me and Larry, so I swallowed my pride with reluctance and called my brother John for help. He had no idea I was in Vegas with "a friend," but by God's grace, he provided his credit card details over the phone to a ticketing agent for a new ticket. And I was soon on my way home with much to reflect upon.

A couple of months after Vegas, Larry visited me in Calgary for a few days, but it was clear our relational dynamics had begun to shift. We seemed more like naughty friends than glitter-covered lovers of destiny. Inner turmoil about being in a gay relationship had been escalating, and I'd recognized the primary lure was the comfort and safety of familiar intimacy.

Another revelation was that the convenient distance barrier of about two thousand miles prevented our relationship from fully blooming or becoming an obsession, which may not have been such a bad thing. Meanwhile, Larry wrestled with coming out to his family and grew more aware of my internal struggle that made for shaky ground in a relationship. Before he left to fly home, we agreed to call it quits and cut off contact cold-turkey style to help each other move on more quickly.

\* \* \*

In reflection, I've often marveled at God's gift of free will. By the time Larry entered my life, I had gained a deep understanding of the root causes of my same-sex attractions, fully accepted Christ, participated actively in church life, underwent baptism, and completed a semester of Bible college.

Then, almost seven years into my healing journey, I had attempted reconciling my faith with a gay identity. Ever patient with me, I trusted that God allowed me to explore my options, always aware of the eventual outcome. Perhaps experiencing the consequences of my choices would evoke more authentic yielding to Him and His plans for my life, but only God knows.

After a period of intense soul searching, I was convinced in my repentant heart that God's will for me included neither a gay identity nor an erotic same-sex relationship. As I surrendered it all, my heart nearly burst as I received His loving forgiveness with immense joy! *How can I thank you Lord?*

One of the most powerful epiphanies in my journey resonated throughout the years as solid truth: I am not defined by my feelings, or my past. What's more, the Bible tells us our hearts are deceitful above all things (Jeremiah 17:9) and we're a fool if we trust in our own mind (Proverbs 28:26). As a follower of Christ, I feel I have no choice but to trust in Him alone and how He defines me, no matter what temptation comes my way to think otherwise or take matters into my hands of flesh.

God's Word also speaks to the matter of idolatry and self-determination by using plain English to illustrate how absurd it is for us to question His sovereignty.

> *"My goodness, how you've turned things around!*
> *You seem to think that the potter is equal to the clay;*
> *Should the pot say about the potter, 'He didn't make me'?*
> *Or does the thing formed say about the one who formed it,*
> *'He doesn't understand anything.'?"*
> —*Isaiah 29:16 (The Voice)*

# My Father Knows Best

A rewarding non-profit administrative job I'd held for three years yielded a unique opportunity to cease being an employee and contract my services back to the charity. The shift allowed me to create additional streams of income through other projects and multiple federal government service contracts. Enduring many years of financial instability and aimless job pursuits, I was reveling in a six-figure income at thirty-two years old.

After nine years in my recovery process, the time had come to part ways once again with Butch, but this time from a much healthier non-enmeshed place, unlike when the television job forced us apart. The Lord's faithfulness had brought us through almost a decade of healing and recovery, along with the inherent challenges of same-sex friendship and same-sex struggles. Butch's influence on my life had been unequaled, and his steadfast love and commitment nourished me into a life-changing relationship with Jesus. Our friendship felt rock-solid, and we were both ready for a new chapter of independence and openness to God's will.

My business earnings enabled me to furnish a two-story condo, and I was so thankful to God for His extraordinary provisions. One of my indulgences was a huge projection TV with a high-end audio system nestled within a small media room in my basement. I frequently enjoyed worship music there, roused by the rich bass resonating deep within my chest. One evening, as I sat absorbed in my favorite tunes and myriad thoughts, something incredible occurred.

The random CD player served up Shania Twain, crooning her hit, "From This Moment," exquisite as it flowed through large speakers to overtake the room. I'd long enjoyed Shania's music and had been surprised with the opportunity to meet her in person at a promotional event before she became a megastar.

At first, I found it peculiar that a romantic wedding song, celebrating the commitment of two lovers, could stir such a wellspring of emotions within me—a single man. Before I knew what was happening, tears cascaded down my face, the feels surged from head to toe as I sat transfixed on the couch, staring into space. *What's going on?*

My poignant upheaval wasn't merely a response to the high-quality recording; something far more intense had me absorbing new meaning behind the song's lyrics, line by line, beat by beat.

"You're the reason I believe in love," clenched my swollen heart. But instead of addressing a significant other, I found myself singing those words to the Lord, my Father in Heaven! It was a love song from my heart to His, and I belted out every word as loud as I could, as my voice cracked with passion. Indescribable transcendence washed over me.

"You're the reason I believe in Love!" I sang out again to Father God, my voice and heart soaring with Him in the music. Throughout the last nine years, He'd shown me time and again He delighted in me as His beloved son… and in every part of me He created.

"All we need is just the two of us," I exclaimed, my voice growing louder still. "You and I will never be apart. From this moment on!" It was true, He has always been with me. Even when I didn't know Him, He was at work throughout my life. In the curiosities, the fear, the secrets, the insecurities, the abandonment, the struggles, the rejection, the anxiety, and the humiliation—all of it—my Heavenly Father was there, loving me through it all. *Oh thank You, always there, my Father God!*

The matchless love and peace of Christ flooded my entire being as if Hoover Dam had collapsed. In that moment, I wholeheartedly received Him as my One and only, knowing in my heart all my affirmation seeking from others pointed me straight to Jesus and what He did for me. Fully alive in Him, I needed nothing from anyone else. I wanted Him alone. *Wow, it's true, thank You Jesus!*

As my heart swelled larger with overwhelming love for Him, my dominant-thinker mind jumped in like an uninvited guest.

> *Now, wait a minute, nobody else, really?*
>
> *What about my dream of a loving wife, wonderful kids, and sharing our beautiful life with my parents and siblings?*

A voice, louder than anything else in the room, pierced me like a pin to a startled balloon.

"Do you trust me?" He asked.

And with that, my heart persuaded my mind to make its best choice ever. Nothing was more meaningful in all creation and life than loving and serving my Abba Father with all I had. And I got it, embracing a life surrendered to singleness and celibacy meant I would be less distracted and more of me would be available to Him for His greater purpose. Perhaps, after all, it was God's will that I wouldn't be like *all* the other boys. This was it! *Yes, my loving Father, my Other, forever… I want to be Your boy!*

> *"So you have not received a spirit that makes you fearful slaves. Instead, you received God's Spirit when he adopted you as his own children. Now we call him, 'Abba, Father.'"*
> —Romans 8:15 (NLT)

*"My old self has been crucified with Christ. It is no longer I who live, but Christ lives in me. So, I live in this earthly body by trusting in the Son of God, who loved me and gave himself for me."*
*—Galatians 2:20 (NLT)*

*"Behold, I am the Lord, the God of all flesh. Is there anything too hard for Me?"*
*—Jeremiah 32:27 (NKJV)*

*"No, Christian brothers, I do not have that life yet. But I do one thing. I forget everything that is behind me and look forward to that which is ahead of me."*
*—Philippians 3:13 (NLT)*

**If you've not yet welcomed Jesus into your heart**, you can begin your journey right now by talking with Him, using these or your own words:

> *"Dear Lord Jesus,*
>
> *I know I am a sinner, and I ask for Your forgiveness. I believe You died for my sins and rose from the dead. I turn from my sins and invite You to come into my heart and life. I want to trust and follow You as my Lord and Savior."*

If you've prayed this today, please tell someone who knows Him so you may continue in the steps of faith, or email me (todd@toddnormanringness.com) so I may celebrate and guide you to your next steps!

There's much more to my story coming soon in the sequel to this book! To receive updates, please visit: notlikealltheotherboys.com

# Get Your Free Audio Book Sample

Receive as a gift the <u>first three chapters of this book as an **audio file**</u>, narrated in the author's own voice. Enter your email address below and instructions will be emailed back to you.

Please visit this website:

gift.nlatob.com

Included in the **free downloadable MP3 audio file**:
- *Introduction (Spoiler Alert)*
- *Roots and Wings*
- *Danny's Lessons*

By providing your email address, you'll also receive **author updates about the book and the upcoming sequel.**

Your email address will be kept strictly confidential and you may cancel at any time.

PLEASE KEEP IN TOUCH!

gift.nlatob.com

# Notes

1. GREASE. Directed by Randal Kleiser. Allan Carr Enterprises, Stigwood Group. Released June 16, 1978.

2. Leanne Payne. THE BROKEN IMAGE. Crossway Books. 1987 (Tenth Printing). Page 46.

3. Max Lucado. "FEAR NEVER WROTE A SYMPHONY OR POEM, NEGOTIATED A PEACE TREATY, OR CURED A DISEASE." Facebook post. February 20, 2024. Accessed May 14, 2024. https://www.facebook.com/maxlucado/posts/fear-never-wrote-a-symphony-or-poem-negotiated-a-peace-treaty-or-cured-a-disease/10158718971705162/

4. Anonymous, "FOOTPRINTS IN THE SAND"

5. Myers-Briggs Type Indicator, Myers-Briggs, MBTI, Step I, Step II, Step III, the MBTI logo, and The Myers-Briggs Company logo are trademarks or registered trademarks of Myers & Briggs Foundation in the United States and other countries.

6. Todd Norman Ringness. SAIT GRADUATION INVOCATIONS ("The Force is With You" 1997; "Titanic Love" 1998; "The Force or Higher Power" 2002. Accessed May 14, 2024. https://archives.toddnormanringness.com#saitinvocations

7. Todd Norman Ringness. DISCOVER PURPOSE COACHING. Retrieved May 14, 2024. https://toddnormanringness.com#purpose

8. David Rogers. REFORMED GAY MINISTER SY ROGERS PASSES AWAY. MyChristianDaily.com. Initiate Media. April 20, 2020. https://mychristiandaily.com/reformed-gay-minister-sy-rogers-passes-away/. Accessed May 15, 2024.

9. Wikipedia contributors, "KINSEY REPORTS," Wikipedia: The Free Encyclopedia, last modified, May 7, 2024, https://en.wikipedia.org/wiki/Kinsey_Reports, last modified: May 7, 2024

10. Andrew Comiskey. PURSUING SEXUAL WHOLENESS: HOW JESUS HEALS THE HOMOSEXUAL. USA. Siloam, A Strang Company. Page 113.

11. Andrew Comiskey. PURSUING SEXUAL WHOLENESS: HOW JESUS HEALS THE HOMOSEXUAL. USA. Siloam, A Strang Company. Page 134.

12. Elizabeth R. Moberly. HOMOSEXUALITY: A NEW CHRISTIAN ETHIC. England. James Clarke & Co Ltd. Page 28.

13. Andrew Comiskey. PURSUING SEXUAL WHOLENESS: HOW JESUS HEALS THE HOMOSEXUAL. USA. Siloam, A Strang Company. Page 20.

14. Edgar A. Guest. KEEP GOING (DON'T QUIT). Detroit Free Press. March 4, 1921 (public domain). https://freep.newspapers.com/article/detroit-free-press-breakfast-table-chat/4988587/. Accessed May 15, 2024.

## Your Opinion Matters

Please consider the gift of **an honest rating** of this book (1 to 5 stars) that you can submit quickly and anonymously. ALL RATINGS are welcome and needed to help keep this book in front of those who may be encouraged by this story.

Please visit this website to **give your star rating**:

### rating.nlatob.com

Also, below are some simple suggestions for your optional review:

*"It's a good book!"*

*"I couldn't put it down... so honest and insightful. Oh, and Todd's humor cracks me up."*

*"I was uncomfortable reading this book."*

*"I don't recommend this book for anyone looking for a light summer read."*

*"I'm glad I read this book."*

## THANK YOU FOR YOUR FEEDBACK!

### rating.nlatob.com

# Acknowledgements

I've so much gratitude for all who've helped shape my life, especially my parents and my siblings. The hundred plus people mentioned in this book all played vital roles in my journey, and I give thanks to God for each one.

My beta readers were so very helpful with excellent feedback and suggestions that made this book better. And sincere thanks go out to my editor Cara for her enthusiasm and guidance along the way, proof positive that very good things can come out of Facebook.

Special thanks to Sandra Gaye for her steadfast, always ready support and assistance. There were many times it seemed that your commitment to this project matched or perhaps even exceeded my own, amidst the emotional ups and downs. I know that Father delights in you even more than I do, and I am grateful beyond measure for the gift of you on this journey.

All praise, honor and glory unto my King Jesus, for His unchanging love, surprising mercy, unmerited grace, and renewing hope. You, Lord God, are why I am, and why this is. As You have Your way, once again, I surrender all.

www.ingramcontent.com/pod-product-compliance
Lightning Source LLC
Chambersburg PA
CBHW030430010526
44118CB00011B/574